African Widows

AFRICAN WIDOWS

An empirical study of the problems of adapting
Western Christian teachings on marriage
to the leviratic custom for the care of widows
in four rural African societies

Michael C. Kirwen

ORBIS BOOKS
Maryknoll, New York 10545

The Catholic Foreign Mission Society of America (Maryknoll) recruits and trains people for overseas missionary service. Through Orbis Books Maryknoll aims to foster the international dialogue which is essential to mission. The books published, however, reflect the opinions of their authors and are not meant to represent the official position of the Society.

Library of Congress Cataloging in Publication Data
Kirwen, Michael C.
  African Widows

  Bibliography: p.
  1. Widows—Africa—Case studies   2. Levirate—
Case studies.   I. Title
HQ1058.5A4K57   261.8'34'286   78-15870
ISBN 0-88344-009-1 pbk.

DEDICATED TO
THE MARYKNOLL MISSIONARIES
WHO HAVE WORKED IN EAST AFRICA

CONTENTS

10 7530

List of Maps

Introduction

In the fall of 1969, forty-five East African Christian leaders were asked in personal interviews what they considered to be the most pressing pastoral problems facing the African Christian churches. These leaders were mostly Africans and they included theologians, directors of pastoral institutes, teachers, education secretaries, rectors of seminaries, pastors and curates of parishes, and bishops. They all responded that one of the most serious problems was the constant confrontation between African marriage customs and the Christian marriage customs taught by Western missionaries.[1] This confrontation, they declared, was threatening the very indigenization of the African churches, was an unending source of anxiety and frustration to both clergy and laity, and was causing the loss of faith and practice for many baptized people, especially the youth and the educated.

In these interviews, they complained that in many parishes throughout East Africa, every baptized person could look forward to being excommunicated from the Church as a result of marriage problems sometime in his or her life. They pointed out how many men and women who are involved in polygynous* marriages are categorized as unworthy of membership in the Christian community despite the fact that some of them show positive signs of faith and are the religious and political leaders of their peoples. They mentioned the injustice involved in the Church's demanding the removal of a second wife in order to allow a polygynist to be baptized. They spoke of the religious fate of the widow who chooses to cohabit with her brother-in-law and is thereby refused communion in the Church even though there is no other acceptable and decent way for her to live.

---

* *Polygyny* is the practice of having more than one *wife* or female mate at one time. Its opposite is *polyandry,* the practice of having more than one *husband* at one time. The general term meaning to have a plurality of spouses of either sex at one time is *polygamy.*

1

They discussed the Church's lack of understanding of the way African marriages begin, thus leaving the Christian youths to fend for themselves with no clear guidelines, except those of a Western courtship model, a model meaningless in the context of the African societies. In Morogoro, Tanzania, for example, they cited the traditional practice of trial cohabitation for several months of the prospective bride and groom. The Catholic missionaries in the area, they said, applied strong religious pressure on Christian parents to ignore this custom, demanding that there be a Church marriage before cohabitation. Two marriages that later ended in divorce were pointed to where there had been no cohabitation, a clear indication to the people that their tradition of "premarital" cohabitation is necessary in order to establish a permanent and stable marriage bond.

These leaders spoke of the conscious and unconscious attempts of the Western missionaries to promote the "nuclear" style Western family as the ideal Christian family, even though the Western family structure is often seen by Africans as dehumanizing, selfish, and far removed from the Christian spirit of fraternal charity. They noticed that some of the Western missionaries, aware of the differences between the African and Western Christian marriage customs and knowing that they were doing violence to African values and social structures, find it impossible to make any positive adaptations.[2] Moreover, they objected to the training programs for Church ministry, which often make their own sons sensitive to *Western* marital values at the expense of their own *African* values.

Further, they commented on how the Church's marriage dispensations and the fictitious domestic living arrangements resorted to in order to solve certain marriage problems, creates the impression in the minds of many African Christians that a successful solution to a marriage problem depends on the good will of the local pastor. For example, a polygynous man who wishes to be baptized can choose from among his wives the one he wishes to keep as his Christian wife—demanding of course that the other wives (usually the older ones) be sent away and divorced without any concern for the injustices done to them.[3] Likewise a second wife, who is declared to be too old to cohabit sexually with her husband, is allowed to be baptized even though her polygynous marriage is still intact.

In brief, most of these leaders felt that the Christian churches' policy in the area of marriage *often* does not come from the demands of Christianity itself, but comes from both the narrow ethnocentrism of the Christian missionaries, and from a lack of understanding and insight into African values and customs. A number of the leaders said plainly that they know that their marriage customs are intrinsically good, valuable, and compatible with Christianity, but they are unable to articulate and explain, in terms of Western marriage theology, why these customs can and should be integrated into their Christian way of life. As a result they have given little attention as to *how* Christianity can be skillfully adapted to these customs.

Encouraged by these interviews and in light of the Catholic Church's teaching on adaptation, this study asks the question whether or not adaptation to African marriage institutions and customs has been taken seriously in the pastoral order by the Cahtolic Church.[4] This study discusses *one* particular African marital custom, the "levirate,"* as a concrete example of the kind of difficulties and problems present in any attempt to evaluate and understand a non-Western marriage custom in terms of its compatibility with Christianity. The leviratic custom (called variously, "widow inheritance," "levirate," "leviratic marriage") is the cohabitation of a widow with her brother-in-law in which the brother-in-law relates to the widow as a substitute for her deceased husband. This custom has been judged by the Roman Catholic Church (and other Christian churches) to be immoral and incompatible with Christian marital and moral behavior. It was selected for study because it both highlights the problem of adaptation and, with proper understanding, points to certain resolutions that involve a minimum of confrontation with Western Christian morality.

This study proceeds by developing an analysis and critique of the present-day situation of the African leviratic custom vis-à-vis its prohibition by the Catholic Church. The basis of the critique is research data collected in 1971–72 by means of a sociological sur-

---

*The word *levirate* comes from the Latin word *levir* meaning husband's brother. Levirate can pass into an adjective, e. g., levirate custom. Also, leviratic or leviratical, i.e., pertaining to or in accordance with the levirate, e.g., leviratic marriage.

vey from 1,350 African adults and 115 Catholic Church leaders (both African and missionary) in four traditional Tanzanian societies. These data are discussed in terms of anthropological models in order (1) to highlight the radical differences in the ways of caring for widows operating within the African social structures independently of Christian influence; (2) to show the cultural presuppositions underlying the missionaries' negative judgment on this custom; and (3) to determine the meaning, value, and function of this custom within these societies in order to reassess its compatibility or incompatibility with Christianity.

This study, of course, does not pretend to create a new theology of marriage for the African Catholic Church. This is a task best undertaken by Africans themselves.[5] Rather it assumes that a general theology of Christian marriage, or marriage in its essential Christian aspects, if it were clearly known and presented to the African peoples, would be more compatible with African marriage institutions than is presently realized. The hypothesis is that many of the incompatibilities between African marriage institutions and the Christian marriage institutions taught by missionaries (as will be seen in our discussion of the African leviratic institution) arise out of the Church's lack of understanding of and sympathy with non-Western "lineage" marriage* rather than out of true theological conflicts.

---

*"Lineage" marriages are those that are formed by alliances between both the individual partners and their "extended" families.

NOTES

1. This same concern was voiced by missionaries in Africa in a survey conducted in 1913 involving forty-two missionaries. See J. H. Oldham, "The Missionary and His Task," *International Review of Mission* 3 (1914) 512–514.

2. This feeling of frustration on the part of the missionaries is discussed by Adrian Hastings, in *Church and Mission in Modern Africa* (London: Burns and Oates, 1967), p. 163. He comments that almost all missionaries feel that there is something deeply wrong with their approach to marriage.

3. See A. H. van Vliet and D. G. Breed, in *Marriage and Canon Law* (London: Burns and Oates, 1964), pp. 193–195, for details of this kind of legal casuistry.

4. In the area of marriage, especially plural marriage, the experiences and reactions of the non-Catholic "main-line" Protestant churches have often been the same as the Catholic's to the problem of adaptation. (The "main-line" Protestant churches in this East African context are the Anglican, Mennonite, and Lutheran.) Harry Boer, in "Polygamy," *Frontier* 1 (Spring 1968) 24, writes that the churches which have developed out of the missionary services do not permit polygynous husbands to be members, no matter how Christian their witness and character may be. Likewise, Geoffrey Parrinder, in *Religion in an African City* (London: Oxford University Press, 1953), p. 166, says that all orthodox Christian churches have opposed polygyny. On the same point, Adrian Hastings, in "Church's Response to African Marriage," *African Ecclesiastical Review* 13 (1971) 194, writes that the Catholic missionaries in the matter of polygyny took quite as firm a line as Protestants.

5. See Charles Nyamiti, *African Theology: Its Nature, Problems and Method,* Gaba Institute Pastoral Papers, no. 19 (Kampala, Uganda: Gaba Publications), pp. 31 ff., for his practical suggestion to African theologians regarding adaptation. Charles Taber, "The Missionary: Wrecker, Builder, or Catalyst," *Practical Anthropology* 17 (July-August 1970) 151, points out that an indigenous church must not only be self-supporting, self-governing, and self-propagating but also, at the level of cultural forms, *self-designed.*

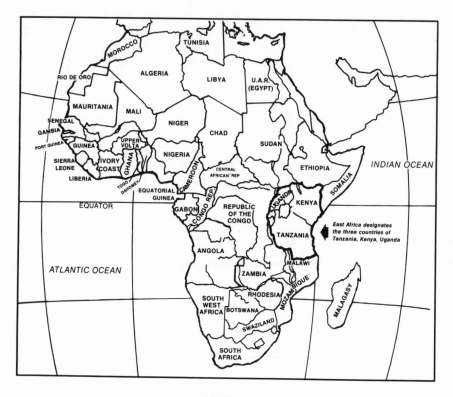

AFRICA

PART ONE

Christianity and the Care of Widows in Four African Societies

CHAPTER ONE

The African Widow's Problem
"Does the Church Understand?"

In 1966 a young Christian mother, Victoria Akech, the woman to whom this study was originally dedicated, lost her husband. At that time she was confronted with a major decision about her life: was she to live maritally with her deceased husband's brother in a leviratic union according to the customs of her people, or was she to reject this custom in the name of Christian moral teachings and either seek out a new marriage or live alone without a designated marital partner? (A leviratic union, as will be shown, does not entail a new marriage; rather, it is a temporary adjustment in a continuing marriage in which a brother-in-law substitutes for the deceased legal husband.) Victoria's problems were complicated by the fact that she was both a foundress and an active leader of a small neighborhood Christian community. She knew that if she followed her traditional customs regarding widows, she would be forbidden the sacraments of the Church, expelled from her leadership role, and declared to be living in a "state of sin."

I can recall arguing with her as to how simple it would all be if she would just remarry (whether or not she could remarry was never discussed), for her husband Joseph had died and as far as I was concerned there was no longer any bond with him; furthermore, there was no reason to feel obligated to his family's wishes and desires, and finally, the leviratic custom was bizarre and unworthy of a woman of her caliber and Christian faith. Her response was, "You white men do not understand the black man's ways."

To Victoria's way of thinking, the only decent way for her to live and support her children, despite the opposition of the Church, was in a leviratic union with her brother-in-law. She asked, "Does the Church really know what it is asking? Does it really want me to

9

remarry, thus abandoning my children, or to live alone without a marital partner?" "No", she said, "the Church doesn't know! Indeed it is better to live in peace with one man according to custom than either to divorce and remarry or to live alone and play the prostitute. And [she added, with a thoughtful look on her face] you know I still believe firmly in Christ and his Church, and once I have raised my family and am past childbearing age, you'll see, I'll return to my role as a Christian leader." Victoria attended Mass for several more months and then dropped out of sight. She was said to have entered into a leviratic union with her brother-in-law.

The African leviratic custom arises in the context of certain presuppositions about the nature of marriage institutions. Its strangeness to Westerners is due to the fact that they do not share these presuppositions, hence they have no comparable custom. custom. The major presupposition is that marriage involves both individuals and their lineages; marriage is both a personal and a social alliance. Evidence for this is that, at the time of marriage, the lineages involved exchange expensive gifts of livestock and money—often equal to a life's inheritance—as a sign and proof of the marriage, to seal the alliance, to "buy" the bride, to determine the lineage of the children. Thus the bride is both the wife of an individual and, in a real sense, the wife of the lineage. Likewise the children are both the children of their individual parents and the children of the lineage. The result is that the obligations and relationships entwining a woman and her children with her husband's lineage do not cease automatically with his physical death. Indeed she is able to continue on in the lineage as a functioning wife through the ministrations of her brother-in-law in a leviratic union.

The story of Victoria Akech is not an isolated case. It represents an ongoing serious pastoral problem within the African Christian Church. To begin with, more than 20 percent of the four hundred and seventy-two married women surveyed had been widowed—thus we are dealing with a significantly large segment of the population.* Secondly, in many areas the widows are usually cared for like Victoria. That is, a widow enters into a leviratic union

---

*See Appendix A, Table 25.

with a brother or male relative of her deceased spouse, who acts as a "surrogate" (also described as a "proxy" or "substitute") for her deceased husband.* The final complication arises from the fact that not only the Catholic, but also the Anglican and other mainline Protestant churches proscribe this custom.[1] These churches, through their Western missionaries, reject the leviratic custom as a practice incompatible with the Christian way of life, declare it to be an unlawful type of sexual union, a type of polygyny, and oppose the custom by placing sanctions on Christians who practice it. These churches insist that a woman is "free" either to remarry or to live alone without a marital partner on the death of her husband.

The Catholic Church's prohibition of the leviratic custom was sharply debated in a 1968 meeting of Tanzania Church leaders at the Catholic mission station at Kowak, North Mara. In the meeting, the African leaders pointed out how the Church, in the name of charity, enjoins on all the support and care of widows and their children, quoting James 1:27: "The kind of religion which is without stain or fault in the sight of God our Father is this: to go to the help of orphans and widows in their distress." The conflict over this issue, the Africans declared, arises over the question of how one can best help a widow in her needs. The Church, they noted, officially encourages the Christian communities to take care of all the widow's needs except that of procreation (*uzazi*). The Africans argued that the widow's procreative needs are as important and as real as her needs for food, clothing, shelter, gardens, and school fees, for it is only through her continuing fertility that she can maintain the integrity and continuity of the family begun with her husband, fulfill her sacred obligation to participate fully in the procreative process, and in addition, that she can look forward to care and support in her old age. The meeting concluded with the statement that the Luo leviratic union cannot be construed as either immoral or incompatible with Christian charity, and that the custom should not continue to be proscribed unless it can be clearly demonstrated that Christ himself in the New Testament had forbidden it.

---

*These terms are used by anthropologists in describing the relationship between the widow and her leviratic partner. See Chapter VII, p. 164, where these terms are formally discussed.

The thought that "procreation" is a basic and fundamental human need may seem strange to non-Africans: even a sociologist friend expressed surprise at this phrase. It illustrates the African's orientation towards life as a reality received and shared through a corporate group—a common motif of their artists—and their belief that the fullness of human development must entail personal participation in the total physical, social, psychological, and spiritual growth and development of this group. The inability or unwillingness to procreate is seen by the community as a tragic failure to become involved in life at its deepest level, and usually creates in the individual personal feelings of rejection as well as a sense of loss of ultimate meaning in life.* (Notice that the widow's sexual needs do not enter into this discussion: the focus of the problem is on procreation and not on fulfilling personal sexual needs.)

This dilemma of the Christian churches' neglect of widows' procreative needs in their program of support and care for widows becomes clear when one looks for ecclesiastically *acceptable* alternatives to the custom of the levirate, alternatives which are also in harmony with African marriage institutions and customs. One alternative promoted by some Catholic Church leaders is to have the widow build a house (mud and wattle) outside of the compound of her brother-in-law's homestead as a sign that she is not cohabiting with him, although he is still her official guardian.† An unfortunate consequence of such a situation is that the widow in fact loses the protection of a designated marital partner. Promiscuity either by design or by default becomes a real possibility. As Victoria Akech reflected: "It is better to live with one man in the homestead in peace than live outside the homestead and play the prostitute."

Another alternative to the custom of the levirate allowed by many Catholic missionaries is to allow the Christian widow to move

---

*The reality of this concept is clearly illustrated in the Luo language. There are no specific terms for an unmarried adult. Consequently the "celibate" Catholic religious are often referred to as "Boys" or "Girls" and are addressed with Westernized terms such as "Sista," "Padri."

†This same solution is sometimes imposed on junior wives in order that the polygynous husband would be seen as free to receive baptism.

to the mission compound, where she builds a house and is given land for growing food. (Almost all the Catholic mission stations in the areas surveyed have taken in widows under this arrangement.) The major problem with this solution, besides reducing the widow to the status of a welfare recipient, is that it offers only temporary relief: sooner or later the widow has to settle up with her husband's lineage, especially in matters regarding the inheritance of her children. For example, the widow Helena, who lived at the Masonga Catholic Mission for many years, was eventually forced to return to her husband's homestead by her two sons who needed her presence there in order to receive their rightful inheritance, i.e., land and cattle for marriage. Furthermore, as in the previous solution, the widow loses the protection of a designated marital partner. This leaves her open to promiscuous relationships with casual friends, causing her to be known as a prostitute or the pastor's woman, since to the eyes of many it looks as if he were the man "inheriting" her. In a number of cases where a widow living at a mission station became pregnant, the Church leaders considered it a scandal to the Christians and required her to move off the mission property. The unspoken rule seems to be that widows living at Catholic missions are not to have sexual relations or at least are not to get pregnant.

Another alternative to the custom of the levirate presently fostered by the Catholic Church is that a widow should be allowed to remarry as a new wife in a new lineage, but this alternative, as will be shown, depends for its implementation on factors such as one's ethnic group, the descent and inheritance rules followed, the presence or absence of children, and the age of the widow (only 10 percent of the 106 widows interviewed had actually remarried).*

The final alternative proposed by the Catholic Church is that the widow should be allowed to continue to live in her husband's homestead, or in the homestead of one of his male relatives, or in her father's homestead as a single person without a designated marital partner.† Again, this alternative leaves the widow in an

---

*See Appendix A, Table 26.

†Both the Sukuma and Kwaya people studied in this research allow this practice.

undefined and insecure position within the society, especially if she is still young, for it allows her no stable marital relationship in which to fulfill her procreative needs with all their major social ramifications.

The consequence of the Church's pastoral opposition to a widow's leviratic union is such that the unattached widow is able to continue to be a practicing Christian, whereas her leviratic counterpart is judged to be in a state of sin (i.e., in a permanent condition of sin) and so is excluded from the sacraments of the Church. The distinction here is that the unattached widow, since she does not have a permanent "unlawful" sexual partner, can always have a firm purpose of amendment not to sin again; hence she can always be forgiven and reunited with the Church. On the other hand, the widow in the leviratic union is willingly cohabiting with her inheritor, and for her to confess her sexual involvement with him would have no meaning, for she has no desire to cease this involvement; hence she has no purpose of amendment and cannot be forgiven. * Ironically the impact of the Catholic pastoral policy is to favor the unstable situation of the unattached widow with its potential for promiscuity over the relatively stable and responsible situation of the leviratic widow.

Finally, it should be noted that the widow's conflict with the Church happens independently of her will and without consideration of the quality of her Christian witness and involvement in the Church prior to the death of her husband, as we have seen in the case of Victoria Akech. Usually the widow wants to continue in the Church as a full practicing member but is hindered by an event outside of her control, i.e., the death of her husband. It is axiomatic among some African Christians that a woman can be a practicing Christian only until she becomes a widow, unless old age intervenes.

In the light of the prohibition of the levirate by the Catholic Church, it seems important that this custom, as well as all other customs, should be evaluated from *within* its African context by

---

*This is a direct application of the principles of Christian sexual morality taught in the standard textbooks used in the Catholic seminaries prior to the Second Vatican Council. These principles are discussed in detail in Chapter IX, pp. 185ff.

people who are indigenous members of these various African cultures. Moreover, their evaluations should be given major consideration in the formulation of pastoral policies. Foreign missionaries cannot and should not be the sole guides in judging the fitness or unfitness of particular customs in the life of the African Christian Church. Since they are only partially at home in African cultures, they, of necessity, often use their Western values and social structures as norms for interpreting the morality of African customs and institutions.[2]

Thus, in order to approach this "widow" problem as well as other problems from an African point of view, a sociological research project was designed to collect empirical data on contemporary marital attitudes, values, and structures of four different African peoples living in northwest Tanzania.* It was felt that this kind of empirical data, drawn from African people themselves, would provide an entirely new basis for assessing, evaluating, and discussing the theological problem of adapting Christianity to specific African marriage customs and institutions.

There were four questions of major interest in the design of the research project. The first question was: Have new influences, especially the preaching of the Christian religion, had any measurable impact on traditional African marriage customs and institutions? Second: Have the distinct African ethnic groups responded similarly or differently to the Christian marriage customs taught by missionaries, especially Catholic missionaries? Third: Are the Christian churches' marital teachings based on an understanding of local culture, are they clearly taught to the people, and are they capable of being assimilated without unreasonable difficulty? Fourth: Where there is apparent acceptance of Christian teachings regarding marriage, is this due to (1) support of an already established pattern that had the backing of traditional wisdom, law, and mores; (2) conversion to the Christian faith; (3) exposure to economic and educational influences; or (4) a combination of these factors?

---

*On the basis of the data collected, two additional studies are projected: one on polygamy, the other on "trial marriage."

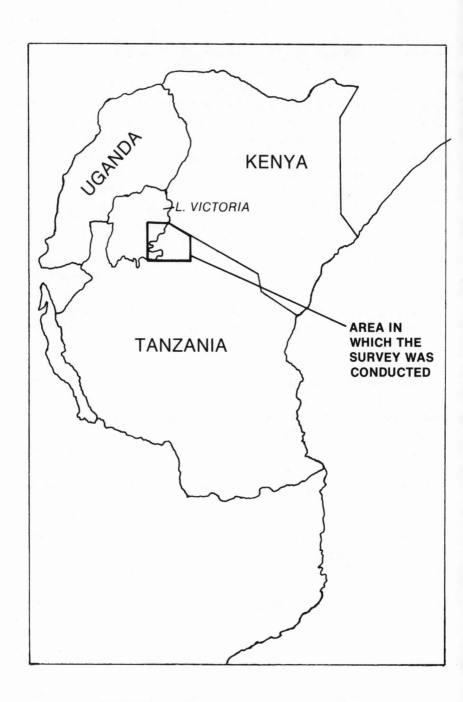

TANZANIA AND NEIGHBORING COUNTRIES

Tanzania, a nation of more than 15,000,000 (1978 estimate) has been politically independent since 1961. It lies south of the equator, and borders on Kenya and Uganda to the north, Rwanda, Burundi, and Zaire to the west, Zambia, Malawi, and Mozambique to the south, and the Indian Ocean to the east. The 1967 census reported that there were 3,700,000 people whose household heads were Christians; 3,362,000 whose household heads were Muslims, and 4,200,000 whose household heads followed traditional beliefs. The United Republic of Tanzania, *1967 Census*, III, 251.

With these questions in mind, several criteria were used in the selection of the specific African people for the research. These criteria were intended to accentuate the differences in the responses of each people to Christian teachings on marriage, differences due to varying cultural presuppositions about marriage. The first criterion was that the peoples selected should represent distinct cultures: language was considered one of the important indicators of the distinctiveness of each culture.[3] The second criterion was that the peoples selected should include a mix of those following patrilineal and matrilineal rules of inheritance and descent: such rules, as will be shown, have far-reaching implications for marriage institutions and customs. The third criterion was that the peoples selected should have been in pastoral contact with Catholic missionaries from the Maryknoll mission society,[4] a U.S. based organization, for at least a generation: this would give both an element of continuity as well as a certain consistency to the type of Christianity preached and enforced and the type of pastoral approach employed.*

On the basis of these criteria, the following three peoples were selected: The Luo, a "nilotic" *patrilineal* people; the Kuria, a "Bantu" *patrilineal* people, and the Kwaya, a "Bantu" *matrilineal* people.† All three had been in contact with Maryknoll missionaries

---

*The Maryknoll society accepts only North Americans into its membership, and even though there may have been different theological preparation, the members share a common pastoral approach learnt from the American Church. The same may not be true of the multinational missionary societies such as the "White Fathers" or the "Mill Hill Fathers" who have no shared pastoral approach learnt from a common "home" Church.

†The terms "Bantu," and "nilotic," are extremely general linguistic classifications based on some similarity in structure and sound. See Roland Oliver and Gervase Mathew, *History of East Africa* (London: Oxford University Press, 1963), pp. 60–61.

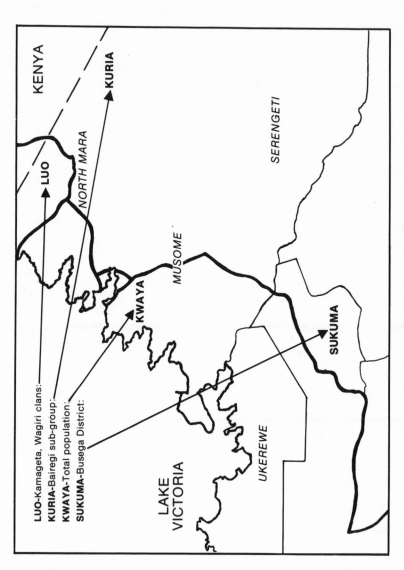

LUO-Kamageta, Wagiri clans:
KURIA-Bairegi sub-group:
KWAYA-Total population:
SUKUMA-Busega District:

KENYA

LUO

KURIA

NORTH MARA

MUSOME

KWAYA

SERENGETI

LAKE
VICTORIA

UKEREWE

SUKUMA

AREAS OF TANZANIA SURVEYED

The sociological survey concentrated on the Mara region of Tanzania where three of the four peoples surveyed reside. Geographically the Mara region, which takes in the Musoma and North Mara districts, is situated like a rectangle. To the north lies the Kenya border along which the Juria and Luo people reside; to the east and south the vast plain of the Serengeti, and to the west the shore of Lake Victoria: the homeland of the Kwaya. This section of Tanzania is one of the most linguistically diverse areas of the whole country. The people of Mara represent twelve or more distinct ethnic groups, adding an unparalleled cultural richness and variety to the whole region.[5]

South of the Mara region, along the southern and southeastern shore of the Lake is the territory of the Sukuma people—the fourth people selected. The part of Sukumaland surveyed, the sub-district of Busega, is along the extreme southeastern corner of Lake Victoria.

The history of the Catholic Church in this part of Tanzania began with the opening of a mission among the Sukuma by the "White Fathers," in 1878 at Bukumbi near the present port city of Mwanza. In 1911 they started a mission 135 miles to the north among the Kwaya people at Nyegina in the Musoma district. Twenty-five years later, in 1936, they crossed the Mara Bay and opened a mission among the Luo people at a place called Kowak, about 25 miles north of Nyegina. In 1946 the White Fathers were joined in the Mara region by four Maryknoll missionary priests from the United States. Two of the missionaries, Frs. Collins and Bayless, were assigned to Nyegina; the other two, Frs. Brannigan and Good to Kowak: Good to work among the Luo and Brannigan among the Kuria. Three years later, Brannigan opened a permanent mission among the Kuria at a place called Rosana. In 1954, four Maryknollers, including the veterans Bayless and Brannigan, took over pastoral responsibility for the Busega district—the Sukuma area covered in the survey.[6]

since 1946. A fourth people, the "Bantu" *patrilineal* Sukuma, were later added to the project in response to a request from the Mary-knoll Fathers—the sponsors of the research.[7]

These four peoples made the following contrasts and comparisons possible.

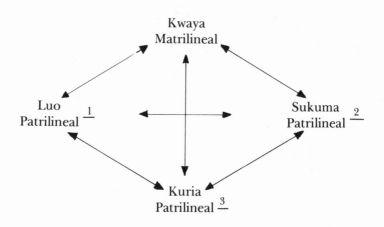

It may appear strange to the reader that there would be in Africa these kinds of radical differences among neighboring peoples. Yet this is the case in many areas. For example one can walk through an area like Nyabirongo (see map, p. 42) where the Kuria and Luo lands intersect and find them living side by side despite major differences in language and customs. One effect of this is to make the African very aware of the pluralistic nature of human societies. Thus instead of being a "tribalized" man in a closed society, as he is so often pictured by tourists, popular fiction, and even reputably scientific monographs, he tends to be open to novelty, and very sophisticated culturally. The ironic thing is that, contrary to popular belief, it is the African, not the Westerner who is more understanding and respectful of diverse points of view, and more pluralistic in outlook. The Westerner is often so narrowed by his mass culture that he is hardly aware of the bigger and infinitely

more complex world surrounding him; consequently he is closed
to being influenced by it. The charm of the African to so many
Western people is that they feel immediately accepted by the Africans as human beings and treated as such: an acceptance that is
often misinterpreted as due to the childish and unsophisticated
nature of the Africans rather than to their deep understanding of
the human condition and their openness to novelty. Actually sometimes it is the Western man who is the childish and unsophisticated
one, for he often cannot reciprocate and accept the African on
even the most basic human level, nor is he open to learning from
him even after many years of personal contact.

Once selected, each of these peoples was studied in four related
but separate projects. The first was through all available literature
and monographs, the second through a sociological survey using a
questionnaire, the third through special interviews with selected
people, and the fourth through personal interviews with the
Catholic Church leaders, both indigenous and missionary.

In the second phase, the sociological survey phase, a questionnaire, the source of the new empirical data, was administered to
1,217 adults (selected on a random basis) by trained interviewers in

1. Luo interviewer Adriano Onyando at work

the four vernacular languages.[8] The questions asked relating to widows are as follows:*

1. *"In this country can widows remarry?" "Why?"*
2. *"Do widows want to remarry in this country?"*
3. *"If a widow cannot remarry who can best take care of her?"*
4. *"Are widows who are cohabiting with their brothers-in-law always taken care of just like wives?"*
5. *"Why do the Christian churches forbid the practice of inheriting a dead brother's wife?"*
6. *"Do you approve or disapprove of the Christian churches censuring widows who are cohabiting with their brothers-in-law?" "Why?"*

(The following two illustrations, featuring the first and sixth questions give a brief preview of the differences among the responses of the people surveyed and their reactions to the Church's prohibition of the levirate.)

ILLUSTRATION 1—OPINIONS REGARDING THE POSSIBILITY OF WIDOWS REMARRYING

Can Widows Remarry?	(%) Ethnic Group				% Total
	% Luo	% Kuria	% Kwaya	% Sukuma	
Yes.....................	2	16	74	91	46
Depends	1	17	19	7	11
No......................	97	67	7	2	43
Total % Number	100 (297)	100 (301)	100 (309)	100 (300)	100 (1207)

This table shows the radical differences among the four peoples surveyed. At the one extreme there is the Luo with over 97% responding that a widow *cannot* remarry. At the other extreme there is the Sukuma people with over 91% responding that a widow *can* remarry. Between these extremes, there are the Kuria people who are similar to the Luo in their responses and the Kwaya people who are similar to the Sukuma.

---

*For responses to these questions, see Appendix A, Tables 27–36.

**ILLUSTRATION 2—ATTITUDES REGARDING THE CHRISTIAN CHURCHES'
PROHIBITION OF THE LEVIRATIC UNION**

Attitudes	Ethnic Group				%Total
	%Luo	%Kuria	%Kwaya	%Sukuma	
Approve	17	35	74	34.5	40
Disapprove....................	74	54	26	64.5	55
Do not know	9	11	—	1	5
Total %	100	100	100	100	100
Number	(304)	(302)	(308)	(301)	(1,215)

This table shows that 55% of the people surveyed disapproved of the churches' prohibition of the levirate. Interestingly, it is the matrilineal Kwaya people, who do not have a traditional leviratic custom, who are the most approving of the churches' prohibition (74%)

In the third phase of the research, the special interview phase, these same questions were asked of approximately 120 adults (30 per area) selected according to age group, marital status, sex, religious affiliation, and education. These interviews, known as in-depth interviews since they probe into the background and context of each answer, encouraged the respondent to fully explain all his or her answers and add any information or comments deemed relevant. They were both a check on the validity of the *Questionnaire* responses and a help in interpreting those responses. (Questionnaire responses are, by nature, short and to the point.) For example, I can recall thinking that the survey response: "a widow cannot remarry because her deceased husband didn't divorce her," was a meaningless and irrelevant answer until the in-depth interview pointed out how a widow is not seen as free to remarry until her husband's lineage actually institutes divorce proceedings and sends her away.

In the fourth stage of the project, the personal interviews with Catholic Church leaders, empirical data on the Catholic Church's pastoral position was obtained by means of in-depth interviews conducted with 115 leaders, both clerical and lay, missionary and

African, living and working in the areas surveyed.* These interviews consisted of thirty-six questions concerning Catholic Church
marriage discipline and teachings.† These questions were aimed at
discovering (1) the official pastoral policy of the Catholic Church
regarding marital issues such as polygamy, divorce, the leviratic
union, widow remarriage, cohabitation, etc.; (2) the leaders' personal opinions about this pastoral policy; i.e., whether they agreed
with it and whether they saw it as fitting and necessary for the
African Church; and (3) the changes the leaders wished to see
made in this pastoral policy. The questions asked of the Catholic
leaders relating to widows are as follows:

1. *"Can widows usually be remarried in this area?"*
2. *"Do (should)‡ you allow widows in leviratic unions access to the
   sacraments?"*
3. *"Is the levirate really a marriage in the full sense or is it a way of
   caring for widows?"*
4. *"What pastoral changes should be made for widows?"*§

(Illustration 3 gives a preview of the way the leaders responded to
question four.)

In the analysis of these interviews, the responses of the catechists
(African lay religion teachers and leaders), since they do most of
the teaching of Christian doctrine, were given equal weight with
the responses of the ordained leaders of the Catholic Church, i.e.,

---

*A total of twenty-seven Maryknoll missionaries, four African priests, and
eighty-four African lay religious teachers, called "catechists," were interviewed.
Seventeen of the catechists had had a special two-year training course in religious
education and community leadership.

†These questions were translated into the four vernacular languages; the same
care was taken as with the survey questionnaire to ensure that the translations
were accurate and correct.

‡By mistake, this question was translated into the four vernacular languages in
two different ways. One meant: *should* you allow widows . . . ; the other meant: *do*
you allow widows. . . . The different meanings will be pointed out when the
material is discussed in the text.

§See Appendix A, Tables 37–39 for the responses to these questions.

ILLUSTRATION 3—CATHOLIC CHURCH LEADERS' SUGGESTED PASTORAL
CHANGES REGARDING WIDOWS

Changes Suggested	Areas Surveyed				% Total
	% Luo Leaders	% Kuria Leaders	% Kwaya Leaders	% Sukuma Leaders	
Work to enable widow remarriage	10	30	44	59	34
Reinvestigate the leviratic problem......	7	—	38	—	4
Accept the levirate fully............	48	56	13	14	39
Accept the levirate with qualification	13	14	—	17	12
Help widows spiritually and temporally......................	22	—	6	10	11
Total %	100	100	100	100	100
Number	(31)	(27)	(16)	(29)	(103)

This table shows that 39% of all the Catholic Church leaders call for a full acceptance of the leviratic custom, with another 12% calling for a qualified acceptance. Thus a total of over 50% do not see this custom as radically incompatible with Christian moral teachings.

the local African and foreign missionary priests. *It was felt that the catechists' opinions on these marital issues would be an excellent indicator of what was taught to the African Christians. Interestingly, the interviews with the Catholic leaders showed that there was, in general, close agreement between the opinions of the missionaries and African priests on the one hand and those of the catechists on the other.

---

*The catechists also do the recruitment, preparation, and presentation of the people for baptism into the Catholic Church; the teaching role of the ordained priests in most cases is and was supervisory.

2. Kwaya interviewer
Mara Bay on Lake Victoria visible in background

During a three-week training period each of the sixteen interviewers conducted 25 to 30 practice interviews using an intermediate version of the
questionnaire. They were instructed to make corrections and changes in the
questions as they saw fit. These corrections and changes were evaluated at
the close of the training session and many were incorporated into the final
form of the questionnaire.

Once the four phases of the research had been completed, the
data collected was coded, computerized, and then subjected to
critical analysis, beginning with the material relating to widows.
(For those interested, the details of the methodology and tech-
niques employed in the data collection and computer program-
ming can be found in the Ph.D dissertation written from this
research.)* It was not the purpose of the analysis to delineate
precisely fine distinctions between categories of answers or to de-

---

*Michael Kirwen, "The Christian Prohibition of the African Leviratic Custom,"
Ph.D. Dissertation, St. Michael's College, University of Toronto, 1974. (Available
on microfilm from the University of Ottawa, Canada, and the University of
Michigan, Ann Arbor, Michigan, U.S.A.)

scribe in detail all the customary rites; it sought only (1) to present the general attitudes, practices, and opinions regarding the institutions for the care of widows; (2) to highlight the differences between the four peoples in ways of relating maritally to widows; (3) to measure the changes (if any) in practices and attitudes regarding widows that can be attributed to new influences, especially those of Christianity and education.* We now turn to a discussion of the Luo customs for the care of widows.

---

*In the analysis of the data, particular attention was given to the influence of the following independent variables: (1) ethnic group, (2) descent pattern, (3) membership in a Christian religion, (4) education, (5) sex, and (6) marital status. These variables were automatically cross-tabulated with all the responses. Other independent variables such as mobility, wealth, leadership, skills, and wage work were also considered and, if found to be statisically significant, were included in the analysis.

NOTES

1. See M. G. Whisson, "The Will of God and the Wiles of Men" (paper read at a conference of the East African Institute of Social Research, Makerere University College, held at Limuru, Kenya, January 1962), p. 19. Also G. Wilson, *Chik gi Tim Luo* (Luo Customary Law) (Nairobi: Government printers, 1961), pp. 134–45.
The independent Protestant Churches, in general, do not prohibit this custom.
2. See Alyward Shorter, *Theology of Mission* (Notre Dame, Ind.: Fides, 1972), ch. 2 *passim*, esp. p. 23.
3. See Benjamin Lee Whorf, "Science and Linguistics," in *Make Men of Them,* ed. Charles Hughes (Chicago: Rand McNally, 1972), pp. 132 ff. Also Charles O. Frake, "The Ethnographic Study of Cognitive Systems," in *Readings in Anthropology,* ed. Morton Fried, (New York: Thomas Y. Crowell, 1968), p. 86.
4. The author, a Maryknoll missionary, was first assigned to Africa in 1963 to work among the Luo-speaking people of North Mara, Tanzania.
5. Joseph Carney, "The History of the Functional Structure of the Maryknoll Mission in Musoma and Shinyanga, Tanzania" (Ph.D. Dissertation, St. John's University, New York, 1973), pp. 25–26 (mimeograph copies available: Maryknoll Fathers, Maryknoll, New York).
The president and founding father of Tanzania, Julius Nyerere, is from the Musoma district.
6. Ibid., pp. 104, 395.
7. Since one-third of the Maryknoll personnel in Africa in 1972 (about thirty-

six priests and brothers) were working among the Sukuma, the Society felt that including the Sukuma in the research project would be worth the extra time and expense and would be of value to the missionary effort.

8. An extra thirty questionnaires were administered to Kwaya people living in Musoma Town in order to have data for comparing people in urban and rural situations.

CHAPTER TWO

Luo Attitudes and Customs Regarding Widows
The Patrilineal Pattern

The Luos of East Africa, the patrilineal* nilotic society of our widowed friend Victoria Akech, in 1972 numbered close to two million people—most of whom resided in Kenya. Since it was neither feasible nor desirable to sample this entire population,[1] two Luo clans, the Wagiri and the Kamageta, were selected for the study after careful consideration. These clans, living side by side along the Kenya-Tanzania border, constituted the Luo "universe" for the purposes of the research. Their combined population in 1971 was estimated at 23,500 with the Kamageta being twice the size of the Wagiri. The place of the Luo in the model is as follows. (They alone are nilotic in language and culture.)

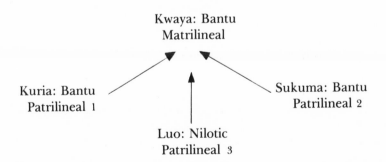

Kwaya: Bantu
Matrilineal

Kuria: Bantu
Patrilineal 1

Sukuma: Bantu
Patrilineal 2

Luo: Nilotic
Patrilineal 3

---

*Patrilineal means that the children are recruited into the clan or lineage of the father: Pater-lineal.

29

The Luo people allow a woman two legal choices upon the death of her husband: (1) she may remain in her deceased husband's homestead in a leviratic union, or (2) she may return to her father's home to remarry, provided she severs her connections with her late husband's clan. A meeting of Luo lawyers in 1972 gave these rules legal articulation as shown in the following illustration:

ILLUSTRATION 4—LEGAL EXPRESSION OF RULES RELATING TO LUO WIDOWS

When a husband dies his widow may either: (A) continue to live in her deceased husband's home, in which case she may cohabit with either (1) one of her dead husband's brothers, (2) one of her husband's male relatives, or (3) any man who has been adopted into the deceased husband's clan, though originally a stranger, e.g., a *Jadak Mocham Musumba.* However, her choice is subject to the approval of the family and clan elders (*Jodong Anyuola*) of her deceased husband. If she cohabits with a man of whom they do not approve, the man may be sued by the *Jodong Anyuola* for adultery.

The children of a levirate union belong to the family of the dead husband.

(B) return to her father's home. In such a case the *Dho Keny* (bridewealth) may be returnable according to the number of children the widow has . . . However, a widow may *not* return to her father's home before she first cohabits (even though for a very short period) with someone under (A) above, i.e., a leviratic union must be formed before a widow can sever her connections with the late husband's clan, and go back to her father.[2]

It is clear from the survey that even though the second option (returning to the father's home) is legally possible it is not seen as a viable or realistic option by over 94% of the Luo respondents. For them, a widow's remarriage is contingent on breaking the alliance between the two families by the return of the bridewealth*—an unreasonable and unnecessary action.

The force of these attitudes is clearly illustrated by the cases of two widows (known to the author) who remarried with single men in Catholic Church ceremonies with government marriage

---

*The amount of bridewealth paid varied from six to twenty cows; the majority paid around fifteen. See Appendix A, Table 40.

3. Luo polygynous family

The rate of plural marriage for the Luo area was 45%—the highest of all the four peoples surveyed (see Appendix A, Table 44). This high rate indicates clearly that plural marriage is still a viable, strong, and central institution within their social structures.

licenses. Both husbands later on rejected their marriages as not being true marriages. This happened even though the situation had been carefully discussed with the parties concerned, and all had agreed to act against the traditional practices regarding widows. When challenged on the fact that they had clearly agreed to marry the widows as their legal wives, both husbands responded that the widows could never become their legal wives as they were still the wives of their dead husbands. The men stated that they had been pressured by the widows to go through with the church ceremony so that the women could be reconciled with the Church. Their true feelings came to light when they had collected sufficient bridewealth to marry their own legal wives: then they wanted new church marriages.

A strong confirmation of the fact that widows do not remarry in these Luo clans is found in both their marital histories and in the in-depth interviews. In the marital histories, twenty-five of the

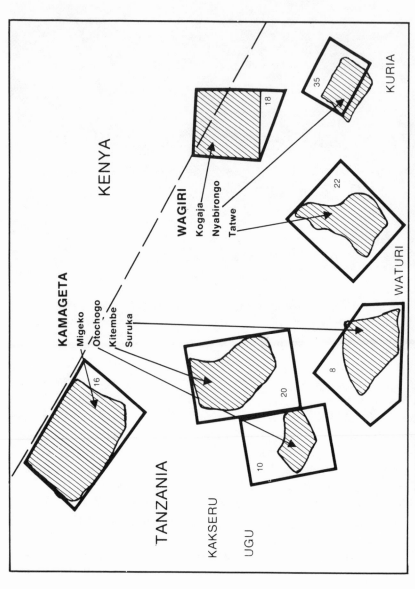

SELECTED CENSUS ENUMERATION AREAS IN THE LUO AREA

The northern limits of the Kamageta and Wagiri territory is the Tanzania/Kenya border. On the south they share a common border with the "Luoized" Wategi people; to the east the Wagiri share a border with a Kuria subgroup, and to the west the Kamageta share a border with the "Luoized" Kakseru and Ugu clans.

KAMAGETA, WAGIRI HISTORY

The remote history of the Wagiri and Kamageta clans is unknown. It appears that they were living in South Nyanza, Kenya (a large region just north of their present homeland) when it was invaded by the migrating Luo people about 150 years ago. They, along with other clans, were unable to resist the invasion as a group and were gradually absorbed, losing their Bantu languages and customs. About seventy years ago they began to migrate south, eventually settling in their present location.[3] The Luoization of the Kamageta people is such that they no longer speak anything but the Luo language and they no longer circumcise or follow Bantu initiation rites; whereas

the Wagiri people have only recently stopped following Bantu circumcision initiation rites and many of them are still bilingual.

AGRICULTURE

Agriculture is still on a subsistence basis. Food is grown for consumption and it is sold only if there happens to be a surplus. The main food crop cultivated is the cassava (manioc) root. This root can survive long periods of drought and ensures a source of food if the other crops fail. Formerly this root was cultivated only as a starvation food. Corn along with finger millet, sorghum, beans, bananas, and sweet potatoes are cultivated on a limited basis.

The major source of wealth is in the raising of livestock (cattle, sheep, and goats), and the men spend a great deal of their time in pasturing and taking care of their herds. The importance of livestock is magnified by its role and function in the payment of bridewealth. Without possession of livestock there is no possibility of marriage.

twenty-six widows (22% of the married women) reported that they had not remarried (there was no response recorded for the twenty-sixth) and all but four stated that they had cohabited in leviratic unions.* At the same time 18% of the married men reported that they had cohabited with widows at one time or another.† In the in-depth interviews there was overwhelming support for the survey's negative response to the possibility and desirability of widow remarriage.

When asked the reasons why a widow cannot remarry, half of the Luos responded that, "she is already married and cannot be married twice as she is someone's wife"[4]—a response clearly at odds with accepted Western attitudes and customs regarding multiple marriage and ways of relating to those deceased. For the Luos, a person physically dead is still considered alive, present, and capable of influencing the living. These relationships are seen to continue on intact through the barriers of physical death. Table 1 shows the major reasons cited by the Luos against widow remarriage.

TABLE 1

REASONS LUOS GAVE WHY WIDOWS CANNOT REMARRY (%)

Reasons Given	% Luo
She is already married, cannot be married twice; she is someone's wife	50
The bridewealth has already been paid; it is not right to take cows twice to a girl's village	22
A widow is always just taken by a brother-in-law or she should find someone to take care of her	23
Other	5
Total %	100
Number	(286)

---

*See Appendix A, Tables 26, 41.
†See Appendix A, Tables 42, 43.

These three reasons appeal to the traditional attitudes that (1) a widow is still considered married even though her husband has physically died; (2) the continuation of the marriage is determined by the fact that the bridewealth paid by the husband's lineage had not been returned; (3) a widow is cared for by her brother-in-law, who cohabits with her in a levirate union substituting for the dead husband. The remaining 5% of the Luos, grouped into the "other" category, gave low frequency responses such as, "She (widow) would not want to leave her children"; "she did nothing that would cause her to be removed from her husband's lineage"; "the dead husband would put the evil eye on her."*

The thirty in-depth interviews indicated that the three reasons given in Table 1 are closely associated in the minds of the people, i.e., almost all the respondents cited these three factors when pressed for more explanation as to why widows cannot remarry. The following additional comments were made: "The widow is in the midst of her brothers-in-law who are now her husbands"; "they (her brothers-in-law) stand in the place of the dead husband"; "the cows with which her husband married her didn't die, all his things are still alive."

The phenomenon of paying bridewealth to the father of the girl is a very involved and complicated part of Luo social structure. The Luos themselves described it in terms of "payment," "gift," "sign of real marriage," "security and identity of children." It is intimately bound up with the creation of alliances between the lineages; it assures the paternal inheritance and identity of the children. One must be careful, therefore, not to interpret the "payment" of bridewealth as a purely economic transaction, a real "buying"—in a Western economic sense—of the bride. For it is also a highly symbolic action, perhaps akin to the Western custom of giving an engagement ring or expensive gifts to one's prospective bride. Notice that the Western version of bridewealth, i.e., the exchange of expensive gifts, involves only individuals, whereas the African version involves whole lineages (clans).[5]

When asked why widows themselves do not want to remarry

---

*These responses are too few in number to be significant statistically, but they sometimes give added information and insight on an issue.

4. View of Luoland
The Otochogo market is seen in the background

There are no high schools in the area covered by the survey but there are six government-supported primary schools (grades 1 to 7). Three of them are sponsored by the government and one each by the Catholic, Mennonite, and Seventh Day Adventist school agencies. (According to the figures supplied by the government, primary education in 1971 was available to about 50% of the eligible children.)[6]

(Table 2), over 50% gave basically the same reasons as to why widows are unable to remarry, namely the widows know that they are still wives—they are not free for remarriage. This points out how the English term "widow" when applied to an African woman is not used univocally; the African "widow" is still considered to be a functioning, legal wife. In the Luo language, for example, the technical term for a widow is *chi liel* literally a "wife of a grave." (Not "*widow* of a grave" but "*wife* of a grave.")

Other respondents said that the widow could not remarry because of the traditional sanction that the dead husband would put the "evil eye" on her, i.e., cause her sickness and misfortunes (19%). Others observed that it is just bad luck that the husband died—his death does not mean that the widow had been divorced (15%). A few mentioned that a widow would not want to be parted from her children (6%)—a necessary condition for remarriage. Luo children, as already indicated, belong in perpetuum to the lineage of their fathers.

TABLE 2

REASONS LUOS GAVE WHY WIDOWS DO NOT WANT TO REMARRY (%)

Reasons Given	% Luo
She knows she is the wife of a family; she is already married	55
The dead husband would put the evil eye on her and the "men" would stop her	19
It is just bad luck that her husband died, he did not divorce her	15
She would not want to leave her children	6
Other	5
Total %	100
Number	(269)

Again the in-depth interviews on the question of widows wanting to remarry indicated the interrelatedness of the four reasons stated above in Table 2. Moreover they added the following comments: "who would agree to take on the responsibilities of a wife with children if not the brother-in-law?"; "she stays in her husband's place so the name of the husband won't be lost"; "if married with cows, no other family could begin to marry her."

Thus we see that the main reason for widows not wanting to remarry is the same reason why widows cannot remarry: i.e., that widows are still wives and hence are not free to remarry. In addition, two important sanctions were indicated that operate against those who break with this custom: namely, bewitching by the dead husband and separation from one's children.

When asked who could best take care of a widow if she could not remarry, the overwhelming majority of the Luo respondents stated that it was the brother-in-law (86%), with the remaining few saying it was a relative of the dead husband (9%).* The reasons given in the in-depth interviews for the choice of the brother-in-law were: "this is Luo custom"; "he is like her husband"; "a woman with children knows that her people (husband's lineage) will always help her if her husband dies"; "the wealth which married her came from the joint efforts of her husband's lineage."

The fourth question asked was whether a widow is cared for just like a wife: 11% said that she is "frequently" or "always," 21% said "sometimes," and 68% "rarely" or "never."† The one reason given in the in-depth interviews for the category of "frequently" was that "the widow would leave to cohabit with another if not properly cared for, especially if she was still young." The reason for the "sometimes" category was that it "depended upon the wealth of the widow." The reasons for the "rarely" or "never" category were "her husband was dead and no one will care for her like he did"; "it is not necessary for anyone to help her as she is a 'wife of troubles' "; "there is jealousy with his (the brother-in-law's) wife."

In summary, we see that the Luo people maintain and insist upon the levirate union as the preferred and ordinary way in which to care for widows. Over 94% of them do not see how widows can remarry, and do not feel that they *want* to remarry. Conformity to this pattern of behavior is ensured: by the threat of the dead husband's "evil eye," by the necessity of parting with one's children, by the difficulties of persuading one's lineage to pay back the bridewealth, and by the fact that no Luo man would marry a widow who is still regarded as someone's legal wife. Furthermore, there is no evidence of any change in attitude regarding the levirate, on the part of Christian Luos, that would indicate an acceptance of the new "Christian" way to care for widows, even though their churches have declared the traditional leviratic practice to be immoral. Given these circumstances it is not surprising that Victoria Akech wondered whether the Church knows what it is doing when it promotes for widows either remarriage or the single state.

---

*See Appendix A, Table 32.

†See Appendix A, Table 33.

5. Young Luo mother and sister

Luo Reaction to the Christian Prohibition
of the Leviratic Custom

Given the fact that the Luos not only practice the leviratic custom but also strongly defend it as reasonable and fitting, one cannot help but wonder what they think about the churches' opposition to this custom and what they understand it to mean. To investigate this, the Luo were asked *why* they thought the churches opposed the levirate. Not surprisingly, 20% said they did not know why, while 43% responded that it was purely a matter of "ecclesiastical" custom, i.e., a rule or regulation without specific moral content. Another 18% explained that the churches are opposed because the widow is "not the brother-in-law's wife but like a polygamous second wife"; 8% claimed that the levirate was "forbidden by God."* Cross-tabulation with the independent variables showed

---

*See Appendix A, Table 34. Luo widows stressed that the prohibition was due to church custom; only two said that it was due to the fact that the widow is "not his wife."

*6. Luo (Wagiri) monogamous family: the husband is a
catechist at the nearby Catholic mission*

The Catholic mission was built at Tatwe in the Wagiri clan area in 1959 and
intensive evangelization was then undertaken. By 1971 there had been over
2,600 adults and 3,700 children baptized and 350 marriages officially recorded.

that the reason that the leviratic widow is like a polygamous second
wife was given only by those who belonged to a Christian religion.
This is the first and only case in which African Christians articulated a specific reason that was not also stated by African non-
Christians. This indicates that this reason has been taught by the
churches as an explanation for their opposition to the levirate. As
we shall see, the absence of any leviratic institution in Europe and
North America led the theologians to interpret this custom as a
type of polygamy.* But the levirate is not polygamy. The Africans
clearly indicate this by saying that the leviratic widows remain
married to their deceased (legal) husbands.

---

*See Chapter VII, pp. 166ff., where this point is fully discussed.

Table 3 shows the differences in the reasons given by the Christians and non-Christians as to why the churches forbid the levirate.

TABLE 3

REASONS GIVEN FOR THE CHRISTIAN PROHIBITION OF THE LEVIRATE
BY RELIGIOUS AFFILIATION (CHRISTIAN/NON-CHRISTIAN) (%)

Reasons Given	RELIGIOUS AFFILIATION		% Total
	% Christian	% Non-Christian	
It is a custom of Christians......................	46	29	43
Widow is not his wife; like a second wife..........	22	—	18
God forbids the levirate	8	8	8
Do not know church discipline	14	49	20
Other	10	14	11
Total %	100	100	100
Number	(255)	(49)	(304)

The independent Protestant Church members gave a significantly different response to this question. Close to 30% of them said that they did not even know of this prohibition—an indication that this custom does not cause much difficulty within their communities. Furthermore, six of them stated that the prohibition of the levirate by certain Christian churches was a result of "pride in seeking to make themselves appear as better Christians." These different denominational responses correlate with the general thesis that the independent Christian churches often arise in opposition to rigorous pastoral policies, especially in the area of marriage, of the institutional Christian churches. Furthermore, the independent churches generally proclaim a brand of Christianity that is compatible with traditional African values and customs. Evidences for these differences are illustrated in Table 4.

TABLE 4

REASONS GIVEN BY LUO CHRISTIANS FOR THE PROHIBITION OF THE LEVIRATE
BY TYPE OF CHRISTIAN AFFILIATION (%)

Reasons Given	Types of Christian Affiliation			% Total
	% Catholic	% Mainline Protestants	% Independent Protestants	
It is a custom of Christians.....................	51	49	24	46
Widow is not his wife; like a second wife..........	23	25	12	22
God forbids the levirate	9	6	5	8
Do not know church discipline	13	10	27	14
Other	4	10	32	10
Total % Number	100 (124)	100 (49)	100 (83)	100 (256)

The in-depth interviews' distribution of responses as to why the Church forbids the levirate was similar to that of the survey's. The comments added to the answer that it is "merely Church custom" were: "it is the rule of the Church"; "the custom breaks the matrimony of the Church"; "it is said to be sinful"; "Christians just follow what they are taught"; "if one has one wife and takes another, one becomes like a pagan." The comments on the second answer, that the "widow is not his wife; but like a second wife" were: "it is a sin before God"; "the woman is merely a prostitute"; "if he takes her he will start to desire her again (sexually)"; "Christians know yet break the laws of Christ and religion."

ILLUSTRATION 5—RELIGIOUS AFFILIATIONS OF LUO ADULTS*

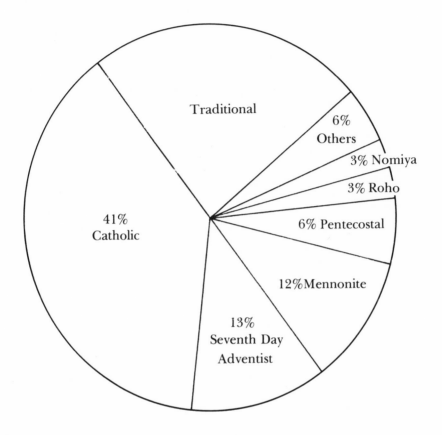

This illustration shows that the Luo areas surveyed have been heavily proselytized, with more than 80% of both the Wagiri and Kamageta adults claiming membership in a Christian religion—this makes them an ideal group with which to assess changes due to possible Christian influence—although the religious affiliations of each clan were quite different. The Kamageta Christian people were 40% Catholic, 20% Mennonite, and 20% Seventh Day Adventist, whereas the Wagiri were 65% Catholic, 10% Pentecostal, and 7% Seventh Day Adventist. The greater percentage of Catholics among the Wagiri can be explained by the fact that the Catholics built their mission center in Wagiri territory while the Mennonites and Seventh Day Adventists built their schools and churches in Kamageta territory.

The Luos were then asked whether they approved of the Christian churches' prohibition of the levirate and, as might be expected, only 17% said "yes" while 74% said "no."* All but one who said "yes" were members of a Christian church, four-fifths attended religious service at least 2 to 3 times a month and two-thirds were women.† (The latter indicates that the proscription of the levirate is more attractive to Christian women than men, although a plausible reason for this is not apparent from the survey data.) Here we have clear evidence of Christian influence on the attitudes of active Christians regarding the morality of a traditional custom. This influence is shown in Table 5.

TABLE 5

LUO ATTITUDES REGARDING THE CHRISTIAN PROHIBITION OF THE LEVIRATE
BY RELIGIOUS AFFILIATION (CRISTIAN/NON-CHRISTIAN) (%)

Attitudes	Religious Affiliation		% Total
	% Christian	% Non-Christian	
Approve	20	2	17
Disapprove.....................	77	59	74
Do not know	3	39	9
Total % Number	100 (255)	100 (50)	100 (305)

The reason most frequently given for approving the churches' prohibition was that the widow is like a second wife—an un-Chris-

---

*See Illustration 2, p. 22. The in-depth interviews showed five respondents approving and twenty-five disapproving the churches' prohibition of the levirate.

†See Appendix A, Table 45. Other considerations showed that those respondents with more than a year's residence in an urban area and those who had studied in schools sponsored by both government and Christian agencies were less likely to approve of the prohibition. This may indicate that wider and more varied experiences tend to make the African more sensitive to traditional values.

7. View of Luoland showing how the homesteads were dispersed before the people were resettled in 1974 into village communities of 250 to 500 families.

tian situation (31%).* Others (26%) stated that this practice is against Christian teaching; 18% stated that the widow destroys another's sacrament of matrimony (the mutual pledge of monogamy); 8% said that the widow had sinned.† Representative comments in the in-depth interviews were: "the levirate custom always brings clashes with someone else's husband"; "levirate breaks up the church-style monogamous marriages."

The reasons given by those who did *not* approve of the churches' prohibition can be grouped into two categories: religious and moral. The religious category includes: "God did not forbid this custom (20%)";‡ "she is still a member of the Church and should be given her freedom (13%)"; "she still loves God and should be allowed to pray (8%)." The moral category includes: "she is in need and in difficulty with her family and she should be helped by her brother-in-law to make her house grow (16%)"; "she did not kill her husband—there is no reason to reject her; the Church brings troubles and gives people bad ideas (12%)"; "the widow is not a prostitute but she will become one if she does not stay with her brother-in-law (12%)"; "the Church law would have us throw away the bridewealth, give up the children, and drive away the women, who would be left to play the harlot (9%)." In the "other" category there were two responses of interest. One was: "It is necessary that the children of the dead brother be cared for (3%)"; the other: "failure to care for the widow shows a lack of love for the brother (3%)."§

The in-depth interviews indicated that these moral and religious reasons are not mutually exclusive, and that most of those who opposed the churches' prohibition would accept all of them as either primary or secondary reasons for their opposition. The comments in the in-depth interviews centered on the observation that failure to care properly for a widow will mean the loss of her dead husband's wealth and will lead to prostitution. (The plight of

---

*Nowhere is the widow called a second wife. She is always said to be *like* a second wife.

† See Appendix A, Table 35.

‡In a number of instances a comment was added to this response that God's approval of this custom is evident in the Old Testament.

§See Appendix A, Table 36.

the widow living under the care of the missions is cited as an example of this.) Likewise, it was stated that "no one will marry a widow anyway." Moreover, "she should be allowed to help herself" and "the rejection of traditional customs is tantamount to a rejection of the widow herself."

The marital histories of the Luo widows demonstrated that nine of the twenty-two *Christian* widows had been punished by their churches because of a leviratic union.* All of the punished widows had not remarried, and all had children under their care. Furthermore there was an age difference between the punished and unpunished widows. The unpunished widows tended to be over 45 years of age. This coincides with the fact that once a Luo woman is past menopause she no longer cohabits with a marital partner, hence she cannot be faulted for having a permanent "unlawful" relationship.†

Three of the censured widows agreed that their punishment was just and gave the following reasons: "God's laws were broken"; "the laws of the Church were not followed"; "I knowingly broke the laws because I still wanted a husband." The remaining six said that their punishments were unjust and gave their reasons: "I still love God and pray"; "I was inherited in order to have children—God wants us to have children"; "I followed our own customs"; "I can't be called a sinner as I didn't kill anybody"; "this punishment is bad in the sight of God"; "I don't agree with this prohibition."

Thirty of the Luo men were cohabiting or had cohabited with widows. Twenty-one of them were members of Christian churches and fifteen of them admitted to being censured by their churches because of the levirate.‡ They reported that they had been under a ban for ignoring this prohibition for periods of one to fifteen years: over half of them claiming five years or more, and all but one were still under the censure. Four said that their punishment was just;

---

*The Christian churches punish their members for failure to observe the ban on the levirate by refusing them the sacraments, e.g., Holy Communion; by expelling them from any position of leadership, e.g., position of church elder; and by stigmatizing them as sinful in the sight of God.

†As will be shown in Chapter IX, the churches' specific objection was to what they considered to be an unlawful sexual union and not to the institution as such.

‡See Appendix A, Table 46.

twelve said that it was unjust. Those who said it was just gave the following reasons: (1) "it was my mistake, I am a sinner"; (2) "I did not follow church law"; (3) "Jesus has already changed those pagan customs which overcame me." Those who said it was unjust gave these reasons: (1) "I took the widow in order to have children —God wants us to have children"; (2) "I still love God and pray"; (3) "I followed our customs"; (4) "I don't agree with this prohibition"; (5) "I did it to have a helper"; (6) "without me these women would be in trouble"; (7) "when I die I'll be buried alone (i.e., each man has to make his own decisions about his life)."

In summary we find that in the responses to these questions about church discipline, there is evidence for the influence of Christian teachings on a few Christian adults. However, the magnitude of this problem for the Christian Luo is clear: close to half of all the Christian widows and three-quarters of all the inheriting Christian brothers-in-law had been censured by their churches because of the levirate. These figures represent 12% of all the Christian men and women in the Luo areas surveyed—about 1,500 adults.

Responses of the Luo Catholic Leaders

In the face of this Christian/levirate conflict involving hundreds of baptized Luo Christians, many questions arise as to how this issue is dealt with in the pastoral order. That is, how do local Church leaders understand and justify the expulsion or the exclusion of leviratic widows and leviratic brothers-in-law from the Church? Do they see this as an unavoidable clash between the forces of paganism and Christianity? Do they hope to bring about the demise of this custom, at least for Christians? Do they preach a viable alternative to the levirate? Do they truly understand the nature of the leviratic custom?

In order to find answers to these questions, the following Luo Catholic Church leaders were interviewed: seven Maryknoll missionary priests,* one African priest, eight trained catechists (those who had completed an intensive two-year course in pastoral theol-

---

*Four of these men had more than twelve years of experience working among the Luos.

ogy) and fifteeen regular catechists. These men represent the formal leadership within the rural Luo Catholic Church and are the ones who explain Catholic doctrine and morality and enforce Church discipline.

The first question asked concerned the possibility of a widow remarrying. Six of the seven missionaries responded that a Luo widow could not remarry (the seventh made it clear that remarriage was possible only in a church ceremony). Twenty of the twenty-three catechists also said that widows could not remarry. Two of the remaining catechists said that remarriage is *now* a possibility and the final catechist stated that remarriage is possible only for a young widow.* Thus all but a few leaders are in agreement that remarriage for a Luo widow is not a real option.

The reasons given by the catechists for the widow's inability to remarry were the same traditional reasons as given in the survey: namely, "a wife of bridewealth is a wife of a lineage and is cared for by her brother-in-law," and "those who remarry are like prostitutes." It is clear from this that the catechists were fully aware of the traditional meaning and force of this custom.

The second question concerned the access of a widow to the sacraments of the Church while cohabiting with a leviratic partner. This question was asked only of the ordained priests, because the Luo language version of this question, used with the catechists, had a different meaning.† Five of the priests stated that a cohabiting widow cannot receive the sacraments. The reasons were: "the widow is living in the state of sin (two priests)," "the people (the congregation) are opposed to them receiving the sacraments (two priests)," "she is refused so as not to cause scandal (one priest)." Another priest said that the reception of the sacraments depends on whether the widow is in good faith, but generally "no," another that he would like to allow them so as to provoke a confrontation and thereby force a more acceptable solution to the problem. In these responses we see clearly expressed the Catholic Church's official *moral* objections to the leviratic custom, even though many

---

*See Appendix A, Table 37.

†The original question was mistranslated. The verb *yie* (to be in favor of) was used rather than *nyalo* (to be able).

of these leaders, as will be demonstrated, do not agree with these objections.

The mistranslated question asked only of the Luo catechists was: "Are you in favor of widows in leviratic unions receiving the *sacraments*?" Ten of the catechists gave an unqualified "yes." Of these, four gave the reason that, "the widow has no fault, she didn't kill her husband"; two others that "the widow is in much trouble and the reception of the sacraments would help her spiritually and materially." Seven of the catechists responded that the leviratic widow's reception of the sacraments depends on certain conditions. Their conditions were: (1) that the partner be single; (2) that he be a Christian. (Whether or not they envisaged a church marriage for the two is not clear from the data. Often one would look for a single man, usually old and poor, who could be persuaded to go through a church marriage with a widow to maintain the pretense that she was truly married even though the marriage was not accepted as real by the people.)

The remaining six catechists gave an unqualified "no" to the widows' reception of the sacraments, giving as reasons that: "her reception of the sacraments would cause scandal to others [the congregation]"; "the widow is resisting the will of God and not submitting to the laws of the Church"; "she is involved with another's husband in an un-Christian union"; "she cannot receive the sacraments, for there is no way to straighten out her marital status." The Luo catechists are clearly divided as to whether it is possible to reconcile leviratic widows with the Church. These differences are illustrated in Table 6.

When asked whether the leviratic union is seen as a way of caring for widows, or as a real marriage, the overwhelming majority of the leaders (29) responded that it is "a way of caring and not a marriage."* One exception, a missionary, said that it was "in between," and another missionary said that it was a marriage as it "sought to produce children—the purpose and meaning of marriage." From this question it is clear that the Church leaders do not view the leviratic union as a new polygamous marriage for either

---

*See Appendix A, Table 39.

TABLE 6

LUO CATECHISTS' ATTITUDES TOWARDS WIDOWS IN LEVIRATIC UNIONS
RECEIVING THE SACRAMENTS (N=23)

Attitude	Luo Catechist N.
Approve	10
Depends	7
Disapproves	6
Total	23

partner even though they might apply phrases such as "like a second wife" in describing the relationship.

The major reason given by six of the leaders for not calling the relationship a marriage is that the situation is unstable; i.e., the widow can leave whenever she wants, or she can be dismissed by the brother-in-law even after having had children by him, since the children take the name of the dead husband. Other reasons given were that "there is no bridewealth paid," "that this custom is the taking on of the burdens of the deceased brother," "that the widow is still called the wife of the dead husband," "that a single man is not considered married even if he is cohabiting with a widow."

When asked what changes should be made for widows in the Church's pastoral policy, half of all the Luo leaders said that the Christians should be allowed to follow this custom while remaining practicing Christians (see Table 7 below). Two leaders commented that the Church should still encourage remarriage but not force remarriage, since (1) "no one would marry a widow anyway"; (2) "widows in a leviratic union can live well"; and (3) "leviratic widows are not guilty of any fault and so can continue to be good Christians."

Moreover, three of the leaders would allow a widow to receive the sacraments under certain conditions. These conditions are: if she cohabits with a pagan—stipulated by one of the missionaries so as not to put a Christian brother-in-law in bad faith—or, just the opposite, if she cohabits with a Christian—stipulated by two cate-chists who were concerned about protecting her Christian faith. Six other leaders felt that ways should be found by which the Church could help a widow in her temporal and spiritual needs, e.g., training in a skill, etc.; two missionary leaders called for more investigation and three catechists said that the widow should be allowed to remarry, since the Church teaches that "death ends marriage." These suggestions are illustrated in Table 7.

TABLE 7

Proposed Pastoral Changes Regarding Leviratic Widows
by Type of Luo Catholic Church Leadership (n=29)

Changes Proposed	Luo Catholic Leadership		Total
	N. Missionary	N. African	
Accept the levirate fully	3	12	15
Accept the levirate with qualification	1	2	3
Help widows spiritually and temporally	1	5	6
Reinvestigate the leviratic problem	2	—	2
Work to enable widow remarriage	—	3	3
Total	7	22	29

Taken together these suggestions show the confusion, frustration, and indecision that exist on the part of the Catholic Church leaders trying to come to grips with this problem. One missionary com-plained that he would not unilaterally change the discipline regard-ing widows, even though he felt it to be wrong, because of the threat of ecclesiastical censure and because he could not guarantee to the parties involved that his decision would be final and that they would be left in peace. Thus he continued to enforce a policy that he personally found unacceptable.

The final question asked of the Church leaders was a general question regarding changes they would like to see in the current pastoral policies on marriage. One-third of the Luo leaders gave responses that related directly to the leviratic union.* This was the highest percentage among the leaders of the four peoples surveyed, indicating the seriousness and magnitude of the "widow" problem for the Luo people.

In summary, we find both the missionary and indigenous Christian leadership among the Luo unhappy with the Catholic Church's official stand on the custom of the levirate. Over half feel that this custom is compatible with Christianity and should be accepted (15), and a few others said that they would be willing to accept the custom under specific conditions (3). This means that close to two-thirds of the local Catholic Church leaders among the Luo are in the ambiguous position of enforcing a discipline with which they are not in sympathy and which they would like to see changed. Only three of the leaders supported the Church's policy that a widow should remarry if she wants a new marital partner. These objections to the Church's policy of proscribing the leviratic custom are held by both African and non-African leaders, indicating a similar assessment of the issue.

In conclusion, the reasons for the confusion and conflict between the official stand of the Catholic Church on the custom of the levirate and the role and function of this custom in the Luo society are now apparent. Three-quarters of the Luo people surveyed, together with two-thirds of their Catholic Church leaders, reject the official assessment of the Catholic Church regarding the nature and morality of this custom. They feel that the Church has not taken into account their patrilineal rules of inheritance and descent, the fact that they exchange bridewealth and that their marriages involve alliance between lineages (clans), not just individuals, and that the wife is both a wife of an individual and of a lineage. Furthermore, the Church has failed to see how this custom has

---

*See Appendix A, Table 55.

many positive values: it protects the widow against divorce and it enables the family of a widow to maintain its identity and achieve its goals in continuity with its origin.

Thus over 70% of the people questioned, people who are intimately involved in the Luo culture, judge that this custom is both morally and religiously *compatible* with the demands of Christianity. And they judge that the Catholic Church's prohibition is both unnecessary and without valid reasons. They therefore ask that this custom be allowed to function within the Christian community and not be made a stumbling block for widows and their brothers-in-law. Furthermore, the majority of leaders and people find objectionable the Church's teaching that remarriage or the single state is the only acceptable Christian solution to the dilemma of the widow: first because the Luo widow (usually) does not want the single state, and second because her freedom to remarry must presuppose a *divorce* settlement between her husband's and her father's lineages—a settlement that always separates her from her children. Ironically, the Church, in violation of its teachings on the indissolubility of marriage, promotes divorce when it promotes the remarriage of widows. For, as we have seen, the widow's marriage to her deceased husband is seen as continuing on despite his death and can only be broken or terminated by a traditional divorce—this point will be discussed fully later on. We now turn to a presentation of the Kuria customs for the care of widows.

NOTES

1. The aim of the research was to compare Luo marital customs, attitudes, and opinions with those of other African peoples—the smallest being the Kwaya with a population of 22,000. Thus to make the research "congruent" as already pointed out, it was only necessary to select a homogeneous group within the Luo-speaking population that approximated the Kwaya population in size.

2. Luo Law Panel, "The Law of Marriage and Divorce," Meeting held at Kisumu, Kenya, April, 1972, p. 1 (mimeographed).

For a description of the traditional inheritance ceremonies, see Paul Mboya, *Luo Kitgi Gi Timbgi* (Luo Customs and Traditions) (Kendu Bay, Kenya: African Herald Publishing House, 1965), pp. 126–27. Also E. C. Baker, "The Ba-Girango," (manuscript available in the Africana Collection, Library, University of Dar es Salaam, Tanzania), pp. 48–49.

3. This brief history was pieced together from the following sources: Bethwell A. Ogot, *Peoples of East Africa: History of the Southern Luo* (Nairobi: East African Publishing House, 1967), I. 41,200. Carole E. DuPre, *The Luo of Kenya,* (Washington, D.C.: Institute for Cross-Cultural Research, 1968), p. 15; Baker, "The Ba-Girango," pp. 4–6; H. Huber (manuscript on the customs of the Kwaya, Fribourg, Switzerland, c. 1966), p. 10.

4. The English phraseology of each response accurately represents the four vernacular African languages *(Dholuo, Kikuria, Kikwaya, Kisukuma)* used in the interviews. A literal English translation of each language would show slight differences in idioms.

5. Marcel Mauss, in *The Gift*, trans. Jan Cunnison (New York: W. W. Norton, 1954), presents the theory that the giving and receiving of gifts, in all societies, always entails reciprocal obligations and is the basis of all economic activity.

6. The United Republic of Tanzania, *Tanzania Second Five-Year Plan for Economic and Social Development, 1st July 1969–30th June, 1974* (Dar es Salaam: Government Printers, 1969), I, 149.

8. View of Kurialand
In background: the Myamwaga Catholic Mission

The Kuria, like the Luo, did not live in villages until 1974. At that time the government moved them into village communities of 200 to 500 families. There are four government-supported primary schools in the Bairegi area but no secondary schools.

CHAPTER THREE

Kuria Customs for the Care of Widows
The Importance of Initiation Groups

The eastern neighbors of our Luo people are the Kuria: a people radically different from the Luo in language and in many social customs, such as age groupings and initiation rites. However, the Kuria are very similar to the Luo in terms of the patrilineal rules of inheritance and descent and the payment of bridewealth, factors which would lead one to expect that they also have a leviratic custom for the care of widows: this is in fact the case. The vernacular languages of these two peoples are so different and difficult that practically no missionary has been able to learn both of them. Hence a missionary either works with one or the other of these people but not with both. Since 1972 a few new missionaries, trained in only the national language, Kiswahili, have been assigned to the Luo and Kuria Catholic missions without any understanding of the vernacular languages. This has unnecessarily complicated the pastoral work and caused a great deal of frustration for all concerned, since only 14% of the Kuria and 32% of the Luo have any fluency in Swahili.* The missionaries stereotype the Luo as a noisy and aggressive people who openly speak their minds, whereas they stereotype the Kuria as a quiet and submissive people who are reluctant to let one know exactly that they are thinking.

These percentages are from data gathered in 1973. However, there is increased comprehension because of the education of the youth in a Kiswahili medium.

The Kuria population in 1971 was estimated at over 200,000 people with 140,000 of them living in Tanzania.[1] As with the Luo, it was not desirable to sample the entire population. Accordingly, a

---

*See Appendix A. Table 57.

Kuria "sub-group," the Bairegi, was selected as the homogeneous group, the "universe," for the purpose of the research.[2] (The Bairegi had been bisected by the Tanzania-Kenya border when it was created in 1905. In 1972 it was estimated that only 15% of the Bairegi were living on the Kenya side of the border, but it proved impossible to do any interviews among them.)[3] The place of the Kuria in our model is as follows. (They together with the Sukuma represent a Banto-patrilineal language and culture.)

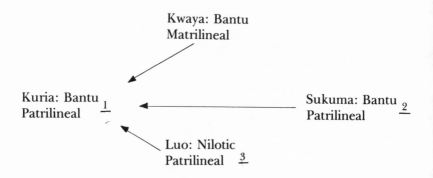

Kwaya: Bantu
Matrilineal

Kuria: Bantu [1]
Patrilineal

Sukuma: Bantu [2]
Patrilineal

Luo: Nilotic
Patrilineal [3]

As we have seen, the Luo in fact have only one viable option for the care of widows; i.e., a leviratic union, even though they legally recognize a second option, i.e., remarriage. By contrast, the Kuria recognize *four* legal options, all of which are real possibilities. They are as follows: (1) a widow can return to her father's home and be remarried; (2) a widow can cohabit with her brother-in-law in a leviratic union; (3) a widow can be leviratically *inherited* by her brother-in-law but choose to live alone and not cohabit with him; and (4) a widow can be leviratically inherited by her brother-in-law but choose to cohabit with a friend. (Two sources indicated that the latter two options are possible only if the widow is older and has adult sons.)[4]

The widow usually continues to reside in the homestead of her deceased husband. If her leviratic cohabitor happens to reside in a different place, he visits her periodically. However, under special circumstances, the Kuria widow will move to the homestead of her leviratic partner. The legal articulation of the rules relating to the care of widows is shown in Illustration 6:

ILLUSTRATION 6–KURIA RULES REGULATING WIDOWS

Widows are inherited by the brothers or, if there are no brothers, by the nearest relatives of the deceased, but only if they agree. If a widow refuses to be inherited, the bridewealth paid for her can be reclaimed . . . If the widow agrees to be inherited she does not necessarily become the wife of the heir. She can live near him but he cannot force her to become his wife.

If the widow wishes to return home and marry again into another family, the whole bridewealth, including the offspring of the bridewealth cattle, must be repaid whether she has children or not.

Legitimate children always belong to their father and their status cannot be altered by the payment or repayment of bridewealth.[5]

It is clear from the survey that the first option of returning home and being remarried is *more* than just a legal possibility for Kuria widows: three of the thirty widows in the Kuria sample reported that they had actually remarried.* This flexibility is apparent in the responses to the question of whether or not a widow *can* remarry: close to 33% responded that it is possible in general or under certain conditions; the remaining 67% gave an unqualified "no." These responses are illustrated in Table 8.

TABLE 8

Possibility of Widow Remarriage among Kuria People (%)

Can Widows Remarry?	% Kuria
Yes	16
Depends	17
No	67
Total %	100
Number	(301)

---

*See Appendix A, Table 26.

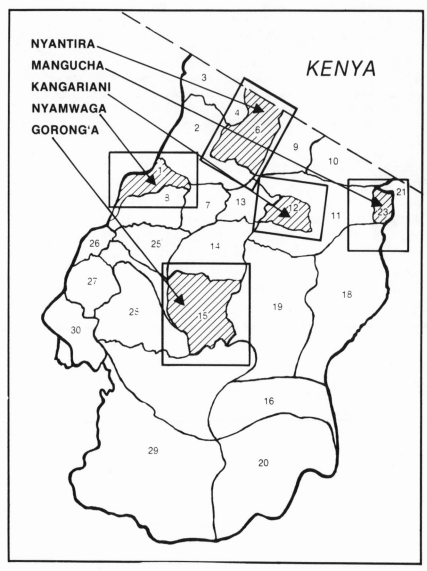

NYANTIRA
MANGUCHA
KANGARIANI
NYAMWAGA
GORONG'A

KENYA

SELECTED CENSUS ENUMERATION AREAS IN THE KURIA AREA

The territory of the Bairegi included in the survey has as its northern boundary the Tanzania-Kenya border, on the east it has a no-man's land inhabited by the Masai, on the south the Mara River, and on the west several different sub-groups of Kuria-speaking people. The beautiful Isuria escarpment cuts through this area, as can be seen in the photograph on page 69.

The population of this area in 1972, as calculated on the basis of the 1967 census, was 13,303 adults and 10,884 children: a total of 24,187.[6]

Nothing is known of the Kurias' early history beyond the fact that they formerly lived in the southern portion of Kenya and were forced to migrate southward by encroaching Masai and Luo peoples. Baker surmises that at one time the Kuria and the Luoized people of North Mara lived together with the Bantu Kavirondo in South Nyanza, Kenya forming a large political unit. But the invasion of the Nilotic tribes from the north was more than the group could withstand, and and it was broken up. Those who, like the Ba-Kuria, were the first to withdraw, retained their tribal customs, whilst those who remained behind were subjected to the influence of the newcomers.[7]

This divergence of opinion regarding a traditional pattern of behavior seemed at first to be unusual. However, closer scrutiny showed that it was due to a certain ambiguity in the question itself. The majority of the people understood the question to mean *usual or ordinary* behavior, i.e., can widows remarry (usually) and the answer is "no." Others understood the question to mean *exceptional* behavior, i.e., can widows remarry (under certain circumstances) and the answer obviously is "yes."

When asked for reasons why a widow *can* remarry, 41% cited sterility ("if she does not have any children"); 24% cited the need for support ("if she was unable to live on her own"); 21% cited the absence of any taboo ("there is nothing to oppose remarriage as her husband had died"); and 10% cited personal preference ("if she wants she can"). In these responses, surprisingly, we find a third of the Kuria people speaking as if traditional customs for the care of widows were not important; i.e., they see the death of the husband as "freeing" the widow for remarriage rather than seeing the original marriage as continuing. These answers are illustrated in Table 9.

TABLE 9

REASONS KURIA PEOPLE GAVE WHY WIDOWS CAN REMARRY (%)

Reasons Given	% Kuria
If she does not have children	41
If she wants to she can	10
There is nothing to oppose it as her husband has died	21
If she cannot live on her own	24(35)[a]
Other	4
Total %	100
Number	(99)

[a]Given as second reason by 10% of the respondents.

The question arises as to why this difference between the Luo and Kuria; i.e., why do the Kuria allow widows to remarry but not the Luo? The best answer, drawn from the data, appears to be an economic one. The Luo lineages, exchanging only fifteen cows for bridewealth, can "afford" to maintain barren widows in leviratic unions while marrying other wives to compensate for the widows' infertility. Furthermore the barren widows are seen as valuable allies in domestic work and activities since they are not encumbered by the care of children, and there is always hope that they will become fertile. The Kuria lineages on the other hand, since they exchange an average of thirty cows for bridewealth, often do not have the means (bridewealth) to marry other "compensatory" wives while maintaining barren widows. Hence there is pressure to recover the bridewealth by divorcing the barren widows (as has been indicated, bridewealth can only be recovered by means of legal divorce even though the husband is deceased) and initiate new marriages which, hopefully, will produce progeny for the lineage. Evidences for this explanation are as follows: (1) over 40% of the Kuria cited sterility as the major reason for the remarriage of widows; (2) 15% of the Kuria again cited sterility as the major cause of divorce as opposed to only 5% of the Luo; (3) only 28% of the Kuria were able to "afford" second wives as opposed to 45% of the Luo.

When those who responded that a widow *cannot* remarry were asked *why*, they reasoned exactly like the Luo, namely, that she is already married and can't be married twice (79%), that the bridewealth had already been paid and it isn't right to take cows twice to a girl's village (26%).* The in-depth interviews again confirmed that these two reasons are closely related: a woman is seen as being married only once in her lifetime no matter what happens to her husband. And, as long as the bridewealth given for her has not been returned, it is as senseless to speak of a second marriage as it is to speak of paying bridewealth twice.

When asked whether or not widows *want* to remarry, 86% of the respondents gave negative answers together with 100% of all the in-depth interviewees. The reasons being: she knows she is the wife

---

*See Appendix A, Table 28.

of a family (63%), it is just bad luck that her husband died—he did not divorce her (20%), she would not want to leave her children (18%). The only difference from the Luo responses to this question was the emphasis on the sanction of being separated from one's children and the de-emphasis of the sanction of the deceased husband's "evil eye." These answers are illustrated in Table 10.

TABLE 10

REASONS KURIAS GAVE WHY WIDOWS DO NOT WANT TO REMARRY (%)

Reasons Given	% Kuria
She knows she is the wife of a family; she is already married	63
The dead husband would put the evil eye on her and the men would stop her	2
It was just bad luck that her husband died, he did not divorce her	20(24)[a]
She would not want to leave her children	6(18)[a]
Other	9
Total %	100
Number	(257)

%Given as a second reason by respondents.

The principle reasons stated above are similar to the reasons given previously as to why widows *cannot* remarry. Taken together these reasons reinforce the attitude that the death of a husband neither terminates a marriage (thereby freeing a widow for remarriage) nor causes an automatic divorce where the widow would be forced to leave her husband's family and her children.

When asked who could best take care of a widow if she were not remarried, 46% said the brother-in-law, 38% said a relative of the husband, 14% said a friend—if there is no understanding with the

9. Kuria girls winnowing corn

The Kuria raise livestock, their major source of wealth. They also grow coffee as a cash crop and, owing to the fertility of the soil and the abundance of rainfall, are able to be prosperous farmers, harvesting corn, millet, bananas, sorghum, potatoes, and beans in surplus quantities for marketing.

husband's relatives.* The in-depth interviews added these comments: "the brother-in-law or the clan can best take care of a widow as they see her and treat her as a brother's wife"; "she was left in her husband's home"; "one cannot allow an outsider to care for a widow"; "the brother-in-law is the same as the husband of the widow."

The interesting aspect of this question of who can best care for a widow is that a significant number of Kuria respondents (14%) felt that it would be a friend of the widow rather than a blood relative of her deceased husband. This reponse flows from the fact that the Kuria distinguish in the leviratic relationship two functions: that of

---

*See Appendix A, Table 32.

inheritor and that of sexual partner. Thus a widow can agree to accept a brother-in-law as her leviratic inheritor while accepting a friend as her leviratic sexual partner (the third option of the Kuria widow). The Luo on the other hand do not make such a distinction. For them the leviratic inheritor and sexual partner are always one and the same person.

There was no obvious answer found in the data as to why this inheritor/cohabitor distinction is made by the Kuria. One explanation, advanced by Baker,[8] is that this distinction arises so as to furnish domestic and sexual partners for the many young men whose marriages are delayed (sometimes for years)* due to the high bridewealth demanded. Thus relationships with widows as leviratic cohabitors enables them to be partially integrated into the adult life of the community—an arrangement that is conducive to the good order and harmony of the society. This explanation, however, does not seem to me to be adequate. It stands or falls on whether in fact the leviratic cohabitors of widows are unmarried men—a fact not substantiated by the data.

A second and more plausible explanation is that the distinction between a leviratic inheritor and leviratic sexual partner is due to the existence of circumcision or initiation groups called *esaiga* within the Kuria social structures. These groups are formally constituted at the time when the young men and women are initiated into adulthood through the circumcision ritual.† Usually the participants are about twelve years of age when they undergo these rites, although there are presently many exceptions to this rule. During the time of preparation for circumcision, the boys and girls pair off, establishing "platonic" friendships. The girl is the one who choses her boy friend; intercourse is strictly forbidden. At the time of marriage, the girl leaves her own initiation group and joins the group of her husband.

The members of a circumcision group are mutually obligated to help one another in work and in need. For example, a girl who has been told to weed a garden by her parents can call on her

---

*The situation is such that often when one long-awaited marriage takes place, the same bridewealth cows are quickly used in several successive marriages before they finally come to rest in the paternal homestead of the last bride.

†In the Kuria tradition, both the men and the women are circumcised.

initiation-group friends for help. Furthermore, interactions between members of an initiation group are given special interpretation. Thus one could take food, without asking, from a member of one's circumcision group without it being considered stealing. The reason for this special bond and responsibility is that the members of these groups consider themselves related by blood, since their blood was mingled together at the place of circumcision. The Kuria, therefore, have *two* networks of blood relationships, one by birth, the other by circumcision ritual.

According to the Kuria tradition, therefore, both the blood brother by birth and the blood brother by circumcision are seen as capable of substituting for a deceased man in a leviratic relationship with his widow. This is so because a man has communal identity with both his lineage and his circumcision-group fellows. Thus there is the possibility of a true leviratic relationship between a widow and a "friend," a nonrelative of her deceased husband, provided he is a member of her husband's circumcision group. The role of the brother-in-law as the legal leviratic inheritor arises so as to ensure that the widow's wealth and children continue to remain in the lineage of the deceased husband and not switch to the lineage of the leviratic "friend." (It is interesting to note how the institutionalized initiation group relationships are in addition to and in competition with the demands of the blood group (lineage).*

Finally, in response to the question of whether a widow is cared for like a wife, we find that 38% of the Kuria (three times that of the Luo) said "frequently" or "always." This is a clear indication that the Kuria widow (generally) receives better treatment than the Luo widow. This, no doubt, is due to the fact that the Kuria widow has a larger number of men from which to select a compatible leviratic partner: she is not limited, like the Luo widow, to her husband's lineage. Of the remaining Kuria, 35% said that a widow is "sometimes" cared for like a wife and 23% said "rarely" or "never."†

The one reason given in the in-depth interviews for the "always" or "frequently" category was that she lives like a wife and works in

---

*There is a similar kind of competition in North American society between the demands and pressures of one's peer group over against the demands and pressures of one's family (parental) group.

· †See Appendix A, Table 33.

the village. The reasons for the "sometimes" category were that the care she receives depends upon whether she is obedient, has a good character, and does not have bad habits. The reasons for the "rarely or never" category were that it is not her husband's homestead, and that widows behave badly and are proud.

In summary, it is clear that there are two major patterns of marital behavior possible to Kuria widows: they can either choose to divorce and remarry or choose to enter into a levirate union. If the latter, they can either cohabit with a brother-in-law, live alone, or cohabit with a friend. The option of remarriage, dependent as it is on the return of the bridewealth, is in fact the least attractive option: only three of the thirty Kuria widows in the sample had actually remarried.* (The major reason for wanting to remarry appears to be the sterility of the original marriage.) The second option, the leviratic union, is the usual and preferred way of caring for widows, just as in the Luo tradition. However, the Kuria differ significantly from the Luo in this option in that they distinguish the role of leviratic inheritor and cohabitor. Thus a widow can be inherited by one man (usually the brother-in-law) while cohabiting with a "friend": eight of the thirty Kuria widows were in this type of leviratic union.† The apparent reason for this is the initiation groups of the Kuria society. Moreover a Kuria widow can be inherited but choose to live alone without a marital partner: fifteen of the widows were in this kind of arrangement. This left only four Kuria widows cohabiting in leviratic unions with their brothers-in-law—the ordinary situation of the Luo widows. The marital histories of the men, meanwhile, showed that 7% had cohabited or were cohabiting with widows.‡ As a final note, there was no measurable influence on the Kuria responses to these questions derived from membership in a Christian religion.

Kuria Reactions to the Church's Prohibition of the Leviratic Custom

Since Kuria widows can and do remarry as well as live alone without marital partners even though legally in a leviratic union, it

---

*See Appendix A, Table 26.
†Ibid., Table 47.
‡Ibid., Table 42.

10. Kuria interviewer and view from the Isuria escarpment

The Isuria escarpment drops in stages from 6,000 feet until it reaches the level of Lake Victoria at about 3,500 feet.

is possible for them to reconcile their state with the teachings of the Christian churches. Thus one would expect that there would be greater tolerance for and understanding of the churches' position and less opposition to their prohibition of the leviratic union. This proved to be the case.

To the first question of why the Christian churches are opposed to the leviratic custom, 54% of the Kuria (three times that of the Luo) gave the church-sponsored moral reason that the "widow is not his (the brother-in-law's) wife." At the same time only 4% of the Kuria gave the major Luo reason that the prohibition is merely the custom of the Church; 26% of the Kuria said that they did not know the reason for the churches' position.* (This same distribution of responses was found in the in-depth interviews.) These

---

*See Appendix A, Table 34.

ILLUSTRATION 7—RELIGIOUS AFFILIATIONS OF KURIA ADULTS

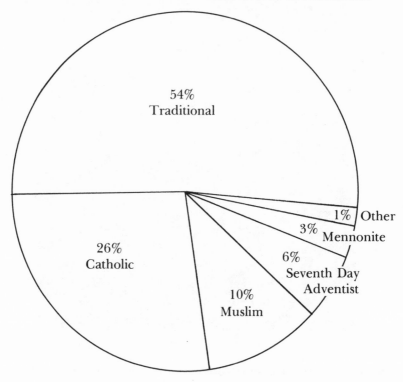

54%
Traditional

26%
Catholic

10%
Muslim

6%
Seventh Day
Adventist

3% Mennonite

1% Other

CATHOLIC CHURCH HISTORY

The history of the Catholic mission in the Bairegi area began in the early 1950's when an outstation was started near Nyamwaga, a small administrative center. This outstation was part of the Catholic mission of Rosana (opened in 1949) located about eight miles to the west. In 1960 a church, unregistered primary school, and rectory for the Maryknoll missionaries were constructed, and the area began to be administered separately with a resident pastor. The first baptisms took place in June 1961, with twenty-three adults and twenty-two children being received into the Church. By 1971 a total of 1,734 adults and 270 children had been baptized, while 308 marriages, 191 of which were between practicing Catholics, had been duly recorded in the official marriage register.[9]

MUSLIMS

No one seems to know why there were so many Bairegi Kurias who claimed affiliation with the Muslim faith. Some speculated that it was due to the fact that many Kuria men have at one time or another been members of the police forces or armies of the Tanzanian and Kenyan governments, and were converted by the strong Muslim communities located in the urban areas where they lived and worked. This hypothesis was not substantiated by the survey data. The Muslims were distributed throughout the five survey areas and half were women.

responses may indicate either that the Christian teachers of the Kuria have been much more efficient than their Luo counterparts in making clear and explaining the churches' teaching on widows, or that the understanding and acceptance of the new teaching is correlated with the possibility of it's being put into practice—the latter seems to be the more plausible explanation. In the case of the Luo teachers, it would be hard for them to be convincing on the widow issue since the majority of them did not accept the churches' teachings on widows in the first place.

In the in-depth interviews there were the following comments opposing the churches' prohibition of the levirate. Five people said that to neglect the care of a widow is not "to finish a brother's house"; another stated that this leviratic custom is "from our grandfathers and must be followed." At the same time there was a comment supporting the churches' stand given by six respondents: "the widow is still somebody's wife, as bridewealth has been paid [and so] the brother-in-law cannot become a proper husband." The reasoning behind this latter comment is an example of Africans interpreting a Christian position in terms of traditional attitudes and beliefs. The churches' opposition, in fact, is based on the lack of a proper church marriage—making the sexual union unlawful—and not on the fact that the bridewealth has been paid by the dead man's lineage and still binds the widow.* For the Church, death is the end of a marriage and the widow by that very event is free to marry. (About one-third of in-depth interviewees also accepted as valid the reason that this custom was forbidden by God—an obvious Christian interpretation.)

To the second question, concerning approval or disapproval of the Church's practice or stand on the levirate, 54% of the respondents disapproved, 35% (twice as many as the Luos) approved, and 11% did not know the problem.† (The in-depth interviews showed a similar distribution of responses.) These responses, as expected, were positively correlated with Christian membership. Fifty percent of all the Christians (two-and-a-half times the number of Luos)

---

*In Chapter VII and IX a full discussion of the reasons for the Church's opposition is presented.

†See Illustration 1, p.

agreed with the churches' prohibition, as compared with only 28% of the non-Christians.

When breaking down the Christians into the different Church memberships, no difference was found between the Catholic Church respondents and those belonging to two Protestant sects —Mennonite and Seventh Day Adventists.[10] (The Kuria are not attracted to the independent Christian sects the way the Luos are. Consequently there was not a significant number of "independent" Christians in the area surveyed. However, there was a large Muslim community embracing 10% of the Kuria adults.) Likewise there was no significant correlation between the frequency of attendance at religious worship and the type of response to this question.* Table 11 illustrates the differences in attitude regarding the prohibition of the levirate between the Christians and the non-Christians.

TABLE 11

KURIA ATTITUDES REGARDING THE CHRISTIAN PROHIBITION OF THE LEVIRATE
BY RELIGIONS AFFILIATION (CHRISTIAN/NON-CHRISTIAN) (%)

Attitudes	Religious Affiliation		% Total
	% Christian	% Non-Christian	
Approve	50	35	28
Disapprove....................	43	54	60
Do not know	7	11	12
Total %	100	100	100
Number	(106)	(195)	(301)

The reasons given by the Kuria for their approval of the Church's prohibition were as follows: "The widow is like a second wife (43%)"; "the widow destroys another's sacrament of marriage (21%)"; "the levirate is forbidden by church law (15%)"; "the

---

*There was statistical significance, although weakly associated, between the students attending schools under different agencies. The students attending the Catholic and Mennonite schools tended to approve the prohibition, whereas students attending government and Seventh Day Adventist schools tended to disapprove it.

widow has sinned (8%)"; "she is like a prostitute (4%)."* Again, as with the Luo people, all of these reasons represent moral judgments about this custom which were *not* present in the traditional attitudes and beliefs of the Kuria people. Interestingly, these reasons were randomly distributed throughout the population.

The Kuria people who were opposed to the Christian churches' position cited both moral and religious reasons for their objections. These reasons are as follows: the widow is not a prostitute, she is a widow (64%), the widow did not kill her husband, there is no reason to reject her (19%), the Church would have us throw away the bridewealth and the widow play the harlot (11%), God did not forbid this custom (11%). These reasons for opposing the Church's prohibition of the levirate are illustrated in Table 12.

TABLE 12

REASONS GIVEN BY KURIAS FOR OPPOSING THE CHURCHES'
PROHIBITION OF THE LEVIRATE (%)

Reasons Given	% Kuria
Widow still loves God	2
Widow still a member of Church	4
God did not forbid this custom	11
She is not a prostitute, she is a widow	64
Widow did not kill her husband, there is no reason to reject her	12(19)[a]
Church would have us throw away the bridewealth and the widow play the harlot	1(11)[a]
Other	6
Total %	100
Number	(163)

[a]Given as a second reason by respondents.

*See Appendix A, Table 35.

The in-depth interviews confirmed that the major reason for opposing the churches' stand was that the widow is not a prostitute; that is, a leviratic union is not a type of prostitution (13 out of the 18 "opposing" interviewees gave this as their first reason). Twelve of the eighteen also accepted the second reason as valid: namely, "the widow had not been at fault, she did not kill her husband"; that is, his death arose independently of her will. Other comments were that "no one can keep a widow as well as her brother-in-law, who will be sympathetic to her situation, will make the brother's house grow, and will give the widow everything she needs."

The marital histories of the Kuria widows show that half of them, fifteen in number, were Christians and two of them had been censured by their churches because of the leviratic custom. One of them, a Catholic, claimed that her punishment was unjust as she still "loves God and prays." There were only two Christian men who at one time or another had cohabited with widows, and neither had been punished, the reason being that their cohabitation with widows predated their baptisms.

It is clear that the extent of the leviratic problem for the Christian Kuria widows is much less than that for the Luo widows—only two of the Kuria widows had been censured by their churches. The reasons for this are that there are two acceptable and possible ways for a Kuria widow to satisfy both her traditional obligations and her Church obligations, ways that are not possible to a Luo widow. She can remarry (10% had actually remarried) or she can enter into a type of leviratic union that does not entail cohabitation with either her inheritor or with a friend (this was the choice of half of the Kuria widows). Thus, what might appear to the reader to be an insignificant distinction between a leviratic inheritor and leviratic cohabitor, turns out to be the major reason for a certain harmony between traditional Kuria customs and Christian teachings. Moreover, it is evidence that the stumbling block for the Church is the sexual union, the unlawful cohabitation, and not the leviratic institution as such. For if it were the institution, then every leviratic widow, whether cohabiting or not, would have to be excluded from the Church—this is clearly not the case.

The position of the Kuria people regarding the Christian churches' prohibition of the custom of levirate can be summarized as follows: the majority of the people have understood that the churches' opposition is based on a judgment that a widow in a leviratic union that entails cohabitation is in fact living *like* a second wife—a situation that is immoral from the Christians's perspective. As expected, agreement with the churches' judgment is positively correlated with church affiliation. Moreover, those in accord articulated this moral judgment of the churches as their own principal reason why this custom is wrong—a clear indication of Christian influence. The majority of those who oppose the Church's position on the levirate (64%) attack the Church's assessment of the custom, holding that a leviratic widow is not in an immoral situation and is not a prostitute. Furthermore they stress that she is not guilty of any wrongdoing that could condemn her, such as killing her husband or violating a law of God.

The success of the Christian churches in explaining to the Kuria the reasons for their opposition to the leviratic custom is probably due to the fact that Kuria widows have ordinary ways for remaining active in their Christian churches while satisfying traditional obligations. Consequently, they are able to hear and understand Christian teachings about the levirate, teachings incomprehensible to Luo widows, who have no real options for keeping ecclesiastical discipline. Furthermore, the Kuria customs for the care of widows makes it clear that the Christian churches' real objections to the levirate are centered on what is considered to be unlawful cohabitation and not on the institution as such.

Response of the Kuria Catholic Leaders

Since there are ordinary ways for a Kuria widow to satisfy both traditional and ecclesiastical obligations, one would suspect that the Kuria church leaders would be less concerned about this issue than their Luo counterparts. Questions arise, therefore, as to how the Kuria leaders would view the leviratic conflict. Would they dismiss it as an unimportant peripheral problem? Would they have the same insight into it as the Luo leaders? Would they suggest the same changes as the Luos in ecclesiastical discipline? To answer these and other questions, the following Kuria Catholic Church leaders were interviewed: five Maryknoll missionaries, five specially trained catechists, and nineteen regular catechists.

The first question asked was whether widows could remarry in the Kuria tradition. Nine of the leaders said categorically "no" while nineteen others gave a qualified "yes," pointing out that they do not like to remarry.* The reasons given by over three-quarters of the *catechists* as to why widows either cannot or do not want to remarry were: "she is already married," "she is the wife of bridewealth," "she is cared for by her brother-in-law." Two others reasoned that marrying a widow is difficult since she is the wife of a lineage, and another two that the widow would not want to leave her children. Thus, it is clear that the Kuria catechists, like the Luo catechists, were aware of the meaning and function of the leviratic union within their society.

To the question of whether widows cohabiting in leviratic unions *could* receive the sacraments of the Catholic Church, over four-fifths of the leaders (23) responded "no"; five said that it depended on certain factors, and one said "yes."† Those who answered no justified the policy with the same moral objections to the custom as given by the Luo leaders, namely, that the widow is living in a state of sin, and there is no proper marriage. However, one missionary replied that the policy was merely a church custom with which he disagreed. Those who answered that "it depends" explained that reception of the sacraments was contingent on the widows' living like unmarried girls—the case of inherited widows who choose not to cohabit.

Again, as with the Luo leaders, the Kuria leaders judge the leviratic union *not* to be a real marriage but a way of caring for widows. Six of the catechists further described the leviratic union as a "way of bad friendship." The reasons given for it *not* being a marriage were: "there is no sign of marrying with bridewealth (six leaders)," "the woman is still called the wife of a dead person (two leaders)," "the relation is only a friendship (five leaders)."

When the Kuria Catholic Church leaders were asked what changes should be made in the pastoral policy regarding the custom of the levirate, about half (15) replied that this custom should be accepted; four, that it should be accepted with certain qualifications, and eight, that a widow should be enabled to remarry. The number of leaders requesting full or partial acceptance of the levirate were about the same as for the Luo leaders. There were,

---

*See Appendix A, Table 37.
†See Appendix A, Table 38.

however, some differences between the African and the missionary responses, but the number of respondents involved is too small to draw any conclusions. These differences in proposed pastoral changes are illustrated in Table 13.

TABLE 13

PROPOSED PASTORAL CHANGES REGARDING LEVIRATIC WIDOWS
BY TYPE OF KURIA CATHOLIC CHURCH LEADERSHIP (N=27)

Changes Proposed	Kuria Catholic Leadership		Total
	N. Missionary	N. Catechists	
Work to enable widow remarriage..........	2	6	8
Accept the levirate fully..........................	2	13	15
Accept the levirate with qualification...........	1	3	4
Total	5	22	27

The final general question about desired change in Church discipline on marriage elicited specific responses about the levirate from only two leaders—both missionaries; they repeated their demand that widows in levirate unions should be allowed to continue to be practicing Christians.* The fact that only two leaders mentioned the levirate specifically in answering this question indicates that the levirate does not have a high priority among marriage problems affecting the Kuria Christian people. This is also apparent from the marital histories of the Kuria widows. By way of contrast, the levirate was mentioned specifically by eleven Luo leaders when answering this question.

In summary, we find among the Kuria Church leaders the same concern as among the Luo leaders over the prohibition of the leviratic custom. The majority of the Kuria leaders do not find the levirate to be incompatible with being a practicing Christian even though they, in fact, refuse cohabiting widows the sacraments.

---

*See Appendix A, Table 55.

11. Prosperous Kuria monogamous family

The rate of plural marriage in 1972 was around 28%–the second highest among the four peoples surveyed. The amount of bridewealth paid was considerably higher than that paid by the Luo, with a range between sixteen and forty cows: the majority paying twenty-five to thirty.[11] These high bridewealth payments make marriage difficult for the sons of a man poor in cattle and lacking in daughters. As a result, one finds middle-aged men in the Kuria society who are not yet married owing to their poverty.

They justify this refusal on the grounds that technically the widow is living in a state of sin; i.e., she is in a permanent unlawful sexual union. Many of the leaders, therefore, are in the peculiar situation of supporting a policy *publicly* with which they disagree *privately,* and of enforcing a discipline that they feel is based on a misunderstanding of African values and traditions.

The Kuria Church leaders recognize that the levirate union is not a marriage, but a way of caring for a widow and of continuing her family, and most of them ask that the custom be accepted by the Christian community. Thus, despite a less pressing leviratic pastoral problem in the Kuria Church, we find, surprisingly, that the Kuria leaders, in general, are of one mind with the Luo leaders on the leviratic custom. That is, they have the same general understanding of the custom itself and of the conflict engendered by the Church's prohibition of it. Furthermore they offer the same suggestion for pastoral changes that would help alleviate the conflict.

In conclusion, we see how the leviratic custom of the Kuria, despite many similarities with its Luo counterpart, does in fact have significantly different characteristics. These characteristics are derived from factors which may seem to the reader to be somewhat minor, i.e., the amount of bridewealth paid and the institutionalization of initiation groups. However, these factors appear to be the basis for three marital options for Kuria widows which are not shared by Luo widows. First of all Kuria widows do remarry, Luo widows do not. Secondly, Kuria widows can exploit initiation group relationships in order to *cohabit* with a friend while being *inherited* by a brother-in-law—Luo widows have no initiation group relationships to exploit. Third, a Kuria widow can choose to be inherited by a brother-in-law but live alone without a cohabitor—an impossibility for a Luo widow. This latter option, no doubt, is derived from the fact that the role of inheritor and cohabitor are seen as distinct in the second option.

The effects of the Kuria version of the leviratic custom flow into the pastoral order. There we find that the churches' teachings proscribing the levirate are more acceptable and understandable because there is a way for a Kuria Christian widow to avoid its sanction. That is, she can agree to be inherited leviratically by her brother-in-law but decide to live alone without a cohabitor—thus avoiding what the Church considers to be an unlawful sexual union. The Luo widow cannot do the same, hence, she has no ordinary way for avoiding ecclesiastical censure. One cannot claim, therefore, that the Kuria people make better Christians or have more faith because a greater number of them accept the Church's prohibition of the levirate. Rather one must claim that the Kuria can accept the prohibition because there is a customary pattern of behavior that has the backing of traditional wisdom which enables the Christian widow to satisfy both traditional and Christian obligations.

Ecclesiastically, the interesting part of the Luo/Kuria comparison is that the majority of the Catholic Church leaders (missionary and African alike) among both peoples have the same assessment of the levirate custom and see it as compatible with a Christian way of life. And this is so even though the Kuria leviratic problem is not exactly the same as the Luo problem. Furthermore the Kuria data clarify that the real pastoral objection to the levirate custom is not to the institution as such, but to what is considered to be the unlawful cohabitation connected with it.

Finally, we are beginning to see how change in social structure, however minor, can radically modify patterns of behavior within a society. Thus the major difference in terms of the leviratic custom between the Kuria and Luo (both of which follow patrilineal rules of inheritance and descent) is the institutionalization of initiation groups. Whereas the Luo is only himself by identity and his lineage by virtue of blood, the Kuria is also his initiation group by virtue of the rites of initiation into adulthood. Consequently, the Kuria is involved in a *second* network of people that share a communal identity and that can be mutually exploited. This second network complexifies Kuria social relationships; and, since conflicting claims of the two communities can be played off one against the other, it tends to give a greater measure of freedom to the individual—witness how the Kuria widow, as compared to her Luo counterpart, has been able to work out a more compatible and human solution to her problem. We now turn to a presentation of the Kwaya customs for the care of widows.

NOTES 3

1. Republic of Kenya, *Kenya Population Census, 1969* (Nairobi: Government Printers, Nov. 1970), I, 69. The United Republic of Tanzania, *1967 Population Census*, III, 398–403.

2. E. C. Baker, in "The Bakuria of N. M. Tarime, Tanganyika Territory" (manuscript, in the Library of the East African Institute of Social Research, Makerere, Kampala, Uganda), p. 65, writes that the Kuria *sub-groups* (sub-tribes) are totemic units which owing to peculiar circumstances in the past have failed to maintain territorial unity and became independent units governed by their own councils of elders. All members of the same totem are potential allies and will, at worst, maintain a neutral attitude in wars in which members of their own totem are engaged. The totem of the Bairegi people is the leopard. Moreover, according to Baker (p. 4), there is a second Bairegi sub-group which he calls Bairegi II, which lives south of the Mara river. It was not included in the Kuria "universe."

The author has avoided the use of the term "tribe" because of its objectionable ethnocentric connotations.

3. These figures are based on an unpublished report of the distribution of Kuria sub-groups in Kenya shown to the author in August, 1970.

The Kenyan chief (Kenya does not have a ten-cell grass-roots political organization like Tanzania) living at Ntimaru was unwilling to cooperate and give permission to conduct interviews with any of the Bairegi living in his district.

4. Two sources indicate that age and the presence of adult sons determines whether or not a widow will agree to cohabit with a brother-in-law. The one is a report of a meeting of the Kuria Law Panel—"The Kuria Law of Succession" (unpublished report of a meeting, June 1963, held at Kisii, Kenya, and available in the East African Institute of Social Research Library: Kampala, Uganda), p. 221—which states that if a widow has adult sons, she normally does not enter into a leviratic union. The other is E. C. Baker ("The Bakuria," p. 151), who states that if a woman is older she will choose her own friend rather than cohabit with a brother-in-law.

5. Hans Cory, "Kuria Law and Custom" (unpublished paper, Tarime, Tanzania, 1945, re-edited E. B. Dobson, 1952, available in the Cory Collection, Library: University of Dar es Salaam, Tanzania), ch. 5, pp. 9–10, ch. 1, p. 6 (mimeographed). See also H. Cory, "Kuria Bridewealth" (unpublished paper, Mwanza, Tanzania, 1958, available in the Cory Collection, Library, University of Dar es Salaam, Tanzania), p. 10.

6. The United Republic of Tanzania, *1967 Population Census*, I, 88–90.

7. Baker, "The Bakuria," p. 6.

8. Baker, "The Bakuria," p. 110.

9. Figures were taken from the official records of the Nyamwaga Catholic Mission.

10. Figures were taken from the survey data. See Appendix A, Table 48.

11. See Appendix A, Table 40.

12. Kwaya Muslim family (polygynous)

The Kwaya people who follow patrilineal rules of inheritance and descent pay bridewealth. The amount paid varies from one to thirty cows with the majority paying six to ten cows (see Appendix A, Table 40). The rate of plural marriage among the Kwaya was 13%—the second smallest of the peoples surveyed.

CHAPTER FOUR

Kwaya Traditions for the Care of Widows
The Matrilineal Pattern

We now begin a discussion of the third member of our model—the Bantu-speaking Kwaya people. The Kwaya reside in Musoma district about sixty miles southwest of the Luo and Kuria. It was realized in the very beginning of the research that the marital traditions of the Kwaya would be the most unfamiliar to the Western observer and the most unique of the four people studied. This, supposedly, was due to the fact that their principle of inheritance and descent is matrilineal. This means that Kwaya children are recruited into and given inheritance through the lineages of their mothers—hence, *mater*-lineal. The place of the Kwaya in our model is as follows:

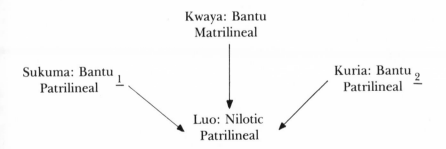

Kwaya: Bantu
Matrilineal

Sukuma: Bantu $_1$
Patrilineal $^{-}$

Kuria: Bantu $_2$
Patrilineal $^{-}$

Luo: Nilotic
Patrilineal

The effect of the matrilineal principle is that it is the brother of the mother, the maternal uncle, and not her husband, the father of her children, who gives the children identity and inheritance. Identity and inheritance, therefore, are passed on to the children

83

through a brother-sister relationship rather than through a husband-wife relationship. A father, in this system, is not the source of either lineage identity or inheritance for his own progeny, but he fulfills this function for the children of his sister.

After having classified the Kwaya as matrilineal—the sister's children ensuring the continuance of the group and being regarded as inheritors of the clan land—there appear to be so many exceptions to this rule that one wonders whether they are in fact matrilineal.* For example, the principle did not hold in practice if the mother of the children was bought as a slave, or if she came from a patrilineal society that demanded bridewealth; likewise if both husband and wife belong to the same clan, the children will stay with their father's lineage and inherit through his clan. Moreover there is a preference for cross-cousin marriage; i.e., marriage to the daughter of one's paternal aunt, which has the effect of bringing the grandchildren back into the lineage of the maternal grandparents.

Despite these obvious exceptions, Professor Huber of the University of Fribourg, Switzerland, who researched the Kwaya traditions in the 1960s, felt that one is still justified in classifying the Kwaya as matrilineal. According to his analysis, the root of the matrilineal tradition is the custom of *kukyuka* meaning "to change sides." It denotes the practice in which a Kwaya who has been raised and cared for in his father's family turns later on to his mother's side. The basis of this practice, says Huber, is the Kwaya attitude towards bridewealth; i.e., since they do not demand cattle for their marriageable daughters, they conclude that children should not belong to and inherit in the lineages of their fathers: only bridewealth payments can secure the children for the father's lineage.[1]

Unfortunately, Huber was unaware of the frequency distribution of marriages following the old matrilineal principle. The survey showed clearly that in 1972 only one-third of the Kwaya marriages were in fact based on the matrilineal principle in which there was no exchange of bridewealth. The remaining two-thirds of the

---

*An obvious exception is the "Bueri" clan, which immigrated into Kwayaland from North Mara and has continued to follow its patrilineal principle of inheritance and descent.[2]

marriages were based on the patrilineal principle involving the exchange of bridewealth.* On the basis of this data, I would argue that the Kwaya can no longer be classified as a matrilineal people as Huber would have us believe. They are in fact a people in the midst of a major social revolution in which the majority have already rejected the old matrilineal tradition in favor of a patrilineal one for reasons that will be discussed. Consequently, they can now only be described as a mixed society following both matrilineal and patrilineal principles of inheritance, with the matrilineal principle being on the decline.

Evidence for the matrilineal decline is the distribution of the bridewealth and nonbridewealth marriages as correlated with age groups: 43% of the Kwaya adults over forty-five years of age were in nonbridewealth marriages (matrilineal principle) as compared with only 30% of those under forty-five.

Another interesting aspect of the data is that the marriages following the matrilineal principle were not equally distributed in all of the interview areas. The areas of Kumugongo, the homeland of the original Kwaya clans (the three that claim common ancestry) and the neighboring areas of Kakisieri had a nonbridewealth rate of around 55% (both of these areas are in the "center" of Kwaya-land). The three other outlying interview areas had much lower rates: Efurifu with only 8%, Kamatico with 21%, and Mumuhari with 26%.† On reflection, this unequal distribution makes sense. One would expect that the matrilineal principal of descent would be most resistant to change in the oldest and most traditional part of Kwayaland. This appears to be the case.

Why are the Kwaya so undecided as to what their principle of descent should be? What moved them to begin to adopt patrilineal structures? The answers to these questions must take into account the active intervention of the Catholic mission authorities. Since the early 1940s, these authorities have been working towards changing the Kwaya's traditional patterns of matrilineal inheritance and succession. One reads in the diary of the White Father missionaries at the Catholic mission station of Nyegina (dated April

---

*See Appendix A, Table 54.
†See Appendix A, Table 49.

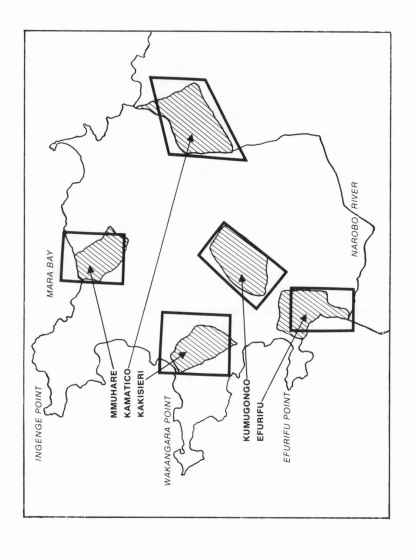

SELECTED CENSUS ENUMERATION AREAS IN KWAYALAND

The Kwaya people occupy a tract of country along the eastern shore of Lake Victoria extending from Mara Bay to the Narobo River, with the three peninsulas of Igenge, Wakangera, and Efurifu. Their neighbors on the east are the Bakairoba and the Bazanaki, and on the south the Bashora.[3] The total population in 1971 was approximately 22,000 people: 12,000 adults and 9,900 children under fifteen years of age.[4]

KWAYA HISTORY

The Kwaya, as regards their historical origins, are a very mixed people. This is apparent in their traditions about the various places from which the first ancestors (or more often the first ancestresses) are said to have come. Some supposedly came from the south, from the country of the Sukuma, others from Ukara Island in Lake Victoria, others from the north—North Mara.[5]

The Kwaya can be divided into six subgroups. Three of them, the Abagitwa, Abang'oma, and the Abahanyisi, claim common ancestry through a man named Magwa. The remaining three are composed of different, only partially related subgroups.[6]

One tradition claims that the first group to reach present-day Kwayaland were the Abang'oma and that they found the country inhabited by the Abakangara —half-nomadic cattle keepers and warriors related to the Masai.

MUSOMA

The town of Musoma, founded in 1921, is located in Kwayaland. It is the capital of the district region as well as the center of Indian commerce. In 1971 it had a population of 14,600 people, of which 2,000 were Kwaya. The Catholic bishop of the Mara region has his residence and diocesan headquarters in this town.

6, 1940) how all the heads of the Catholic Action groups had decided to fight against the wicked customs of *bumama,* i.e., the custom by which children do *not* inherit their fathers' goods (i.e., the matrilineal pattern).[7] But why would they want to change the matrilineal pattern of inheritance and descent?

Western missionaries, as pointed out by Hastings,[8] have always been uncomfortable with the matrilineal tradition since it gives great freedom to women and seemingly violates a most basic human principle, that sons should inherit through their natural fathers—this principle, of course, seems "basic" to the missionaries only because they themselves come from and are familiar with the patrilineal tradition; it has yet to be proved that the patrilineal principle of inheritance and succession is in any way superior or more human and basic than the matrilineal one. In view of this innate lack of sympathy with things matrilineal, it was an easy step for the Kwaya missionaries to blame the alleged marital instability of the Kwaya people on their matrilineal traditions. As a result they began to campaign against the matrilineal customs in an attempt to "stabilize" Kwaya marriage, their main weapon being the obligatory introduction of bridewealth.

How did the missionaries believe that the obligatory introduction of bridewealth would "stabilize" Kwaya marriage? They were, no doubt, following the model of the neighboring patrilineal people. In this model the payment of bridewealth secures children for the natural fathers' lineages, as well as "ties up" wives into marriages in such a way that it is very difficult for them to change marital partners no matter how desperate their living situation. This latter is due to the permanent alliance created between the lineages of the partners through the exchange of bridewealth. However, in all fairness to the missionaries, it must be pointed out that the Kwaya people were not entirely unfamiliar with marriage following the patrilineal principle, as has been indicated. Thus the missionaries' action did not involve inculcating an entirely unknown foreign custom.

In the effort to introduce bridewealth, the missionaries enlisted the help of the government. There is an entry in a White Father's diary, dated January 11, 1945, which states that all the elders (government leaders) of the kingdoms of Busamba, Munguru, and Mugango had unanimously decided to abolish all the "deadly" (matrilineal) social customs of the Bakwaya, namely, *kukyuka,* in which children at the age of puberty are declared the children of their maternal uncles, and *bugabi,* in which a man's legitimate heirs are his sister's children and not his own children.[9]

There was apparently so much opposition to the Church's demands for introducing bridewealth that it was felt necessary by 1947, in a meeting on December 20, to spell out the following pastoral instructions:*

1. No Christian marriage will be celebrated without a dowry.
2. Those who are responsible for refusing to accept a dowry will be forbidden the sacraments.
3. This penalty will last as long as they continue to refuse to accept a dowry.
4. If a man already married, but without dowry, wants to pay dowry for his wife, she has to consent and her family has no right to refuse; otherwise the same penalty as above will be applicable.

The reasons given for these instructions were: (1) that the frequent breakup of marriages is mainly caused by the absence of any dowry (bridewealth), (2) that many of the young men want to marry with a dowry. The first reason betrays the simplistic mentality and patrilineal prejudice of the author of the instructions. How could he be so certain that the absence of bridewealth in itself could be the cause of marital breakups? Did he really think that the mere imposition of bridewealth would solve a problem relational in its roots? Did he ever consider that maybe the breakup of Kwaya marriages was really due to other things, such as the lack of compatibility of the partners and infidelity (these were the major reasons given by the Kwaya when asked in the survey what causes the breakup of marriages) or did he in fact deny the Kwaya an emotional and psychological life governing their marital relationships? Future events proved that the mere payment of bridewealth did not stabilize Kwaya marriages as the missionaries had hoped. Rather it became a factor in even greater instability.

Huber points out that in principle bridewealth could have been introduced into the Kwaya matrilineal structure without effecting

---

*Huber feels that these instructions, attached to the Nyegina diary, were probably written by Bishop Blomjous, a Dutch White Father (Huber, "The Wakwaya of Musoma," p. 83).

a change of that structure.[10] In such a case a man, according to the old custom, would accept only his first daughter's bride-cattle in order to recover what he had spent for her mother, whereas the profit of his other daughters would go either to *their* maternal uncles or to *their* brothers. However, the effort of the mission authorities and the local chiefs aimed to introduce both obligatory bridewealth and the changing of the old practice of *bumama*, i.e., inheritance through one's maternal uncle. Furthermore, it does not appear from the records of the White Father's diary, says Huber, that the structural connection of these two projects was ever seen—this is further evidence that the Kwaya missionaries lacked insight into and understanding of the most elementary aspect of traditional African social structures.

Huber concludes that the structural changes in Kwaya society that have taken place during the past decades have largely contributed to the present-day uncertainties regarding inheritance and social affiliation.[11] He writes: "There is today still a period of transition: the young generation, particularly those that have some schooling, are more inclined to advocate the change (to patrilineal rules of inheritance and descent). They plead for the parents to assume full responsibility over their children (according to the new patrilineal tradition). The attitude of the older people, however, is still rather ambiguous."[12]

Huber comments further on how the older people, on the one hand, like the idea that their children will stay with them for good according to the new patrilineal order. But on the other hand, still thinking in terms of the matrilineal categories of the past, they regret the loss of their sister's children to their own kin group.

The mission authorities, apparently, were not aware of the larger social consequences that would follow the introduction of bridewealth in Kwaya society. This was not true, however, of some of the government officials. Hans Cory, the Tanzanian government sociologist, wrote to the district commissioner of Musoma (the Kwaya district) in *1945* warning that: "The introduction of brideprice influences the position of children and the law of inheritance, thus changing the *foundation* of the system. . . . In such a question of fundamental rules of society a number of eventualities lie hidden which make a sudden change a most *dangerous* adventure" (italics mine).[13] Cory understood that the introduction of bridewealth in Kwaya society would cause major structural changes. And he cautions his government colleagues that bride-price should be introduced only through *propaganda* and not through *force*. Would that his voice had been heard!

By the mid and late 1960s, the confusion and turmoil engendered by these changes began to effect all the institutions in Kwaya society. Church attendance itself dropped dramatically. Some missionaries began to speak of the Kwaya as a broken people, claiming that drunkenness, prostitution, broken marriages, infidelity, etc. had sapped their moral fiber and had led to a general breakdown of social discipline. I can recall a Sister saying that the Kwaya people were a sad people, a people without hope. However, she felt that with a little effort on the part of the Church a new Christian enthusiasm and spirit could be infused into their lives. It is ironic that the Sister did not understand that the Church itself had helped create the very social instability that the Church now experiences.

The Kwaya, however, in spite of this social instability remain especially loyal to the Catholic Church, providing a large number of laborers for the Church's institutions even though they make up less than 5% of the diocesan population. The first diocesan priest is Kwaya; four of the six diocesan vocations to the priesthood (up to 1975) are Kwaya; a large number of Catholic school teachers are Kwaya and not a few young Kwaya girls have joined the Catholic sisterhood. Yet the Kwaya have been pushed by the Church into a major structural change, moving from a matrilineal principle of inheritance to a patrilineal one. Then, life being life, they have been blamed during the transition for having no stable social structures shaping their ordinary marital behavior. Recall, now, these changes were introduced by the Church in order to "stabilize" Kwaya marriages!

Meanwhile, there has never been any extensive discussion on the part of the Christian churches' leaders as to the nature of the matrilineal pattern of inheritance vis-à-vis its compatibility with Christianity. There has never been any theological defense of the matrilineal principle of inheritance and descent as a valid and human way for structuring family relationships. In the case of the Kwaya, it was simply assumed that the patrilineal pattern in which bridewealth is exchanged is a better and more stable way to organize marriage and family relationships: a clear violation of the

Church's principle of adaptation, a principle that will be discussed at length in Part II. One has the suspicion that the matrilineal principle of inheritance and descent was so unfamiliar and unintelligible to the Kwaya missionaries that they would have fought against it even if they had considered the family situation stable.

A further complication of the Kwaya problem was that the White Father missionaries, the ones responsible for initiating the changes in Kwaya structure, pulled their personnel out of the Kwaya mission at the very height of the crisis and debate over the obligatory introduction of bridewealth. They turned over pastoral responsibility for the Kwaya Church to the Maryknoll missionaries, a U.S.-based community with no previous African experience. The Maryknollers, relying on the White Fathers' understanding of African cultures, continued the White Fathers' Kwaya policy without ever seriously questioning its underlying assumptions or justifying reasons. The effects of the imposition on the Kwaya of a disruptive pastoral policy eventually began to be felt by the Maryknoll missionaries themselves. Some of them began to express hostility and anger towards the slow progress of the Kwaya church. Neighboring missionaries made it clear that they would refuse an assignment to work among the Kwaya. One Maryknoller, an outstanding missionary with more than ten years of work among the Kwaya, became so frustrated that he quit his post and left the missionary work entirely. He claimed that his missionary efforts had been in vain, that the Kwaya people were impossible to work with, and that Christianity had yet to radically influence Kwaya society despite years of intensive evangelization.

There has never been any concern expressed that the obligatory introduction of bridewealth also introduces into Kwaya society all the marital problems of the patrilineal people, problems such as the leviratic care of widows, the forcing of a marriage by a father in order to pay off a debt, the inability to marry due to a lack of bridewealth. At the same time it destroys a great deal of the economic and social freedom given to women in the matrilineal traditions—a freedom highly prized and struggled for even in Western societies—and makes women totally dependent on the economic and social fortunes of their husbands. Such a change from a condition of freedom to one of dependency clearly cannot be considered a part of the Christian message. Could not one just as well argue that it is the matrilineal principles of inheritance and descent that should be upheld, promoted, and introduced by Christian missionaries since it gives greater freedom and dignity to women: an essential element of Christianity?

Imagine what would happen if the Catholic Church authorities in the United States would arbitrarily decree the payment of bridewealth, say $20,000* as a condition for all Church marriages in order to "stabilize" Western Christian marriages? Who would respond? What confusion would result? Are not Kwaya social structures and institutions as real and complicated as Western structures? Are not Kwaya people just as much entitled to a fair hearing on their social structures as Western people? Indeed how can the mere bartering of goods, no matter in which society, stabilize intimate, personal marital relationships? How can there be merely an "economic" solution to a problem by nature also moral and relational?

Furthermore, it cannot even be alleged that the matrilineal principle of inheritance causes the breakup of the natural family unit. The Kwaya sons, as Huber points out, are not removed from their fathers' homesteads at puberty. Ordinarily, sons stay with their fathers until the fathers die—it is considered disrespectful to do otherwise—or until the sons are initiated into elderhood. Thus it is the case that the natural fathers are the ones responsible for the "raising" and the socialization of their own children.

What is the real root of the Catholic Church's objection to the Kwaya matrilineal principle? The Church has yet to clearly ask, debate, and answer this question! Then what right has the Catholic Church to interfere with such vehemence in the social structure of the Kwaya on the basis of hearsay, prejudice, and ignorance? None at all! The whole episode must be considered a tragic mistake! (Obligatory bridewealth, historically, did not "stabilize" Kwaya marriages to the satisfaction of Church authorities.)

Against the background of this Kwaya social revolution, we now begin our analysis of the way(s) Kwaya society ordinarily cares for

---

*This figure was arrived at by calculating that the purchase price of twelve cows by the average African man would require his total income for a period of two years. (Based on 1973 prices.)

its widows. We say "ordinarily" with some hesitation, for with the confusion regarding rules of inheritance and descent one would expect a corresponding confusion regarding the care of widows—a problem intimately linked with one's descent system. This proved to be the case. The care of widows in the Kwaya society takes its form from the kind of marriage alliance entered into by the lineages of the two partners. If it is an alliance based on the matrilineal principle, then, the widow ordinarily goes back to her maternal home upon the death of her husband, together with her children. If her marriage was based on the patrilineal principle, and bridewealth had been exchanged as with the Kuria and the Luo, she can either be inherited by a brother-in-law or, if her kin group (lineage) agrees to return the bridewealth, she can return to her father's home.

The result is that the Kwaya, by combining both systems, have at least seven options for the care of widows—by way of contrast, the Luo have *one* and the Kuria *four*. Under the *matrilineal* principle, a Kwaya widow can (1) return to her paternal home with her children and be remarried; (2) be inherited by her brother-in-law in a leviratic-type union if her maternal homestead no longer exists (this is probably due to an analogy with the patrilineal family tradition; children remain members of the maternal lineage); and (3) remain in the care of the husband's family. Under the *patrilineal* principle the widow can (1) be inherited in a leviratic union; (2) if bridewealth is returned, can be remarried; (3) be officially inherited but cohabit with a friend; and (4) be officially inherited but live alone. The following illustration is a partial legal statement of the traditional law of the Kwaya for the care of widows:

ILLUSTRATION 8—KWAYA LEGAL RULES FOR THE CARE OF WIDOWS

If no brideprice is paid (in the case of a Mukwaya wife) the widow goes home with her children. (The children are the heirs to the property of their maternal uncle.)

If brideprice has been paid (in the case of a foreign wife): A. *Childless widow* is inherited by the brother of the deceased or by the son of the deceased's sister or, if the widow prefers to return home, the full brideprice is to be returned.

B. *Widow with daughters* is inherited by the brother of the deceased or by the son of the deceased's sister. Half the brideprice is returned, if the widow prefers to return to her father.

C. *Widow with sons* (the son is heir and the widow guardian).[14]

On the basis of these options it is clear that, legally, the widow in either type of marriage alliance could be allowed to return to her father's home, presumably to remarry. One would expect, therefore, that the overwhelming majority of the people would see the *possibility* of widow remarriage: this is borne out by the data: 74% gave an unqualified "yes" to the remarriage of widows; 19% stated that remarriage was possible but dependent upon certain conditions;* only 7% said "no." The Kwaya responses on the possibility of widow remarriage are shown in Table 14.

TABLE 14

Possibility of Widow Remarriage among Kwaya People (%)

Can Widows Remarry?	% Kwaya
Yes	74
Depends	19
No	7
Total %	100
Number	(309)

The central reason for the remarriage of widows given by the Kwaya is the choice of the widow herself (94%). Two other reasons (also mentioned in the in-depth interviews give circumstances in which a widow would choose remarriage, namely, if she does not have children (10%), or if she cannot live on her own (5%). Another reason was that since her husband had died, there is nothing to oppose her remarriage (9%).†

*An attempt was made to isolate those people who gave the qualified response "depends" and it was discovered that two-thirds of them were from the same geographical area (Kamatico) and had been interviewed by the same person. It appears that the "depends" responses are due to the interviewer's bias—he misunderstood the question.

*See Appendix A, Table 27.

When asked whether or not a widow *wants* to remarry the Kwaya people responded in much the same fashion as they had to the question about the *possibility* of widow remarriage: about 94% said "yes" while the rest said "no."*

The main reason given by the Kwaya for widows wanting to remarry is the widow's desire for a new husband (52%). This reason is consistent with the principal response given to the question of why widows can remarry, i.e., "she can remarry if she wants." The second major reason was that she would remarry if there was no one to take care of her properly (35%). A few others said that only young widows would want to remarry (7%), and others said that widows would want to remarry because it is difficult to live without a husband (5%). The in-depth interviews confirmed that all four responses are common reasons why a widow would want to remarry. Table 15 illustrates the reasons for remarriage.

TABLE 15

REASONS KWAYAS GAVE WHY WIDOWS WANT TO REMARY (%)

Reasons Given	% Kwaya
If there is no one to take care of her	35
If she still wants a husband	52
The young ones want to remarry	7
It is difficult to live without a husband	5
Other	1
Total %	100
Number	(291)

Surprisingly, there were no differences in the answers to the previous questions correlated with the matrilineal/patrilineal principles of descent and inheritance; all the Kwaya respondents answered in terms of their original matrilineal traditions. It had been

---

*See Appendix A, Table 29.

expected that the respondents following the patrilineal principle in their own marriage alliances would have opposed widow remarriage like the Kuria and Luo. This was not the case. This shows how the customs for the care of widows flowing from a patrilineal principle of inheritance and descent are reshaped and modified by each society in which they are applied. Thus opposition to widow remarriage, which appeared from the Luo and Kuria traditions to be an essential application of the patrilineal principles, is found to be nonessential in the Kwaya tradition.

Introducing the patrilineal principle into Kwaya society does not totally displace the matrilineal attitudes and custom, but adds a second and new *possibility*. When, therefore, there is a widow in a Kwaya family following the patrilineal principle of descent, the family can fall back on the old "matrilineal" reason for allowing her the freedom to remarry—even though this means the return of the bridewealth. Furthermore, in the case of a pregnancy out of wedlock, the father of the girl can appeal to the old matrilineal principle of descent and claim the child for his wife's lineage rather than marry off the girl quickly according to the patrilineal principle in order to give the child a name. These examples show that these matrilineal/patrilineal patterns of inheritance and descent are not "closed systems" but can coexist and modify each other.

The other side of the question is whether the traditional Catholic (Christian) attempt to promote widow remarriage as a *possibility* in the patrilineal societies of the Luo and Kuria really represents the introduction of a *matrilineal* principle in those societies; i.e., a principle concerned with the freedom of a woman, the nature of the bond between a woman and her husband's lineage and the right of a woman to control the inheritance and descent of her children. Fortunately, unlike the case of the Kwaya, there were only ecclesiastical sanctions available to try to enforce on the Luo and Kuria this new tradition or pattern. If the Luo and Kuria had accepted *widow remarriage,* it could have caused as great a social upheaval as happened among the Kwaya.

Further evidence for the mixing of the two descent principles among the Kwaya is seen in their answers to the question of who could best care for a widow if she does not want to be remarried (recall that according to the matrilineal principle a woman returns to her maternal homestead on the death of her husband). To this question, no one mentioned the widow's family, even though it is a possibility according to the matrilineal tradition. On the contrary, 83% stated that it was the brother-in-law, 15% a relative of the deceased husband—the patrilineal position.* However, it is important to remember that a widow even in a matrilineal marriage alliance, under certain circumstances, could be cared for by her brother-in-law in a type of "matrilineal" leviratic union. It appears therefore that a traditionally *marginal* matrilineal attitude regarding brothers-in-law was reemphasized, and made central by the interaction with the new patrilineal attitudes.

To the question of whether a widow in a leviratic union is cared for like a wife, 27% of the Kwaya replied that she is "frequently" or "always," 47% said "sometimes," 26% said "rarely" or "never."† The distribution of these responses was similar to that of the Kuria: a society that also provides multiple options for the care of widows. The reasons why a widow is always or frequently cared for like a wife, as recorded in the in-depth interviews, were: "she is a wife and therefore you must care for her"; likewise, "what you refuse her you refuse a wife." Those who said, "sometimes" reasoned: "the wife is given him by force, he didn't request her"; "if they love each other he can help her as his wife"; "she will be as a second wife and it is very difficult to live with two wives." Those who responded "rarely" or "never" thought that "she is not a real wife" and "all is dependent on whether or not he [the brother-in-law] loves her."

What is interesting about these latter responses is that we find articulated for the first time a notion of "love" as a reason for the stability and happiness of a marital relationship. It almost appears as if the Kwaya were searching for an alternative reason for marital stability in the face of waning communal pressures and confusion over principles of inheritance and descent. Yet, the root of their ability to discuss marriage in terms of a "love" relationship must be their matrilineal tradition, a tradition which gives women a certain equality with men in marital relationship.

Ironically, of the three peoples studied so far, it is the Kwaya, the ones most disrupted by the pastoral policy of the Catholic Church

---

*See Appendix A, Table 32.
†See Appendix A, Table 33.

and the most threatening to the Western missionaries, who have in their traditional matrilineal attitudes a certain predisposition to understanding and accepting a Western personalist theology of marriage. However, instead of building on this foundation, the Church through prejudice and ignorance systematically sought to destroy the tradition, substituting a patrilineal tradition that promotes a less Christian vision of the role and position of women in society.

13. Kwaya lineal family

There are three high schools in the Kwaya area. One of them is a Catholic seminary for boys who show an interest in studying for the priesthood.[15] There is also a domestic science school for girls who have completed their primary education and four government-supported primary schools.

The marital histories of the twenty-three Kwaya widows showed that three of them had been remarried, while fifteen had not cohabited with anyone since the death of their husbands. Moreover, at the time of the survey, only one widow was cohabiting with a brother-in-law while two others were cohabiting with friends*—these are not to be confused with the initiation group friends of the Kuria; the Kwaya do not have such a tradition. Furthermore, none of the Kwaya men interviewed reported that they were cohabiting with widows, although four of them stated that they had cohabited with widows in the past but that the unions had broken up: one due to the death of the widow, three due to a lack of understanding in the relationship (notice the psychological reason given for the breakup).†

In summary, the Kwaya people, calling upon their matrilineal tradition, accept the possibility and desirability of widow remarriage, maintaining that the choice is up to the widow herself. This is so even though the majority of them are presently married according to a patrilineal tradition which innately struggles against widow remarriage. In marriages where matrilineal rules of descent are observed, there is no question but that the widow can return to her maternal homestead with her children, being free to remarry. In marriages where rules of patrilineal descent are observed, the same general options apply to the Kwaya widows as apply to the Kuria widows: (1)the widow is not free to remarry until the bridewealth is returned, (2) the widow's children always remain within the lineage of the dead husband, (3) the widow can enter into a leviratic union with a brother-in-law or relative of her deceased husband, (4) a widow can be inherited leviratically but either live as a single person or cohabit with a friend. Again there is no evidence of any specific Christian influence on these attitudes, that is, both the Christians and non-Christians answered in the same way.

The story of the Catholic Church's attempt to change the Kwaya matrilineal tradition by the obligatory introduction of bridewealth can only be seen as misguided, unfortunate, and unnecessary. It not only set the stage for greater social instability and dislocation but also took away from the women the greater freedom given them by their matrilineal tradition.

---

*See Appendix A, Table 47. One informant indicated that a widow would be free to cohabit with a friend only if she was seen as the cause of her husband's death and therefore unwanted by his family and if both of her parents were dead.

†See Appendix A, Table 52.

Kwaya Reactions to the Christian Prohibition
of the Leviratic Custom

Given the confused state of affairs regarding marital institutions, it would be difficult to guess what the reactions of the Kwaya people would be to the churches' prohibition of the leviratic union. However, the data presented so far indicates that the Kwaya would tend to answer in terms of their matrilineal traditions—this appears to be the case. Thus, when asked why the Christian churches forbid the leviratic custom, 67% (the highest percentage of all the four peoples) stated that the prohibition was due solely to "Christian custom": an indication of a lack of concern over the prohibition since it rarely arises in the matrilineal tradition.

At the same time a significant number of the Kwaya (27%) said very plainly that the prohibition was due to the fact that the "widow is not his (brother-in-law's) wife," and 3% responded that "God forbids this custom." The comments in the in-depth interviews further elaborated these responses. They emphasized that the leviratic custom is wrong because the woman is like a second wife—the answer of twelve of the thirty in-depth respondents, and that the relationship is sinful and spoils the sacrament of marriage joining the brother-in-law and his legal wife—the answer of nine other interviewees. These in-depth comments are the clearest expression of the Catholic Church's official teachings about the negative aspects of this custom. Thus we have side-by-side a general indifference to the prohibition of the levirate along with a clear understanding of the reasons alleged by the Church for the prohibition.

Further evidence for the predominantly "matrilineal" attitude of the Kwaya regarding the care of widows is that 74% of the Kwaya (again the highest percentage of the four peoples) *approve* of the Christian prohibition of the levirate (the in-depth interviews showing the same frequency distribution of responses.) Moreover, there was statistical significance (at the .01 level)* to the correlation of

---

*The .01 level means that there is a 1% chance that these differences are not real but are due to sampling bias. Herbert Blaloch, *Social Statistics* (Toronto: McGraw-Hill, 1970). p. 159.

ILLUSTRATION 9—RELIGIOUS AFFILIATIONS OF KWAYA ADULTS *

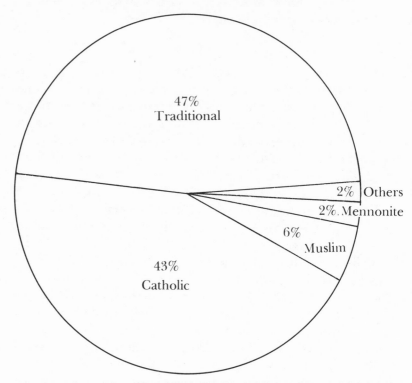

47%
Traditional

2% Others

2% Mennonite

6%
Muslim

43%
Catholic

KWAYA CATHOLIC CHURCH

The Catholic mission work among the Kwaya began with the arrival of the first two White Fathers in 1907. They settled at a place called Nyakatende, but when the superior, Thuet, died six months later, the post was closed until January 1911. In 1912, the missionaries moved to Nyegina near Buramba and started a mission station which has survived until present times. For over twenty-five years Nyegina remained the only mission station in the Mara region. In 1947, the American Maryknoll Fathers took charge of the Nyegina mission. Six years later they created a new parish in Musoma town which took over pastoral responsibilities for parts of Kwayaland.

The most intensive evangelization of the Kwaya took place from 1959 to 1964 when 5,370 people (3,640 adults and 1,730 children) were baptized at the Nyegina mission. During that same period 704 marriages were recorded with 436 of them involving two Catholic partners.†

*See Appendix A, Table 48.
†Figures taken from the official diocesan records.

14. Kwaya polygynous family with a Maryknoll missionary

The Kwaya people are primarily an agricultural people, with fishing, cattle holding, and hunting as secondary forms of economy. Prior to the introduction of cotton in 1924, farming was limited to food crops for subsistence purposes.

attitude towards the prohibition of the levirate with religious affiliation: 82% of the Christians approved of the prohibition as opposed to 68% of the non-Christians. However, because the number of non-Christians who approve is also very large, it is clear that opposition to this custom comes from more than just Christian influence. Hence there must be indigenous cultural factors (independent of Christianity), especially the matrilineal principle of descent and inheritance, that also opposes a leviratic institution. The Kwaya attitudes regarding the Christian prohibition of the levirate in terms of religious affiliation are shown in Table 16.

When the Kwaya were then asked why they approved of the Christian churches' stand on the leviratic issue, 55% gave the reason that the "woman is *like* a second wife" (the highest percentage again of all the four peoples), 30% said that it was "against church law" and 10% said that it "destroys the sacrament of mat-

TABLE 16

KWAYA ATTITUDES REGARDING THE CHRISTIAN PROHIBITION OF THE LEVIRATE
BY RELIGIOUS AFFILIATION (CHRISTIAN/NON-CHRISTIAN) (%)

Attitudes	Religious Affiliation		% Total
	% Christian	% Non-Christian	
Approve	82	68	74
Disapprove...................	18	32	26
Total %	100	100	100
Number	(128)	(178)	(306)

rimony for other people" (i.e. the brother-in-law and his wife). Evidently, these reasons are not mutually exclusive as the in-depth interviews showed that all three reasons were acceptable in explaining why one approved of the churches' prohibition. Table 17 shows the reasons the Kwaya gave for approving the churches' prohibition of the levirate:

TABLE 17

REASONS KWAYAS GAVE FOR APPROVING THE CHURCHES'
PROHIBITION OF THE LEVIRATE (%)

Reasons Given	100 % Kwaya People
Levirate is forbidden by Church law	30
Widow is like a second wife	55
Widow destroys another's sacrament of marriage	10
Widow has sinned	2
Other	3
Total %	100
Number	(229)

The Kwaya respondents (26%) who opposed the churches' policy regarding widows and leviratic unions gave both religious and moral reasons for their position, reasons similar to the ones given by the Luo and Kuria. The religious reasons are: "God did not forbid this custom (22%)," "the widow is still a member of the Church (12%)," "the widow still loves God (6%)." The moral reasons are: "the widow is not a prostitute (21%)", "the widow has no fault, she did not kill her husband (15%)," "she is in need and difficulty and should be helped (11%)."* Again there were no significant correlations of these responses with the independent variables. The in-depth interviews showed, as in the previous question, that all of these reasons are considered valid for justifying opposition to the churches' prohibition.

The marital histories show that ten of the twenty-three Kwaya widows interviewed were Christians. Yet none of them reported that they had been censured by their churches for entering into a leviratic union with a brother-in-law (this is the direct opposite of the Luo widow response). There were also five Kwaya men who said that they had cohabited with widows of which two were Christians, but neither reported that they had been punished by their Church for this cohabitation. It is clear from this that the leviratic prohibition is not a frequent pastoral problem for the Church in Kwayaland. There are so many other options for the care of widows that the levirate does not have the kind of prominance it has in Kuria or Luoland, even though the majority of the Kwaya are marrying according to a patrilineal principle that has a built-in leviratic bias—evidence again that the Kwaya are either shaping and modifying their new patrilineal attitudes in terms of their traditional matrilineal attitudes, customs, and beliefs, or that they are accepting only the outer shell and appearance of the patrilineal structures without its internal value system. If the latter, then one would still be justified in describing the Kwaya as a people with predominantly matrilineal-type attitudes and values, even though the majority presently follow the patrilineal principle of inheritance and descent in their marriage alliances.

---

*See Appendix A, Table 36.

15. Members of a Kwaya homestead: father, son, widow, grandchild.

The Kwaya like the Kuria and Luo did not live in villages until 1974. At that time they were resettled into village communities under a government-sponsored vitalization program.

In summary, the Kwaya's opposition to the leviratic custom is unique. Obviously, it is not derived only from Christian influence but also from their original matrilineal descent tradition. In that tradition there is no bridewealth payment, the woman does not give rights over her procreative powers to her husband's family, and her children always inherit through her own lineage. In such a system there are no compelling reasons of either descent principles or bridewealth payments forcing the widow to remain in her husband's lineage through a leviratic union—the case of the Kuria and Luo widows. If a Kwaya widow chooses to remain in her deceased husband's homestead, she can take on the status of a single woman (if older and with children) or become the leviratic wife of a brother-in-law. There is no obligation or pressure on the part of her brother-in-law to be a surrogate or substitute for her deceased husband.

The churches' reasons for forbidding the leviratic custom have been accepted and understood in an ambiguous manner. Thus, on one question, the majority said that the prohibition of the levirate was merely church custom but when pressed for why they approved of the prohibition, the majority gave the churches' reason that the widow is like a second wife. This ambiguity, no doubt, is partially due to the confusion over the rules regulating inheritance and descent as well as the fact that the leviratic problem for the Christian Kwaya has been infrequent—there was not even one respondent in the survey whose marital history illustrated the problem. Thus one can easily give lip service to a teaching that does not make immediate demands on one's life style thereby forcing a careful examination of the values involved. Likewise, Kwaya widows have many other viable options such as remarriage, returning to their paternal homestead, remaining as a single person in their husband's homestead. Furthermore the acceptance by so many non-Christian people of the churches' discipline in this matter provides a good illustration of how a Christian teaching can reinforce a traditional custom and attitude without changing or challenging the custom's underlying values and social structure.

For Kwaya Christians, the conflict over the prohibition of the leviratic custom may in the future become more frequent if a greater number of people begin to take seriously and put into practice the leviratic implications of their "new" patrilineal principle of inheritance and descent.

Response of the Kwaya Catholic Leaders

Because of a lack of conflict in the Kwaya society over the prohibition of the leviratic custom, it would be hard to predict how the Kwaya Catholic leaders would understand and relate to the issue. Would they be unaware of its nature, seeing it as a foreign custom? Would they be open to accepting it within a Christian context like the Luo and Kuria leaders? Would they call for more investigation? Do they see the potential implications for leviratic types of union growing out of the new, Church-promoted patrilineal inheritance structures? To answer these questions nineteen Kwaya Catholic Church leaders were interviewed: six Maryknoll missionaries and thirteen Africans.

First of all, the greater majority of the leaders stated the obvious, that widows in Kwayaland can indeed remarry. Eight of them gave as the reason the free choice of the widow; others held that a widow can remarry but only in a Church ceremony or that the young widows alone are the ones who can remarry. One missionary commented that even though widows can remarry, he had never seen a widow remarried in a Church ceremony. However, on the other side, three leaders said definitely that a widow cannot remarry and two of them gave the reason of the antiquity of this custom among the Kwaya (they may have been referring to the old patrilineal tradition in parts of Kwayaland).

The question of whether or not a leviratic widow can actually* receive the sacraments, appears to have been misunderstood. There was no distinction made between a single widow and a widow in a leviratic union, nor between whether she *could* or *should* receive the sacraments. Consequently, there was a variety of conflicting responses. An example of this confusion is the response of three leaders that "the widow's reception of the sacraments depends on whether she married a Christian—an obvious misunderstanding of the question.

When asked whether the levirate is a way of caring for a widow or a marriage, suprisingly two of the missionaries felt it was a real marriage and one missionary said it was in between a marriage and caring even though everybody else saw it as a way of caring.†

When asked what changes in the pastoral discipline regarding widows should be promoted, one missionary and six African leaders (a larger percentage than the Kuria and Luo leaders) stated that a widow should be enabled to remarry. One missionary and five Africans (a smaller percentage than that of the Luo and Kuria) thought that the custom of the levirate should be accepted. Two missionaries thought that there should be more investigation and one catechist thought that the widows should be helped temporally and spiritually. Table 18 shows the attitudes towards proposed pastoral changes regarding leviratic widows by type of Kwaya Catholic leadership.

In the final question about Church discipline regarding marriage, understandably there were no direct references to the levi-

---

*See Appendix A, Table 38.
†See Appendix A, Table 39.

TABLE 18

PROPOSED PASTORAL CHANGES REGARDING LEVIRATIC WIDOWS
BY TYPE OF CATHOLIC CHURCH LEADERSHIP (N=16)

Changes Proposed	Kwaya Catholic Leadership		Total
	N. Missionary	N. African	
Work to enable widow remarriage..........	1	6	7
Accept the levirate fully	1	5	6
Reinvestigate the leviratic problem	2	-	2
Help widows spiritually and temporally..............	-	1	1
Total	4	12	16

rate problem by the Kwaya leaders.* However, one missionary said that the Church should generally follow African customs, and one African leader thought that the Church should accept the norms of contemporary society. This silence about the leviratic problem confirms the analysis that the levirate has a low priority among Kwaya marriage problems.

In summary, the responses of the Kwaya Catholic leaders support the position that the conflicts among the Kwaya Christians over the leviratic union are minimal and that this issue is not important or pressing. However, despite the lack of concern and interest in this problem, the overwhelming majority of the leaders still confirm that the levirate is a way of caring for widows and not a new marriage relationship. Moreover, there is a significant number of Kwaya leaders who feel, like the Luo and Kuria leaders, that the levirate can be accepted by the Church. At the same time there also is a significant group that would like to promote widow remarriage. These two groups, perhaps unconsciously, represent

---

*See Appendix A, Table 55.

the matrilineal and patrilineal traditions of the Kwaya regarding the proper way to care for widows.

In concluding the analysis of the Kwaya material, we have come full circle in our study of the leviratic problem vis-à-vis its compatibility with Christianity. At the very time the Church was openly opposing the leviratic custom in the societies of the Luo and Kuria, it was indirectly introducing the same custom into the Kwaya society. In other words as the Church sought to change the Kwaya matrilineal descent structure through the obligatory introduction of bridewealth, which raises the possibility of a leviratic custom, so also it sought to change the Luo and Kuria patrilineal descent structure through widow remarriage, which raises the possibility of a woman controlling the inheritance and descent of her children. The action of the Church in dealing with these three cases is truly contradictory and cannot be justified theologically. The Church, obviously, did not know what it was doing or what it wanted.

The Kwaya material also demonstrates how each society is classified as matrilineal or patrilineal depending on which lineage controls the inheritance and descent of the children. If it is the mother's lineage, e.g. Kwaya, it is matrilineal; if it is the father's lineage, e.g. Luo and Kuria, it is patrilineal. Thus it becomes clear that the leviratic custom is basically only a *patrilineal* institution for the care of widows and their children. It serves two functions: (1) it keeps together widows and their children (whether actual or potential), children that are recruited irrevocably into their fathers' lineages; (2) it continues widows' legal marriages to their deceased husbands through surrogate relationships. As a consequence, in the Kwaya society, where children are recruited irrevocably into their mothers' lineages, and the widows can enter into new marriages together with their children from the previous marriage, the leviratic custom does not make sense.

In view of the logical incompatibility of the matrilineal principle with the leviratic custom, it is no wonder that the overwhelming majority of the Kwaya people would be disposed towards and supportive of the Christian prohibition of the levirate. Thus the Kwaya support for the churches' prohibition, which might be construed as due to Christian influence, is more likely due mainly to the meshing of the churches' position with a traditional matrilineal attitude which finds the levirate meaningless. Indeed, the

Kwaya interviewers complained at how difficult it was to explain to the people the meaning of the questions they were asking about the levirate; so few they said, had any interest in or familiarity with the topic.

Moreover, we see how introducing a patrilineal inheritance structure into Kwaya society did not ensure that the *implications* of this structure would either be understood or accepted the way they are in the Luo or Kuria society. In fact, the data seem to indicate that the new Kwaya patrilineal structure controlling the inheritance and descent of the children has merely overlaid the traditional matrilineal attitudes regarding the care of widows without changing them. Hence, for the Kwaya, payment of bridewealth and widow remarriage can go hand in hand, at least in terms of attitudes, without the kinds of conflicts this would engender in the Luo and Kuria societies. As a result there are so many options possible for a Kwaya widow that at the time of the survey (1972) none of them could be singled out as the preferred option. Too bad that our Luo widow, Victoria Akech, had not been born into the Kwaya society. If she had, she most likely would not have been confronted by the Church, denied the sacraments, and removed from her position of leadership.

Furthermore, control over the children by the Kwaya women and their lineages gives the women greater freedom in their marital relationships, for there is no threat of separation from their children. This not only makes possible greater instability (the Kwaya had the highest divorce rate of the people studied, 28%—no doubt the source of the missionaries' alarm) but also makes possible greater voluntarization and personalization of marital relationships (recall that it was only the Kwaya who spoke of love as a reason for marital stability). Huber tells how the Kwaya father will be especially careful with his sons so as not to alienate them, hoping that they will stay with him as his friends until he dies. (It is amazing how close this is to the Western family's desire for friendship between children and parents.)

The Church appears to have judged the Kwaya matrilineal customs solely on the basis of their negative effects, without taking into account their many positive effects, e.g. voluntarization of marriage relationship, marriage stability based on ties of love rather than payment of bridewealth, care of widows through remarriage.

Are not the many religious vocations from the Kwaya people evidence of the existence of many strong, faithful, matrilineal Christian family units?

The real tragedy of the Kwaya story is that the Church did not recognize and build upon the Kwaya matrilineal traditions, traditions that are in many ways more open to Western Christian teachings about freedom, personal relationships, and the equality of men and women than the patrilineal tradition they tried to put in its place.

A question arises as to what will happen to Kwaya widows if the full implications of the patrilineal tradition take hold? Would the leviratic custom become the ordinary way for the care of widows as with the Luo and Kuria? How would the Christian churches respond to a new Kwaya leviratic problem (a problem they helped create)? Some Church leaders have already suggested the acceptance of the leviratic custom, others have suggested widow remarriage. Would it be *remarriage* for those in marriage alliances following a matrilineal descent principle and the *levirate* for those following a patrilineal descent principle? Let us now turn to a presentation of the Sukuma customs for the care of widows.

NOTES

1. Hugo Huber, "The Wakwaya of Musoma," manuscript, Switzerland: University of Fribourg, c. 1966. p. 39.

2. It is speculated that this matrilineal tradition came from matrilineal peoples of the Eastern Congo—the possible home of the original founders of the Kwaya people. This would explain the reason why this people, together with the Bashora, form a matrilineal pocket in the Musoma district surrounded by patrilineal societies. See Huber, "The Wakwaya of Musoma," pp. 41–42.

3. The Bashora are very close to the Kwaya in customs and language although Huber ("The Wakwaya of Musoma," p. 2.) demonstrates sufficient differences between them to classify the Kwaya as a separate people.

4. The United Republic of Tanzania, *1967 Population Census*, I, 84–85.

5. The tradition of the three major Kwaya clans—Abagitwe, Abang'oma, Abahanyisi—claims that their founder, Magwa, originally came from Bukoba on the Western shore of Lake Victoria, stayed for some time on Ukerewe Island before he arrived in the Ebwayi region, the former habitat of the Kwaya people south of their present location. Another tradition maintains that the original

Kwaya people immigrated from an island in Lake Victoria called "Kome" near Uzinza and that they passed through Sukumaland before reaching Majita and Ebwayi. (See Huber, "The Wakwaya of Musoma," p. 17.)

6. For more information about these sub-tribes see Huber, "The Wakwaya of Musoma," pp. 18–33.

7. White Father's diary for the Catholic mission at Nyegina as quoted by Huber, "The Wakwaya of Musoma," p. 46: "En principe tous les chefs de l'aksi (Action Catholica) se sont déclarés... pour lutter contre cette funeste coutume du bumama, c.à.d. qu'a la mort du père tout, absolument tout, est pris par des parents (maternelles) quelquefois lointains, de sorte que les enfants ne reçoivent rien" (April 6, 1940).

8. Adrian Hastings, *Church and Mission in Modern Africa* (London: Burns and Oates, 1967), p. 172.

9. White Father's diary for the Catholic mission station at Nyegina, Musoma district, Tanzania as quoted by Huber, "The Wakwaya of Musoma," p. 46: "Tous les vieux des trois royaumes de Busumba, Munguru et Mugango sous la présidence de notre roi Pio ont décidé presqu'à l'unanimité... d'abolir les coutumes funestes pour la vie sociale des Bakwaya: le kukyuka qui consiste en ceci: les enfants arrivés a l'age de puberté peuvent quitter définitivement leurs parents propres et se déclarer enfants de l'oncle maternel—et le bugabi qui prive les propres enfants de l'héritage des biens de leurs parents, parce que les cousins, les enfants de la soeur du père, sont les héritiers légitimes" (Jan. 11, 1945).

10. Huber, "The Wakwaya of Musoma," p. 89.

11. Ibid., p. 46.

12. Ibid., p. 89.

13. Hans Cory, "A Few Notes about the General Introduction of Brideprice in Bukwaya," (unpublished letter to the district commissioner of Musoma, September 1945, available in the Cory Collection in the Library, University of Dar es Salaam), pp. 1–2.

14. Hans Cory, "The Customary Law of Inheritance in Mukwaya" (Letter to the District Commissioner, Musoma, Tanzania, 1945, available in the Cory Collection, Library, University of Dar es Salaam, Tanzania), pp. 5–6. Hugo Huber, "The Wakwaya of Musoma," p. 96, indicates that even in the nonbridewealth marriages, the widow could be inherited by her brother-in-law or a relative of her husband and that they (the husband's relatives) would feel responsible for her upkeep in her old age if she would prefer not to stay with her own son or daughter.

15. The other two high schools are government operated, serving the Mara region. Entrance is obtained through competitive examinations.

16. Sukuma monogamous family

The four languages employed in gathering the data for this study are all tonal in structure. The most difficult one, however, appears to be the Sukuma language. Few of the Maryknoll missionaries have learnt it well and most are now studying and speaking only Kiswahili: the national language of the educated elite.

There are nine government-supported primary schools in the Busega area surveyed but no secondary schools.

CHAPTER FIVE

Sukuma Customs for the Care of Widows.
A Patrilineal Variation

The fourth people studied was the Sukuma: a Bantu-speaking patrilineal people. This people is the largest ethnic group in Tanzania, numbering (in the 1967 census) over 1,500,000 people. Their land is situated south and southeast of Lake Victoria; their northernmost boundary reaches up to the famous Serengeti game preserve. As with the Kuria and Luo, it was not intended that the entire population be surveyed. Thus only one section of Sukumaland, the southern half of Busega (a subdivision of the Mwanza district) was selected for the purposes of the survey.[1]

The Sukuma generally follow a patrilineal descent pattern, although Hans Cory sees them as originally following a matrilineal pattern, which has gradually been supplanted by bridewealth payment, permitting the father to control the descent of the children. Evidence for this is seen in the traditional marriage ceremony where there is a custom called *kuhedekwa* in which the groom lives with his in-laws for a period of time. This custom (perhaps) dates back to a matrilineal period and represents an uxor-local residence situation, i.e. the husband resides with the wife's family.[2]

The inclusion of the Sukuma added a further interesting dimension to the study, for it made even clearer how varied these societies are in attitudes and patterns of behavior even though there are some general similiarites in social structures and languages.[3] The place of the Sukuma in our model is as follows. (They are similar to the Kuria in that they speak a Bantu language and follow patrilineal patterns of descent).

In Sukuma tradition, a widow is usually cared for according to one of three major options—by way of contrast, the Luo have only two options, the Kuria four, and the Kwaya seven. The first Sukuma option is to enter into a leviratic union with a brother-in-law or a relative of her deceased husband. The second is to return

115

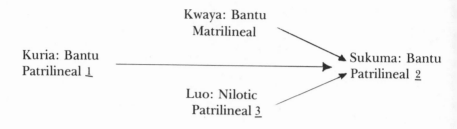

Kwaya: Bantu
Matrilineal

Kuria: Bantu
Patrilineal 1

Sukuma: Bantu
Patrilineal 2

Luo: Nilotic
Patrilineal 3

to her paternal home to seek out a new marriage: this option entails the return of bridewealth and the separation of the widow from her children. The third is to remain in the home of her deceased husband with her children without being inherited and without the status of a legal wife—this option is unique to the Sukuma; it is only possible if the widow has children.[4] Here is a legal interpretation of the rules relating to these options:

ILLUSTRATION 10—LEGAL INTERPRETATIONS OF SUKUMA OPTIONS

A widow *(nchilwa)* must choose the man who is to inherit her from among the brothers of her deceased husband if there are any; if there are none, from among the nearest kinsmen. These and the family council may sometimes agree to a widow choosing another of the deceased's relatives, but they will never agree to her choosing an outsider.

A childless widow is inherited by one of the heirs but only by mutual consent. If she refuses to be inherited, she is allowed to return to her family.

(Widow with children) Such a widow can either agree or refuse to be inherited. In the latter case she can choose to remain with her children, living within her deceased husband's family...

If she remains with her husband's family, she is not free to choose lovers. If she has lovers the family has the right to object and, if the widow does not obey, the family council can return her to her family while the children remain with the paternal family.[5]

The new option for the care of widows introduced by the Sukuma places the widow in a situation where she is neither considered a legal wife nor is she seen as free to remarry. Thus, as pointed out by Cory, if a widow under this third option cohabits with a lover, the man cannot be required to pay compensation for adultery because the widow is not considered a married woman.[6]

However, if she were to have a child by her lover, the child would belong to and inherit in the line of the deceased husband, since the husband's lineage maintains control over the procreative powers of the widow. The advantage of this option to the widow is that it enables her to avoid two things: (1) being inherited in a leviratic union by a relative of her deceased husband, which would require that she cohabit with him, (2) returning to her paternal home, which would separate her from her children and force her family to give back the bridewealth.[7]

On the basis of the Luo and Kuria data, one would expect that the Sukuma, who are also patrilineal, would be more concerned to ensure the continuing fertility of the widow through a designated marital partner as well as to control her domestic services for the lineage. This is clearly not the case. But if the Sukuma, formerly, were matrilineal, one could perhaps argue that this unexpected *freedom* of the widow to avoid these obligations is a carry-over from the earlier tradition (recall how the Kwaya were in a process of interrelating values and priorities of both matrilineal and patrilineal principles; perhaps with the Sukuma, we are witnessing a later stage of this kind of interaction of traditions). At the very least, this unexpected freedom of the widow shows again how each society shapes and modifies the rules relating to the care of widows according to its own inner values and priorities.

This more "matrilineal" approach of the Sukuma to the care of widows ("matrilineal" in the sense of the greater freedom given widows) is forcefully expressed in the responses to the question of whether a widow *could* remarry in Sukuma society. Over 91% of the Sukuma (the highest percentage of all four peoples and completely opposite to the Luo response) gave an unqualified "yes," 7% said that it was dependent upon certain factors, and only 2% said "no." For some reason, the in-depth interviews did not have as high a ratio of positive to negative responses. Still the overwhelming majority gave an unqualified "yes" to the possibility of widow remarriage.

When asked for reasons why a widow could remarry, the Sukuma answered in the same categories as the matrilineal Kwaya namely, that there is nothing to oppose her remarriage as her husband had died (46%), she can remarry if she wants (30%), she can remarry if she cannot live on her own (14%). All these reasons

SELECTED CENSUS ENUMERATION AREAS IN SUKUMALAND

Strictly speaking there is no indigenous name for the Sukuma. The word itself means "north" and probably originated when pioneer travellers passing through Nyawezi to the south were informed about the country to the north, i.e. "Sukuma." Eventually the name came to be applied to the whole area and its inhabitants.

Furthermore, there is no extant tradition about the original inhabitants of present-day Sukumaland. According to the Sukuma themselves, the country (in the beginning) was overgrown with bush and sparsely populated. The scattered human colonies consisted of a hundred odd people under the leadership of an *ntemi*, a name that later became the title for a chief.[8]

BUSEGA DISTRICT

The major reasons for selecting the Busega district for the survey were: (1) the supervision of the Catholic mission in the area by the Maryknoll Fathers since its foundation as a parish in 1954; (2) the support, interest, and encourage-

ment of the Maryknoll missionaries living there at the time of the survey; (3) the area's proximity to the other three survey areas.

There was no information available on the distribution of clans in this part of Sukumaland. The area had been settled relatively recently, and had absorbed people from many clans who had moved out of their paternal homelands in search of land for farming and grazing. Indeed, in the study people claimed affiliation in forty different Sukuma clans. It was impossible, therefore, to select a homogeneous group based on clan affiliation for the Sukuma universe; the selection had to be made on a geographical basis, i.e., all the Sukuma-speaking people living in the selected area.[9]

The approximate boundaries of the Sukuma "universe" were the Duma River to the south, Lake Victoria to the east, the road from Nyahanga to Igalukiro to the north, and a line from Shigara to Nyanguli following census-enumeration area boundaries to the west. The total population included in the survey area was estimated at 23,100.

underscore the freedom of the woman to make her own choice. Table 19 illustrates these Sukuma reasons as to why widows can remarry.

TABLE 19

REASONS SUKUMAS GAVE WHY WIDOWS CAN REMARRY (%)

Reasons Given	% Sukuma
If she does not have children	9
If she wants she can	30
There is nothing to oppose it as the husband has died	46
If she cannot live on her own	14
Other	1
Total %	100
Number	(295)

The marital histories of the twenty-four Sukuma widows interviewed confirmed that remarriage was more than just a legal possibility; five of them had actually remarried.* This was the highest number of all four societies (20%). Of the remaining widows, only two were cohabiting with brothers-in-law, while the rest were living alone, claiming that they had not cohabited with a marital partner since the death of their husbands.†

---

*Tanner ("Marriage and Maturity," *African Studies* 14 [1955] 163) points out how there are no stated sanctions against widow remarriage in the Sukuma tradition, provided the parties to the new marriage ritually purify themselves from the death of the former husband. This same is not true of the Luo society, where the "evil eye" (i.e., malevolence) of the deceased husband warns against remarriage.

†See Appendix A, Table 47.

When asked whether widows want to remarry, again 98% of the Sukuma responded affirmatively.* The reasons given for widows' desiring remarriage all relate to the personal needs of the widows, needs such as the difficulty of living without a husband (56%), the need for a marital partner (11%), the young age of the widow (25%). Table 20 shows the Sukuma reasons why widows want to remarry.

TABLE 20

REASONS SUKUMAS GAVE WHY WIDOWS WANT TO REMARRY (%)

Reasons Given	% Sukuma
If there is no one to take care of her	6
If she still wants a husband	11
The young ones want to remarry	25
It is difficult to live without a husband	56
Other	2
Total %	100
Number	(295)

When asked who could best care for a widow who had not been re-married, 19% of the Sukuma said that it would be the widow's family—an entirely new category. Not even the Kwaya, whom we discussed in the previous chapter, gave this category as a possibility even though it is clear that the Kwaya widow according to the

---

*The in-depth interviews supported this distribution of responses. Only one out of thirty respondents said that a widow does not want to remarry.

matrilineal traditions has the freedom to return to her family on the death of her husband.*

This is clear indication that the Sukuma widow can turn to her family for support, in particular (pointed out by Cory) to those members who received and profited from her bridewealth.[10]

Further confirmation of the Sukuma widow's economic relationship to her family is found in the in-depth interviews. There a very high percentage of respondents answered that it is the mother or father of the widow who could best care for her, helping her with money and clothes and aiding her in times of sickness and difficulties. Another dimension to this question is that the Sukuma (in the area surveyed), unlike the Luo and Kuria, do not necessarily live together with blood relatives. Often they homestead together with friends. Hence, if a widow chooses to remain uninherited in a homestead made up of personal friends, she cannot lobby for their support on the basis of blood ties, the way she might if she resided with relatives of the deceased husband.

The majority of the Sukuma, in fact, gave the expected patrilineal reply to the question of who could best care for a widow if she is not remarried, i.e., 47% said the brother-in-law, and 15% a relative of the deceased husband. A few others replied that if there was no understanding with the husband's relatives, then either a friend (7%) or a single man (6%) could best care for her.†

In responding to the question of whether a widow in a leviratic union is cared for like a wife, we find an ambivalent response on the part of the Sukuma. About 40% say that she is "frequently" or "always," while another 40% say she is "rarely" or "never," and about 20% "sometimes."‡ The comments in the in-depth interviews on the "rarely" or "never" response were that "it is difficult to care for one who is not your real wife," "she is the wife of another,"

---

*A possible explanation for this difference is the economic independence of the Kwaya women. Since no bridewealth is paid for them (matrilineal tradition), there are no corresponding obligations set up with members of their families who would have profited from their bridewealth. The Kwaya women in the matrilineal tradition therefore are presumed to have the wits and means to support themselves; this same is not true of the women in patrilineal societies. The patrilineal women are much more tied to the economic fortunes of their husbands.

†See Appendix A, Table 32.

‡See Appendix A, Table 33.

17. Sukuma polygynous homestead: two wives and married daughter

The rate of plural marriage for the Sukuma people was 12%, the lowest of the four peoples surveyed. The amount of bridewealth payments varied from six to thirty cows, with the majority paying from eleven to twenty (see Appendix A, Table 40).

and "it is difficult to take care of a woman with whom you are not sharing the same bed." This latter comment, perhaps, is a clue to the Sukuma ambivalent feelings about the care of widows. For if the leviratic widow lives apart from her inheritor, as is often the case, and is paid only periodic visits by her inheritor, then of course the widow in such a relationship is not cared for like a wife. The only other in-depth comments were on the "sometimes" response, namely, "it is difficult"; " if the brother-in-law is kind"; "she is not a real wife"; "one only looks after her."

None of the Sukuma men surveyed reported that they were cohabiting with widows at the time of the interview. Two of them reported that they had cohabited with widows in the past, but that the unions had broken up due to the lack of understanding between the parties (notice again that the reason alleged for the breakup is psychological).*

---

*See Appendix A, Table 52.

In summary, we find among the Sukuma, alongside the ordinary leviratic custom, two aspects of widow care that distinguish them from the Luo, Kuria, and Kwaya. First, a significant number of Sukuma widows do in fact remarry. Remarriage, therefore, is not an unusual option, as it is for the Luo and Kuria, nor is it infrequent, as it is for the Kwaya. The reason for this higher rate of remarriage among Sukuma widows may be due to the more "matrilineal" attitudes of Sukuma families towards their daughters. These attitudes would make them more receptive to receiving the daughters back and returning the bridewealth—the social and economic break at the time of marriage between women and their lineages is not as complete and final as it is with the patrilineal peoples such as the Luo and Kuria. However, given the high value traditional African societies place on children, this reason would make sense only if the widow were childless.

Another reason for the high rate of widow remarriage in Sukumaland may be the recent custom whereby a man will agree to the "marriage" of his daughter based only on a promise of bridewealth.[11] However, if the husband should die before having paid any of the promised bridewealth, his lineage would have no legal claim to the children (recall how bridewealth determines the status of the children). The widow, therefore, is free to take her children with her into a new marriage. This custom, apparently, has arisen as a result of the scarcity of bridewealth cattle—the Sukuma cattle have been decimated by epidemics of east-coast fever and sleeping sickness. Many fathers, when faced with the situation of supporting unmarried over-aged daughters, bow to the inevitable and agree to a nontraditional marriage in which there is no actual exchange of bridewealth. They feel that a promise of bridewealth is better than no bridewealth at all. In the meantime, the status of the marital union is in between an elopement and a traditional marriage.

The second distinguishing element of Sukuma traditions dealing with the care of widows is the custom by which a widow with children can remain as a single person in her husband's homestead but cannot remarry. This custom is a "third way" unknown to the Luo, Kuria, and (perhaps) the Kwaya, and is situated in between *remarriage* and the *leviratic* union. It combines both matrilineal and patrilineal attitudes towards widows: matrilineal in that the widow in such a situation can turn to her parents for support, and is no longer considered a legal wife; patrilineal in that the widow's children inherit through their deceased father's lineage, and that the widow herself remains under the sexual control of her husband's lineage, i.e., she is not free to take a lover or remarry.

It was originally felt that the inclusion of the Sukuma in this study would entail a duplication of the traditions, attitudes, and customs of the Kuria since both follow patrilineal rules of inheritance and descent and speak Bantu-type languages. It is now clear that this hypothesis is false. The Sukuma have taken our discussion of traditional customs for the care of widows one step farther. They have introduced a new and novel custom which gives a widow a social status as an unmarriageable single woman and enables her to draw on both her own and her husband's lineage for maintenance and support (there is a remarkable parallel here with the social situation of widows in Western societies). Again there was no measurable Christian influence on these questions and issues.

Sukuma Reactions to the Christian Prohibition of the Leviratic Custom

Since the Sukuma, in fact, permit a significant number of widows either to remarry or to remain in their husband's homesteads as single persons (provided they have children), one would expect a variety of attitudes towards the Christian prohibition of the leviratic union. Some would think in terms of bridewealth and control over children and widows and oppose the Church's prohibition. Others would think in terms of the present situation where widows do remarry or live as single persons and approve the Church's stand on the issue. A divergence in attitude among the Sukuma is borne out by the data: one-third of the Sukuma approve of the leviratic prohibition, two-thirds oppose it (the Kuria were divided in like manner).

Furthermore, a large number of Sukuma (39%) were able to give the Church-sponsored reason for opposition to the levirate, namely, that the widow is not the wife of the man with whom she cohabits: "she is like a second wife." On the other hand, 43% of the Sukuma felt that the churches' opposition to the levirate was due to its conflict with Christian rules and customs. Another 15% said that the real reason for the prohibition was that God had forbidden the custom.*

In the in-depth interviews, the only comment recorded on the reason of "Christian custom" was that this prohibition had come from Europe and was part of European religion. The only comment on the reason of "illicit cohabitation" was that the inheritor had not paid cows for the woman and, consequently, she was not his wife: hence the prohibition of the Church. This comment shows how easily Christian teachings on an issue can be understood in terms of traditional categories, e.g. bridewealth payments, without ever touching on the unique Christian explanation. The only comment recorded on the reason of "God's prohibition" stated that in the beginning God had created one man and one woman: the model for all marital unions.

Moving to the next question of whether or not the Sukuma approve or disapprove of the Christian churches' prohibition of the levirate, we find, as already pointed out, that 35% approve and 65% disapprove. When cross-tabulating the responses to this question with Christian membership, we find that there is very little statistical difference between the responses of Christians and non-Christians.† This suggests that there is opposition in the Sukuma society to the custom of the levirate independent of direct Christian influence. Table 21 shows Sukuma attitudes towards the Christian prohibition of the levirate by religious affiliation.

There was significance at the .05 level for correlation between *urban residence* and disapproval of Church policy regarding the levirate. Of those who had lived in an urban environment for a year

---

* There was a significant difference in these responses between wage workers and nonwage workers. The greater majority of the wage workers gave the moral reason for the churches' prohibition whereas only one-third of the nonwage workers gave that reason. This indicates that the wage workers (mostly men), perhaps due to their greater mobility and wider experience, were more aware of the specific reasons for the churches' prohibition. See Appendix A, Table 50. Also Appendix A, Table 34.

†There was in fact statistical significance to the relationship of Christian and non-Christian responses but only at the .057 level. This means that there is a 5% chance that the statistical differences are not real differences but are due to sampling bias. See Herbert M. Blalock, *Social Statistics,* Toronto: McGraw-Hill, 1972, p. 159.

TABLE 21

SUKUMA ATTITUDES REGARDING THE CHRISTIAN PROHIBITION OF THE LEVIRATE
BY RELIGIOUS AFFILIATION (CHRISTIAN/NON-CHRISTIAN) (%)

Attitudes	Religious Affiliation		% Total
	% Christian	% Non-Christian	
Approve	41	30	35
Disapprove...................	59	69	64
Other	—	1	1
Total %	100	100	100
Number	(123)	(178)	(301)

or more after the age of ten, 87% disapproved of the Church's prohibition.* This data supports the hypothesis that wider experiences as well as education tend to make traditional rural Africans *conservative* and *resistant to change.* One explanation given for this effect is that these factors enable individuals to gain a certain amount of economic and social power in the traditional society. Thus it is to their benefit if the society remains unchanged.

When asked for the reasons why they approved of the churches' prohibition of the levirate, two-thirds of the Sukuma gave reasons that involved negative moral judgments about the custom, reasons that obviously were not present in the traditional understanding of the morality of the custom. These reasons were: The widow is like a second wife (32%), the widow destroys the sacrament of marriage for others; e.g. the married Christian brother-in-law who inherits her (18%), the widow has committed sin (9%), the widow is like a prostitute (6%)—there was a strikingly similar distribution of these responses among the Luo and Kuria. (The in-depth interviewees, likewise, cited negative moral judgments on the levirate as their reasons for approving the Christian prohibition. Their major reason was that the widow is like a second wife.) The remaining third of the Sukuma respondents merely stated that they approved

---

* See Appendix A, Table 51.

ILLUSTRATION 11—RELIGIOUS AFFILIATIONS OF SUKUMA ADULTS *

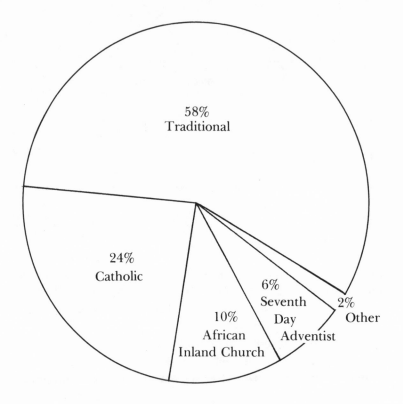

58%
Traditional

24%
Catholic

10%
African
Inland Church

6%
Seventh
Day
Adventist

2%
Other

CATHOLIC CHURCH HISTORY

In 1948 the Catholic Church in the Busega area began as an outstation from Msumbi, a neighboring White Father mission. The first recorded baptisms were in October 1948. In 1954 the outstation was turned over to the Maryknoll Fathers, who made it a regular mission center with a resident pastor. Once again, as with the other three mission centers, the years of 1960–63 were the years of the largest number of baptisms and marriages. In 1971 there was a total of 6,270 baptisms and 484 marriages recorded in the official records of the Catholic mission. (The mission encompasses a larger area than that selected for the survey.) In 1963 a second parish was established at an outstation called Illumia, located about six miles to the south of the original mission.

About 58% of the Sukuma people interviewed claimed membership in the traditional religion. This was the highest percentage for all of the four peoples studied. The African Inland Church, a fundamentalist Protestant denomination founded by North Americans, was found only among the Sukuma people.

*See Appendix A, Table 48

of the churches' prohibition because the leviratic custom was against Christian teachings.*

When those who opposed the churches' position were asked why they felt the way they did, they responded like the Luo, Kuria, and Kwaya with both moral and religious reasons. The major moral reason was that the widow is not a prostitute (45%); i.e., she is not in an illicit sexual union as the churches would have one believe. This response directly contradicts the churches' allegation that the leviratic union is sexually immoral. The other moral reason cited was that the widow did not kill her husband (13%); i.e., the situation has arisen independently of her will, so why should she be penalized for his misfortune. The religious reasons opposing the churches' prohibition were: God did not forbid this custom (17%), the widow still loves God (7%), the widow is still a member of the Church (16%).† All of the in-depth interviewees accepted or cited both moral reasons, and half accepted or cited the religious reasons as valid in explaining their objections to the Christian position on the levirate.

The marital histories of the twenty-four Sukuma widows showed that five of the eighteen who had not remarried were Christian but none of them reported that they had been punished by their churches because of the leviratic custom. Only two widows reported at the time of the survey that they were cohabiting with their brothers-in-law. In addition, two Sukuma men indicated that they had cohabited in the past with widows, but the unions had broken up because of a lack of understanding. One of these men was a Christian and admitted to being punished by his Church for failure to obey its marriage laws.

In summary, the Sukuma like the Kuria have ambivalent attitudes towards the Christian prohibition of the levirate. It would

---

* See Appendix A, Table 35.

†There was significance at the .05 level for the positive correlation between wage earnings and the religious explanations for opposition to the leviratic prohibition. Wage earners tended to give the religious reason that the widow was still a member of the Church. This adds credence to the hypothesis that wage workers are a distinct subgroup within Sukuma society as suggested by their responses on a previous question (see page 126, first footnote). For more statistical details see Appendix A, Table 53.

be hard to explain the support of non-Christians for the churches' policy unless there is already present in the Sukuma tradition a certain dislike of this custom. Evidence for a "traditional" dislike of the levirate can be drawn from the fact that a relatively large number of widows had remarried and that only two out of eighteen widows were cohabiting with their brothers-in-law. Meanwhile, it is still a two-thirds' majority of the people, slightly more non-Christians than Christians, who openly *disapprove* of the Christian prohibition and reject the churches' evaluation of the custom.

For the first time the variables "wage earning" and "urban residence" were statistically significant. It appears that these influences *conservatize* people both from the viewpoint of their own traditions as well as from that of the new Christian teachings, making them more resistant to accepting changes.

The question arises as to the status and care of the majority of the widows who are neither remarried nor inherited but are living as single persons. Should there be a specific response on the part of the Christian churches for the care of these women? Does their "single" status represent a better and more human solution to their problems than either the levirate or remarriage?

Response of the Sukuma Catholic leaders

In the Sukuma area, we have seen how there is already a significant move towards widow remarriage. Furthermore, there does not appear to be any serious confrontation with the Sukuma Christians over the leviratic issue. These factors, therefore, support the Catholic Church's policy of substituting remarriage of widows for the leviratic union. In light of this turn of events, one would expect that the Catholic Church leaders would be happy with the present course of affairs, trusting that the remarriage of widows would become more and more the rule for the Sukuma. To test out these suppositions, nine Maryknoll missionaries working among the Sukuma and twenty-seven Sukuma catechists (four of whom had been specially trained) were interviewed.

When asked whether or not Sukuma widows can remarry, the overwhelming majority of the Catholic leaders (five missionaries and twenty-two catechists) answered in the affirmative. Further, six of these catechists added the following qualifying comments:

18. Sukuma interviewers
View of Sukumaland: Lake Victoria in background

The Sukuma are an agricultural people growing cotton as a cash crop as well
as enthusiastic cattle breeders. A cotton gin built at Mwanangi in the Busega
district has brought some wage employment to the area and created a small
permanent marketing center.

"only young ones remarry"; "it is now possible but I have never
seen it happen"; "the widow can remarry if she wants." In opposition, one missionary and two catechists answered that a widow
cannot remarry in Sukuma society, citing reasons that "no one
would marry her"; "the brother-in-law is the proper one to take
care of her."

The question about the ability of leviratic widows to receive the
sacraments was again misunderstood. No distinction was made
between a leviratic widow and a "free" widow nor between whether
a widow *could* or *should* receive the sacraments. For example, eight
catechists said that the widow's reception of the sacraments depended on whether her "new" husband was a Christian or a single
man—an obvious misunderstanding of the intended sense of the
question. However, two missionaries and one African leader said
that they did not agree with the Church's rule that a leviratic widow
cannot receive the sacraments. One missionary said that he over-

rode the decision of the parish council and made the sacraments available to a leviratic widow. Another missionary said that he had wanted to allow leviratic widows access to the sacraments but had not done so thus far. Here we have a clear indication of the Maryknoll missionaries among the Sukuma taking a stand in favor of the levirate without the full support of African leaders and parish councils. This is the first instance we have found where the Western-trained missionaries were in clear disagreement with the African Church leaders.

The Maryknoll missionaries to the Sukuma, however, are of one mind with the majority of their confreres in the other three areas surveyed as to the compatibility of the levirate with Christianity. The African Church leaders in Sukumaland are the odd men out on this issue. The important question is whether the Maryknollers in Sukumaland are merely articulating a "liberal" attitude of the larger Maryknoll community in East Africa, or whether they are speaking out of serious theological reflection on their Sukuma experience. If the latter, then they have obviously reflected differently than their indigenous African colleagues.

When asked whether the levirate is a real marriage, two-thirds of all the Church leaders stated that it is only a custom for the care of widows.* However, only three of the missionaries answered in this category—the lowest number in comparison to the other three areas. The reasons given for this "care" assessment of the leviratic union were: "it is a way of keeping the children in the family of the husband (one missionary)," "it could not be a marriage as no bridewealth had been paid (one catechist)," "the instability of the situation precludes the levirate from being a marriage (two catechists)."

In the meantime four of the remaining missionaries stated that the levirate was in between a "marriage" and "caring." And the final two missionaries together with four catechists stated that the levirate was indeed a real marriage, contending that this is the way that the Sukuma people understand the relationship. Here again we find a significant number of Maryknoll missionaries (this time two-thirds of those interviewed) taking a position on the nature of

---

* See Appendix A, Table 39.

19. Sukuma polygynous homestead
Man seated at right is a well-known healer, treating
mentally ill people.

the levirate that is out of step not only with the majority of the African leaders in Sukumaland but also with almost all the Catholic Church leaders, both missionary and indigenous, included in the survey. The only possible conclusion is that many of the Maryknoll missionaries to the Sukuma do not understand the nature of the leviratic union.

When asked what changes should be made in the pastoral sphere for Sukuma widows, a surprising seventeen leaders, all Africans, said that widows should be "enabled" to remarry (this was the highest percentage for all four areas, 59%).* Moreover, in light of the previous responses that widows can and do remarry, this can only be taken to mean that in practice it is difficult for widows to remarry (especially if they have children). Thus the African leadership of the Sukuma Church would like to see the Church take a stronger stand in promoting widow remarriage. On the other side,

---

*See Illustration 3, p. 25.

three missionaries and one African leader thought that the custom of the levirate should be accepted by the Church and not made an issue. Another three missionaries and two Africans felt that the custom should be accepted with certain qualifications. And finally three African leaders thought that the widow should be helped by the Church spiritually and temporally. (Notice that the Maryknoll missionaries are again in disagreement with most of the African leaders.) Table 22 shows the proposed pastoral changes regarding leviratic widows by type of Sukuma Catholic leadership.

TABLE 22

PROPOSED PASTORAL CHANGES REGARDING LEVIRATIC WIDOWS
BY TYPE OF SUKUMA CATHOLIC CHURCH LEADERSHIP (N=29)

Changes Proposed	Sukuma Catholic Leadership		Total
	N. Missionary	N. African	
Work to enable widow remarriage....................	—	17	17
Accept the levirate fully	3	1	4
Accept the levirate with qualification...........	3	2	5
Help widows spiritually and temporally..............	—	3	3
Total	6	23	29

In response to the general question about Catholic marriage discipline, only three leaders, two missionaries and one African, mentioned the problem of widows specifically: all three asked that widows be allowed to receive the sacraments even if they are in leviratic unions.* This response indicates again that the Maryknoll missionaries to the Sukuma are more concerned than the African

---

* See Appendix A, Table 55.

leaders with accepting the leviratic custom. Other responses to this question were: the Church should be more lenient in dealing with marital problems (one missionary); African customs should be followed in all marriage matters (one African); these problems should be further investigated (one missionary).

In summary, the Sukuma Catholic Church leaders are not in general agreement, as the Catholic leaders are in the other three areas, over the nature of the leviratic custom and the present pastoral policy towards it. As a result, they are divided as to what the proper pastoral response should be: all of the Maryknoll missionaries who responded to this question felt that the proper response should be acceptance of the levirate, while three-quarters of the Africans felt that the Church should give leadership in promoting widow remarriage.

The apparent reason for the disagreement between the Western missionaries and the African leaders working in the Sukuma Catholic Church is that many of the missionaries have misunderstood the levirate as a type of marriage. Thus they reasoned that if the levirate is already a type of traditional marriage then why not recognize it as such. The pastoral conflicts caused by this kind of misunderstanding are clear in the case at hand: (1) the levirate is being incorrectly promoted with ecclesiastical approval as a "marriage" relationship rather than as a "caring" relationship; (2) no consideration is taken of the fact that the levirate already appears to be in disfavor among the majority of the Sukuma themselves. One cannot help but wonder why the correct understanding of the levirate, known by the Maryknoll missionaries in the Musoma diocese, was not shared with their confreres in Sukumaland. Or, more importantly, why did the Maryknoll missionaries not learn the correct meaning of the custom from the Sukuma themselves?

In concluding the chapter on the Sukuma, the last of the four peoples studied, we are very conscious of how varied the concrete circumstances of each people are, circumstances which must be taken into account by the Christian churches if they are to teach Christianity in an indigenous manner. The Sukuma, instead of being a replica of the Kuria as expected, showed themselves to be uniquely different and added considerably to our discussion in two major areas.

First, the Sukuma, even though they follow patrilineal rules of inheritance and descent, evidenced a number of clearly matrilineal attitudes (very much like the Kwaya) regarding the proper care of widows. These matrilineal attitudes are seen in the fact that remarriage for widows is frequent, and in the custom whereby a widow can remain in her deceased husband's homestead as a single person, relying on her parents for support. These data support Cory's opinion that the Sukuma were at one time matrilineal. It also forces a re-examination of the rigid classification of people into matrilineal or patrilineal categories. It now appears that these categories need not be mutually exclusive—a factor hinted at in the study of the Kwaya and brought to light in the study of the Sukuma. In retrospect one begins to realize that this tension between matrilineal and patrilineal attitudes is present in each society studied in varying degrees and that each society is developing in a specific direction. Here is a graph with arrows indicating the present direction of social development for each.

An example of this matrilineal/patrilineal tension in the Sukuma society is the patrilineal-type marriage alliances in which there are only promises of bridewealth payments. These marriages follow patrilineal rules of inheritance and descent as long as the husbands remain alive. However, if the husbands die before paying bridewealth, the marriages revert to matrilineal rules. Another example is the custom in which the widow remains as a single person in her husband's homestead and seeks support from her parents. This custom is matrilineal in terms of the continuation of an economic relationship between a woman and her family even after marriage, and in the fact that the woman is not required to cohabit with a relative of her deceased husband. It is patrilineal in that the children continue to receive identity and inheritance through their deceased father, and that the widow remains under the sexual control of her husband's lineage, i.e. she is neither free to remarry nor to take a lover.

Second, the Sukuma material also made a significant contribution in the area of the relationship between the missionary and indigenous Catholic Church leadership. In this area, it is clear how a misunderstanding of the nature of the levirate led a large group of missionaries to push for the acceptance of this custom. This was unfortunate on two accounts. 1. These missionaries thought that they were merely recognizing a type of traditional marriage rather

ILLUSTRATION 12—GRAPH OF "MATRILINEAL/PATRILINEAL" ATTITUDES

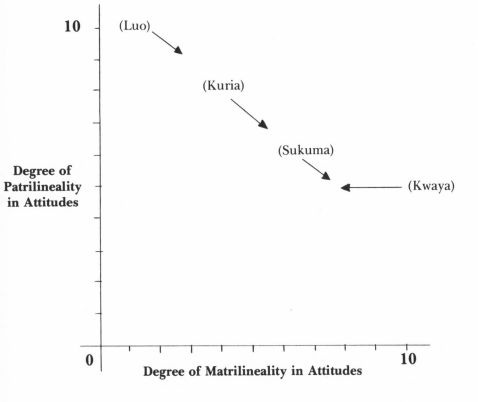

than a unique type of marital union. (One wonders what their opinion would be if they were made aware of the true meaning of the custom.) 2. They were not sensitive to the aspirations and attitudes of the majority of the African leaders, who felt that the best course for the Church would be to promote more strongly the remarriage of widows. What is surprising here is that the African leaders were not further encouraged and supported by the missionaries, especially since they were promoting remarriage of widows in line with the official policy of the Catholic Church. In a sense the Maryknoll missionaries to the Sukuma should have been the most content of all the missionaries with the progress made in the area of widow care. However, a lack of understanding of the true nature of the problem led them to take issue with the African leaders over the proper pastoral response to the levirate and to justify actions such as "overriding" the parish councils in deciding leviratical matters. All of which is contrary to the rule and spirit of adaptation. The reason that missionaries can often get away with this kind of misunderstanding and action is that they continue to control, from the top, local church structures and finance. Hence they need not be accountable to the aspiration and needs of the local Christians. Furthermore, even if the Maryknoll missionaries in Sukumaland had understood the levirate and promoted it for the right reason, would there still not be grounds for deferring to the sensibilities and desires of the local Church?

Once again, two-thirds of the people, many of them knowing explicitly why the churches are opposed to the levirate, reject the churches' position for both moral and religious reasons. Further, there was little indication of any new Christian influence on this issue.

How then should the churches proceed in the Sukuma situation? Should they promote all three options: remarriage, the levirate, the single state? Furthermore, what has caused the possibility of remarriage for so many widows? Does widow remarriage represent a breakdown of traditional patrilineal customs surrounding Sukuma marriages? And what about the marital and moral situation of the widows who are seen as single people but cannot remarry? Does this status represent liberation and new freedom? Oh! If only the Luo widow Victoria Akech had been born a Sukuma, then it would not have been so naive to encourage her to live as a single woman.

NOTES

1. The Busega subdivision of the Mwanza district had a total population of 50,000 people. It was necessary, therefore, to select only half of this population for the "Sukuma universe." The desired number of adults was located and the boundaries defined through the information available on the census-enumeration areas. See the United Republic of Tanzania, *1967 Population Census,* I, 159–60.

2. Aloys Balina, Anthony Mayala, and Justin M. Mabula, *Traditional Marriage* (mimeograph: St. Paul's Senior Seminary, Kipalapala, Tanzania), p. 33.

3. The Sukuma material further illustrated how varied and nonmonolithic the African cultures are, even though they are often grouped together under a single category and treated as if they are members of the one uniform culture. The failure to understand the radical difference among these cultures has, in the mind of the author, doomed many development projects from the beginning.

4. Hans Cory, *Sukuma Law and Custom,* (London: Oxford University Press, 1957), p. 163.

5. Cory, *Sukuma Law and Custom,* pp.163–65, 32, 34. For a description of the ceremonies for the formal handing over of the woman to the dead man's brother, see R. E. S. Tanner, "Maturity and Marriage among the Northern Basukuma, Tanganyika," *African Studies* 14 (1955) 163–64.

6. If a widow who has not been inherited but has remained in her deceased husband's family cohabits with a man, he cannot be required to pay compensation for adultery because she cannot be considered a married woman (Cory, *Sukuma Law and Custom*, p. 68).

7. Cory *Sukuma Law and Custom*, p. 101) states that there are no known cases where a woman with *small* children refused to choose a levirate husband after deciding to remain within her deceased husband's home.

8. See C. G. Seligman, *Races of Africa* (London: Oxford University Press, 1957), p. 192. Hans Cory, in *Sukuma Law and Custom*, p. 3, proposes a theory that Hamitic people (presumably Galla) penetrated Sukumaland and established ruling dynasties over the whole country. Cory, however, admits that there is practically no evidence to support this theory.

9. The bias due to the lack of a homogeneous clan grouping for the Sukuma universe must always be taken into account when speaking of the Sukuma people as a whole in terms of the findings of the survey. The Sukuma universe included nineteen census enumeration areas from the Nyashimo section of Busega, nine from Mazana I, and seven from Nyaluhande.

10. The maintenance of a widow who refuses to be inherited, or who has been refused by the deceased husband's relatives, falls on her paternal family, and in the first instance on those members of it who received her bridewealth (Cory, *Sukuma Law and Custom*, p. 165).

11. A survey conducted several years ago in the Busega district uncovered a significant number of marriages that had been approved by the fathers of the girls with only a promise of bridewealth.

PART TWO

The Adaptation of Christianity
to the African Leviratic Institution

CHAPTER SIX

The Catholic Church and Adaptation
The Principle of Incarnation

The failure of the Catholic Church to come to grips with the leviratic problem in the four African societies under consideration is now apparent. However, despite this present failure, the Church's theory regarding the introduction of Christian religion into non-Western cultures remains open-minded, generous, and adaptive. It is important, therefore, if one is to re-examine the leviratic prohibition, to discuss first the Church's theory of adaptation with a view to delineating its method, meaning, and scope, especially in the area of Christian marriage.

The Catholic Church's official teaching on adaptation is that all cultures have the right to an independent existence within Christianity and that the introduction of Christian teachings in a new culture must involve an "adaptation" that preserves the essential integrity of the culture, its values, institutions, and customs. Adaptation, therefore, is the *process* of the interaction between Christianity and cultures which takes into consideration the total collective religious, social, and moral life as it has gradually taken concrete form in each culture.[1] It is a reciprocal process affecting both the "sending" Church of the missionaries and the "receiving" Church of the new Christians.

This teaching on adaptation is clearly expressed in the documents of the Second Vatican Council. It is stated, for example, in the Pastoral Constitution on the Church in the Modern World that the Church is "not bound exclusively and indissolubly to any race or nation, nor to any particular way of life or any customary pattern of living, ancient or recent"; moreover, the Church can "enter into communion with various cultural modes, to her own enrichment and theirs too" (GS).[2] Likewise, in the decree on missionary activity, the Council Fathers speak of adaptation as an "imitation of the

143

plan of the Incarnation" in which the young local Churches, "in a wonderful exchange" take to themselves all the "riches of the nations which were given to Christ" (AG 22).

Moreover, this teaching on adaptation is reflected by Catholic thinkers in a number of different ways depending on their conception of the Incarnation.[3] For example, the American theologian, Avery Dulles, says that the heart of the Church's position is that the reality of the Church be incarnated in each people to whom the gospel is preached so that the Church becomes an "autochthonous" (indigenous) reality.[4] This incarnational adaptation, according to the German theologian Heinz Schlette, is not, "a simple extrinsic addition of a new element but a *metamorphosis,* which is at once a detachment from the old and dedication to the new, that is, a tension of opposites which is at the same time fulfillment, conversion, and consummation, death and resurrection.[5] Moreover, adaptation, Schlette says, is always conceptualized in terms of the actual self-understanding of the Church within a particular culture. Thus, all theology which is actually thought out and immediately responsible to the faith is necessarily a theology of adaptation.[6]

Pope Pius XII, in his encyclical "Evangelii Praecones," compares the incarnational missionary approach of the Church to an orchardist who engrafts a cultivated shoot on a wild tree so that it yields richer and more tasty fruit. He teaches that when the gospel is accepted by diverse races, it does not "crush or repress anything good and beautiful which they have achieved by their native genius and natural endowments."[7]

In spite of the Church's theological position on adaptation, the Catholic missionary movement from the sixteenth century up to the 1940s has been severely criticized on both theoretical and practical grounds for its *lack* of adaptation, sympathy, and respect for non-European cultures. Critics have charged that during this period the Church largely forgot its policy of adaptation, substituting a narrow, often unsympathetic form of Europeanism or Westernism.[8] Gustav Voss writes:

> The missionaries—true children of their times—shared the intolerant and prejudiced views of the *conquistadores* on the native cultures and religions. Moreover, imbued as they were with the militant zeal of the ancient crusaders, the thought of accommoda-

tion and adaptation could hardly enter their minds. They were unaware of the genuine religious value to be found even in heathenism, ignorant of the sentimental and emotional values bound up with its beliefs and rituals, and equally ignorant of the social structure and racial and psychological peculiarities of their new charges.[9]

Furthermore, says Voss, guided by an utterly unjust superiority complex, missionaries strove to suppress and uproot not only heathen beliefs, but even the cultural traditions because of their variance with the "enlightened" achievements of Renaissance Europe. To all intents and purposes a pagan, no matter what his origin, whether a Brahmin or a savage, had to become a Westerner in order to become a Christian.[10] Likewise, Voss maintains, the oath required of all missionaries going to Asia from the 1740s to the 1940s, not to engage in a controversy over the admissibility of certain practices of accommodation in India and China, served as an effective deterrent against "further attempts at such accommodation."[11]

Another critic, Heinz Schlette, says that since the 1920s it has come to be increasingly regretted that the Catholic (and Protestant) mission since the 1500s was in general European-minded:

> A liturgy and a set of postures in prayer were exported, of Roman, Frankish and Germanic [and ultimately American also] origin, with a similar type of art, forms of piety, customs and social ideals, European philosophy and political ideas. And still more was involved, since this offer of total Europeanization presupposed the condemnation of the indigenous.[12]

According to Schlette, the general development of the Church over the past thirty-five years has brought with it the elimination of "Westernization" as a *theory,* but little real *pastoral* adjustment in Asia and Africa.[13]

The Catholic moral theologian Bernard Häring, speaking of the evangelization of the non-Western world, says that theologians, who should have known better, "did not dare to speak up when ecclesiastical authorities and organizations declared the Latin language and the Latin culture to be *supracultura* and ascribed to the Church the task of civilizing the barbarians with the aid of Latin theology and the Latin liturgy."[14]

The African missionary, Eugene Hillman, cites a number of outstanding African writers and scholars who complain, at times bitterly, that the missionary movement has created half-Christians, and that the effect of the mission work reflects more the glory of European Christendom than it does the glory of God. Hillman concludes, "There is behind all of this [anti-African spirit] an excessive measure of Western cultural arrogance: a naive belief that Western culture is not only superior totally and cumulatively to all other cultures, but that it is also more human and, thus, the only appropriate instrument for the communication and incarnation of Christianity."[15]

Even Pope Benedict XV, in his Apostolic letter, "Maximum Illud," of 1919, rebuked those missionaries who, "display more zeal for the profit of some particular nation than for the growth of the kingdom of God." He taught that the "Catholic Church is not an intruder in any country; nor is she alien to any people."[16] Moreover, he proclaimed that the greatest hope of the new churches lies in having their own local clergy.

These criticisms are not meant to suggest that there were no documents discussing adaptation or positive attempts at adaptation during this long period of mission history, rather that these adaptive attempts and documents do not represent the ordinary approach of the Western missionary to foreign cultures and that their influence was usually limited to particular persons and situations, e.g., the work of De Nobili in India and Ricci in China.[17]

In light of this criticism, we can appreciate the clarity and emphasis with which Vatican II again affirms the principle that the Church's role, vis-à-vis other cultures, is one of accommodation and "incarnation." Indeed, the Council Fathers detail the implications of this teaching. They point out, for example, that the difficulties of harmonizing culture with Christian teachings can "stimulate the mind to a more accurate and penetrating grasp of the faith" and "do not necessarily harm the life of faith" (GS 62). Moreover, they call for new theological investigation into all major socio-cultural areas of concern so that "avenues will be opened for a more profound adaptation in the whole area of Christian life. . . . and Christian life can be accommodated to the genius and dispositions of each culture" (AG 22).

Thus it will be more clearly seen in what ways faith can seek for understanding in the philosophy and wisdom of these peoples. A better view will be gained of how their customs, outlook on life, and social order can be reconciled with the manner of living taught by divine revelation (AG 22).

Even the sensitive areas of Christian morality and doctrine are mentioned explicitly as places where "blending" with modern science is to be considered and studied, so that "the religious practice and morality (of the faithful) can keep pace with their scientific knowledge and with an ever-advancing technology" (GS 62). Thus, teach the Council Fathers, the faithful will be able to test and interpret all things in a truly Christian spirit.

It is in the context of this pastoral call of Vatican II that this study seeks to integrate and blend the findings of the secular sciences with theology so that the "faithful (of the African Church) can be brought to live the faith in a more thorough and mature way" (GS 62).

Second Vatican Council's Statement on Christian Marriage

Vatican II's Pastoral Constitution on the Church in the Modern World, one section of which dealt with Christian marriage, sought to address itself to all men both Christians and non-Christians:

[The Second Vatican Council] now addresses itself without hesitation, not only to the sons of the Church and to all who invoke the name of Christ, but to the whole of humanity. For the Council yearns to explain to everyone how it conceives of the presence and activity of the Church in the world of today (GS 2).

Unfortunately, despite this lofty aim, there was throughout the preparation of the document a lack of communication between the Council Fathers and the world's outstanding lay experts in the secular arts and sciences germane to the topic under consideration. Bishop McGrath, chairman of a subcommission appointed to study the relevance of the Constitution to the non-Western world, complained of how difficult it was to achieve a really universal outlook due to the "absence of theologians from the Third World and from Latin America."[18] Even his subcommission when first formed was seen as too Western and was extended by co-opting bishops from Africa, Japan, India, and Spain but again the major difficulty was finding experts capable of making original contributions.

The lay auditors who were consulted during 1963 and 1964 were Catholic apostolic leaders of broad culture and intimate knowledge of the Church, but they did not qualify as experts in the areas of science, technology, communications media, culture, economics, politics and the arts of war that were touched upon by the schema.[19] Sensing their inadequacies in the area of marriage, for example, Bishop Staverman from Indonesia proposed in the third session of the Council that a larger number of lay experts be consulted who would be more knowledgeable about marriage, conjugal love, fecundity, and the evolution of marriage itself as a historical reality.[20] Furthermore, the laymen consulted were unanimous in saying that for the most part the ecclesiastics they were associated with live in a totally different world, a world of abstractions and theological logomachy.[21]

As a result, the text of the Pastoral Constitution submitted to the Fathers of the Council was criticized for reflecting the spirit of its authors, who were mostly Westerners, and for presenting the issues in ways that were unrepresentative of Asian and African thought. For example, Bishop Proano of Equador, in the third session (1964), in the name of seventy Fathers, declared, "This scheme is too Occidental. It says nothing about illiteracy."[22] Gregorios Thangalathil, archbishop of Trivandrum, India, also at the third session of the Council, speaking in the name of seventy Fathers, said: "The schema deals only in passing with the nations that are not yet within the modern world but are standing in its vestibule, knocking at the door."[23]

In the fourth and final session of the Council, Archbishop Lourdusamy of Bangalore, India, who spoke in the name of sixty-two bishops, and Bishop Abasolo of Vijayapuram, "regretted the absence in the document of a religious message or a natural spirituality."[24] Likewise, Lourdusamy, this time speaking in the name of six Indian bishops, said that the "description of 'man in the modern world' in the text applied mainly to advanced industrialized regions, and would not be recognized by those who constitute the greater part of humanity living in Africa, Asia, and Latin America"; he felt that unless there was a change of emphasis, "the people of India would conclude that the Church is not concerned with her problems."[25] This same point was made by Cardinal Rugambwa with respect to Africa and the viewpoint of people who have recently begun to share world government.[26]

The section of the Pastoral Constitution treating marriage, entitled: "Fostering the Nobility of Marriage and the Family," likewise reflects the general Western orientation of the entire document. Thus it has been justly criticized as presenting only a Western view of marriage and the family; its tone, thought pattern, and idiom have been described as relevant only to a marriage institution which presupposes the Western "nuclear" family as the basic social unit. These criticisms were voiced by both Cardinals Gracias and Slipyj, who openly regretted its excessively "Western approach to marriage."[27] Likewise, Archbishop Djajasepertra of Djakarta declared:

> This schema is too juridical and too Occidental. . . You in the West find it quite natural for those in love to marry. But you are the exceptions if humanity as a whole is considered. Our people love one another because they are married, which is not quite the same thing.[28]

Joseph Ratzinger relates how especially the African bishops in their conversations after the Council discussions on marriage, warned of the danger of overlooking the essential social meaning of marriage in favor of an entirely personalistic view.[29] Ratzinger comments that the personalistic stress in contemporary theology of marriage may sometimes risk overlooking the essentially social significance of marriage. "Thus the personalists can easily slide into their own kind of artificial construction—foreign both to reality and to revelation."[30]

At least three times in the debate on the schema in 1964, African bishops criticized the section on marriage for not having relevance to African problems.

They complained that African issues such as polygyny, the status of women, and dowries were not being included in the scope of the document. For example, Bishop Joseph Nkongolo of Kinshasha, Zaire stated that: "We cannot speak of the indissolubility of marriage if there is no liberty—the father of a family cannot force or supply the consent required for validity. Moreover nothing is said of a terrible evil: polygamy, which is gaining ground while the institution of Christian marriage is being turned more and more to derision."[31] Archbishop Joseph Malula, also of Kinshasha, requested that the schema speak out on the dignity of woman, who should be "neither an instrument of lust nor a slave."[32] Archbishop Bernard Yago of the Ivory Coast regretted that the document did not condemn "Polygamy or the abusive system of dowries and that divorce was not denounced firmly enough."[33]

However, the above statements make the African bishops appear as "Westernized" in their outlook, for they articulate stereotyped viewpoints of Western theologians regarding their own marital customs. Thus, Archbishop Yago describes the system of dowries (bridewealth)* as "abusive." Yet on what basis does he make his claim? Certainly not on the basis of African tradition where bridewealth (dowries) functions to create clan alliances, secure progeny for one's own lineage, distribute wealth, and stabilize marriage bonds. Likewise, is the accusation generally true that in Africa the father of a family forces or supplies marital consent, as the statement of Bishop Nkongolo would lead one to believe?

This Western outlook of the African bishops regarding marriage indicates that adaptation cannot be merely the taking over of an existant viewpoint. Rather adaptation must entail a new creative process that is "incarnational," arising out of the culture itself. Moreover, it illustrates that even though a bishop is from an African country, there is no guarantee that he will be able to speak for the cultures within his diocese. He may be an African who has been Westernized by his educational and social contacts, or he may be a missionary bishop who is insensitive to traditional African cultures. Yet at least these statements show that the African bishops were well aware that Vatican II's statement on marriage was not relevant to their African problems, however they might have conceived them.

---

*The proper technical term in reference to African marriage is "bridewealth," i.e., the wealth given to the father of the bride by the family of the groom. "Dowry" refers to the wealth brought by the bride herself into a marriage.

Vatican II's excessively Western teaching regarding marriage would seem to be inexcusable (1) in light of Vatican II's own recognition of the plurality of cultures and its clearly stated position on incarnational adaptation; and (2) in light of the fact that the African church south of the Sahara, a church of over 30,000,000 Catholics, clearly protested, through some of its native bishops, that the schema did not take into account African problems. This failure is highlighted even more by the fact that there was a sub-commission on the "universal outlook of the shema," that included bishops from Third World countries, which was to submit its criticism of the entire text as to the validity of its observations for the non-European world.[34]

Given the Council's concern to address its Pastoral Constitution to all men, one would have expected that at least the authors of the position paper on marriage would have made it clear that the paper was addressed mainly to the Western world and that it grew out of and reflected a "Western" experience of Christian marriage.[35] Indeed, for the Council Fathers to lump together African, Asian, Western European, Latin American, and North American marriage institutions and treat them as one unit of analysis without acknowledging any differences is sociologically confusing and theologically illegitimate. These diverse peoples are no more united in one common social structure following the same marriage customs than they are united in a common political and economic structure.

Fortunately, there is one sentence, inserted into the section on marriage on the insistance of the African bishops, which points out that conjugal love can take many forms and shapes depending on the culture.[36] The sentence reads: "Many men of our own age also highly regard true love between husband and wife as it manifests itself in a variety of ways depending on the worthy customs of various peoples and times."[37]

This sentence seems straightforward enough, saying that true love is expressed in different ways in other cultures without making any comparative judgments about the quality of that love. Yet, the theologian Victor Heylen (the editorial secretary of a Vatican II subcommission that studied marriage questions) contradicts the very intention and meaning of the sentence (which affirms that conjugal love can take many forms), in his interpretations of conjugal love as having only a Western form. As a result he used the sentence as an occasion to make unsubstantiated judgments about conjugal love and its *absence* among "other" peoples (by "other" one presumes he means non-Western peoples). Heylen makes the following comments:

> Among the majority of people conjugal love has yet to emerge; among them, marriages are sealed by family arrangement, the chief intention being to prolong the line, and *nothing deeply personal* is involved. The woman serves to satisfy the man's desires, and mutual love between the spouses is quite secondary. . . . Taking into account the fact that the culture of love is often underdeveloped in some regions, the Council spoke cautiously of love, "as it manifests itself in the worthy customs of various times and peoples" (italics mine).[38]

One cannot help but be surprised by the above statement. Professor Heylen seems to have a source of information about conjugal love in other cultures unavailable and unknown to the social scientists. How can he be so sure that there is nothing deeply personal involved in an arranged marriage? What is his proof that conjugal love has yet to emerge among the majority of people? How does he account for the growing body of literature written by Africans available in English and French which describes relationships between husbands and wives in highly personalistic, erotic, and even romantic categories?[39]

Bernard Häring, who served as *peritus* (advisor) to the council and was one of the architects of the Pastoral Constitution on the Church in the Modern World, in a commentary on this sentence, also distorts its obvious meaning that conjugal love *has many different valid cultural expressions.* Thus, instead of speaking of conjugal love as it is presently manifested in arranged marriages of the patriarchial family (e.g. in Africa), Häring speaks of such marriages disparagingly, as if they were events of "past" history and mere social and economic affairs that could "hide conjugal love" (i.e., his Western expression of conjugal love).[40]

In another commentary on this same sentence Father Häring again misconstrues the meaning of this phrase and interprets it as an affirmation of the universal validity of the Western personalistic expression of conjugal love. Häring seems to assume that "arranged marriages" ordinarily preclude conjugal love and consent.

He writes: "If parents should assume the responsibility of choosing a spouse, the persons involved still are to be asked whether they consent to a bond and to a vocation which essentially imply mutual love."[41] He illustrates his point by citing the Asian and African bishops, who stated that in their parts of the world marriages are not "made for love but arranged by parents and the young couple trustingly and obediently accept the decisions of their families."[42] Yet, the crucial phrase "not made for love" can be interpreted in two ways. For Häring it is proof that these marriages do not yet entail (Western) conjugal love, but for the Asian and African bishops, in light of their qualifying adjectives, namely, "trustingly," "obediently," it seems to mean only that there is no Western manifestation of conjugal love: it does not directly imply that there is no conjugal love.[43]

A third commentator on the sentence, Peter Riga, misses its point completely. He says that the statement stresses what is common between believers and nonbelievers, namely, "the constituent element of conjugal love and its promotion in marriage."[44] The point is *not* that believers and nonbelievers have conjugal love in common, but that people in different cultures have different legitimate expressions of conjugal love.

In view of the comments on this sentence by these important Western theologians, two of whom were deeply involved in the formulation of the statement on Christian marriage, it is becoming clearer why the Council Fathers from the non-Western parts of the world had difficulty gaining from their Western counterparts an understanding of their own traditions and cultures. The single statement on cultural plurality, which they managed to have inserted into the section on marriage, was immediately misinterpreted and practically rejected by Western theologians. For these reasons, we see that the Second Vatican Council's theology of marriage, dominated as it was by the thought of Western Catholic thinkers, failed to address itself adequately to "all men." The statement on marriage accepted by the Council Fathers failed to take into account in any real way the diversity of marriage forms, institutions, and structures throughout the world. This no doubt is one of the reasons why close to 25 percent of the Council Fathers found the statement only partially acceptable.[45]

This inconsistency in the Second Vatican Council between the clearly articulated theological principle of incarnational adaptation and the practical inability to apply it to a concrete issue such as marriage, focuses our attention on the ethnocentrism of Catholic thinkers, and calls for further discussion of this crucial problem of cultural blindness.

Eugene Hillman, himself a theologian and African missionary of wide experience, speaks of Western cultural arrogance as congenital, however unconsciously it may be expressed by well-intentioned people, and sensitivity to the cultures of non-Western people cannot be regarded, even today, as something that is acquired casually, without conscious effort and persistent care. He feels that the starting point for any meaningful encounter between the members of different cultures is a humble realization that every man is intelligible to himself and to others only in the context of his own culture of origin and experience. And, to reach some understanding of an alien culture requires an unequivocal disposition and willingness to learn and a conscious suppression of the tendency to pass comparative judgments on the ways of others—judgments based on the assumption that our ways are of course superior and more human.[46]

This mentality of Western superiority is expressed by Western *theologians* in many ways, sometimes subtly, sometimes openly. For example, Gustav Voss, in spite of the vigor with which he promotes adaptation, still expresses an exaggerated admiration for Western cultural forms. He feels that European forms of Christianity, if accepted, "will dispose the pagan mind to accept Christianity and will, furthermore, help to advance and refine human living, which is quite in accord with the cultural mission of the Church."[47]

In like manner the missiologist Edward Murphy expresses a certain Western superiority when he says that the emphasis on adaptation should not create the impression that all cultures and civilizations are *completely* equipped to express the fullness of Catholic life.

> The [Church] brings nineteen centuries of experience with the *development* of society, and many elements of Western culture have universal validity. It would be strange if the Mother of the nations [Catholic Church] had nothing to offer to her young members *except revealed truth* and the *source of divine life* (italics mine).[48]

Pope Paul VI, in a message to Africa in 1967, perhaps unaware of the ethnocentric character of his remarks, openly promoted individualistic "Western" family values for the Africans. He began by praising the traditional African family structures and then spoke (mistakenly) as if these communal structures had already changed. He applauded this (supposed) change, calling it "timely," and seeing it as (1) "upholding freedom of action for the *individual*" and (2) allowing the *individual* couple greater freedom and responsibility.[49]

The ethnocentrism of Western missionaries is also expressed in many ways. It is expressed by pronounced antipathy for non-Western customs—cited by the historian Lyndon Harries[50] as a partial reason for the initial failure of the Catholic missions in Africa. It is expressed by a lack of respect and sympathy for local laws and traditions, and by a failure to learn the philosophies, languages, and ideologies prevalent in the countries to which the missionaries are sent.[51] It is expressed by appearing as emissaries of the white race or of Western civilization—a stance that Cardinal Bea sees as giving the new nations an inferiority complex.[52] It means speaking of the "mission" peoples as "barbarians," "uncivilized natives," and seeing only "darkness," "deprivation," "blindness," and "immorality" among them.[53] It means the inability to recognize and trust the faith of the indigenous Christians.[54] It means a belligerency towards other missionary faiths and traditional religions.[55]

Due to ethnocentrism, therefore, the Western theologians and missionaries are usually not aware of the cultural presuppositions underlying their theological and pastoral reflections. Consequently, when faced with non-Western systems and institutions, they are unable to distinguish *cultural* elements from *essential* Christian elements.* Thus the theologians who prepared Vatican II's statement on marriage were not fully aware that they addressed themselves in general to only *one* particular type of mar-

---

*This study makes no claim to clearly delineate just what "essential" Christianity is in terms of a general theology of marriage. Rather it commits itself to an ongoing process of research whereby essential elements are gradually distinguished from nonessential elements within particular cultural contexts.[56]

riage institution—an institution (as described by anthropologists) that is primarily concerned with the "nuclear" family as its basic unit; continuity of the lineage (corporate kin group) over time is not of great importance, and one's relationships with relatives of both the mother's and the father's side are of equal significance.[57]

In conclusion, the Second Vatican Council, despite the difficulties and hazards involved in distinguishing essential Christian elements from particular cultural contexts, strongly affirms and teaches that "Christian life can be accommodated (incarnationally) to the *genius* and disposition of each culture" (AG 22). Therefore, both theologians and missionaries must ask the following questions: What does conjugal love, family, widowhood, and marriage mean for Christians in non-Western marriage systems? What is essential to Christian marriage that must be promoted in each and every marriage system throughout the world? How much of contemporary Western theology of Christian marriage, developed in response to particular problems and social systems in the Western world, is truly applicable or relevant to non-Western cultures and marriage institutions?

NOTES

1. See Jean Piaget, *Six Psychological Studies* (New York: Vintage Books, 1968), p. 8.

2. *The Documents of Vatican II,* "Pastoral Constitution on the Church in the Modern World," ed. Walter M. Abbott, trans. Joseph Gallagher (New York: Guild Press, 1966), p. 264. References to Council documents are hereafter given parenthetically, according to abbreviations of their Latin titles and numbered sections.

3. For the Council Fathers, incarnational adaptation always involves a genuine *exchange* and reciprocal *borrowing.* Dulles has an *indigenization* theory of the incarnation. Schlette thinks more in terms of the *assumption* of a second element in a ("two natures") union with the first which creates a "tension" of opposites. But all these theories of incarnational adaptation presuppose that the missionary accepts a new culture in its integrity.

4. Avery Dulles, *The Dimensions of the Church* (Westminster, Md.: Newman Press, 1967), p. 54. According to Dulles, if accommodation is conceived of only as an expedient for winning converts, it is always tinged with a patronizing attitude, and a dangerous pragmatism.

5. Heinz Schlette, "Theological Problems of Adaptation," in *Sacramentum*

Mundi: An Encyclopedia of Theology, ed. Karl Rahner (Montreal: Palm Publishers, 1969), IV, 82.

6. Another theologian, Gustav Voss, distinguishes Christianity in its "objective" content, the *depositum fidei*, from the assimilation and expression of this objective reality in outward forms and signs of piety. He feels that the innermost essence of all missionary effort is the stripping away of these merely accidental elements in deference to the indigenous culture ("Missionary Accommodation," *Missionary Academic Study* No. 2 [New York: Society for the Propagation of the Faith, 1946], p. 4).

Louis Luzbetak, a priest-anthropologist, points out how the Church must accommodate itself to the local culture insofar as it is a system of interconnected subsystems that are in turn made up of interwebbed functionally organized elements. Thus the accommodation must be to functioning and integrated parts and not to distinct, random items. (*The Church and Culture: An Applied Anthropology for the Religious Worker* [Techny, Ill.: Divine Word Publications, 1963], p. 341).

7. Pius XII, "Evangelii Praecones" (On Intensifying Missionary Effort), *AAS* 43 (1951). English translation by Clarence McAuliffe in *Catholic Missions: Four Great Encyclicals*, ed. Thomas Burke, Incidental Papers of the Institute of Mission Studies, No. 1 (New York: Fordham University Press, 1957), p. 56.

8. See Voss, "Missionary Accommodation," pp. 16–17. Also Schlette, "Problems of Adaptation," p. 82. For a brief survey of mission history see Voss, pp. 44–177. In this work, he indicates that there was a tradition of accommodation throughout the period of ancient and medieval missionary expansion (p. 11). For a more complete history of the mission effort see Stephen Neill, *A History of Christian Missions* (Grand Rapids, Mich.: Eerdmans, 1965), pp. 1–140. Also F. Mourret, *A History of the Catholic Church*, trans. N. Thompson (St. Louis: Herder, 1936); K. S. Latourette, *A History of the Expansion of Christianity*, 7 vols. (London: Harper & Brothers, 1937–45).

9. Voss, "Missionary Accommodation," p. 17.

10. Ibid.

11. Ibid., p. 25. This controversy was sparked by the work of Robert de Nobili (died 1656) in India and Mateo Ricci (died 1610) in China. The occasion and the main subject of the conflict was whether certain Chinese (Confucianist, Buddhist) and Hindu rites, particularly the cult of ancestors, could be permitted in the Church. In 1742 and 1744, Pope Benedict XIV intervened on the side of Europeanization (and colonialism), declaring certain of these practices inadmissible and, by means of the oath, stopped further discussion of the issue. This controversy was known as the Chinese Rites and the Malabar Rites question. See Benedict XIV, Apostolic Constitution, "Ex Quo Singulari," (1742) and "Omnium Solicitudinem," (1744) in *Opera Omnia* (Prate: In Typograpica Aldini, 1839), XV, 216–229.

12. Schlette, "Theological Problems," p. 83.

13. Ibid. This lack of pastoral adjustment is still evident in some Catholic mission literature. For example, Edward L. Murphy, in *Teach Ye All Nations: The Principles of Catholic Missionary Work* (New York: Benziger, 1957), pp. 105–107, speaks of the customs of non-Christian people in the most derogatory terms.

Ronan Hoffman, in "The Council and the Missions," in *Vatican II: The Theological Dimension,* ed. Anthony Lee (Washington, D.C.: Thomist Press, 1963), p. 543, says that the fundamental problem today is the confrontation of the Church with non-Western and non-Christian cultures. He complains that the great need for a theology of mission is frustrated because an *adequate* investigation of missionary problems is sadly lacking. Hence, little serious theological attention is given to missionary efforts.

14. Bernard Häring, *A Theology of Protest* (New York: Farrar, Straus and Giroux, 1970), p. 141.

15. Eugene Hillman, *Polygamy Reconsidered: African Plural Marriage and the Christian Churches* (Maryknoll, N. Y.: Orbis Books, 1975) p. 52. For examples of African writers cited, see Alioune Diop, "Colonization and the Christian Conscience," *Cross Currents* 3 (Summer 1953) 353–355; Bolaji Idowu, *Towards an Indigenous Church* (London: Oxford University Press, 1965), p. 5.

16. Benedict XV, "Maximum Illud," *AAS* II (1919), pp. 440–445. English translation, William Connolly, in *Catholic Missions: Four Great Encyclicals,* p. 15, no. 19; p. 14, no. 16; p. 13, no. 14.

Stephen Neill, (*History of Christian Missions,* p. 523) relates that the apostolic delegate to China, when attempting to implement the directives of "Maximum Illud" in 1922, was told by the superiors of the missions in China that they had not a single Chinese priest qualified to carry the heavy burden of the episcopate. Pius XI responded to this by saying that if they did not know of any qualified priests, they must set to work to find them. This resulted in the ordinations of the first six Chinese bishops in Rome in 1926.

17. Even the great "adaptive" mission work of De Nobili and Ricci is *now* seen as falling short of the ideal approach to other cultures. Their efforts are criticized by Voss ("Missionary Accommodation," p. 18) as being tinged by a "far-reaching but sound Europeanism," and by Heinz Schlette, ("Problems of Adaptation," p. 83) on the grounds that they still understood adaptation as a matter of pedagogy and psychology. For details of Ricci's and De Nobili's work, see J. Schmidlin, *Catholic Mission History* (Techny, Ill.: Mission Press, Society of the Divine Word, 1931), pp. 304, 474, and *passim.* Also Paul Cohen, *China and Christianity* (Cambridge, Mass.: Harvard University Press, 1963), pp. 27–28 and *passim.*

18. Charles Moellar, "History of the Constitution," in *Commentary on the Documents of Vatican II,* ed. Herbert Vorgrimler (Montreal: Palm Publishers, 1969), V, p. 398. See also Moellar, V, 41, for the comment of Cardinal Lercaro, who called the schema "too European" and added that "too much was being expected from it" (conciliar debate: October, 1964).

19. Mark C. McGrath, "The Constitution on the Church in the Modern World," in *Vatican II: An Interfaith Appraisal,* ed. John Miller (Notre Dame, Ind.: University of Notre Dame Press, 1966), p. 408. McGrath's subcommission was called the "Signs of the Times" subcommission.

20. *Third Session: Council Speeches of Vatican II,* ed. William Leahy and Anthony Massimini (Glen Rock, N. J.: Paulist Press, 1966), p. 227.

21. Henri Fesquet, in *The Drama of Vatican II: The Ecumenical Council, June 1962–December 1965,* trans. Bernard Murchland (New York: Random House, 1967), p. 622.

22. Ibid., p. 486.

23. *Third Session,* p. 244.

24. Fesquet, *Drama of Vatican II,* p. 623.

25. Xavier Rynne, *The Fourth Session* (New York: Farrar, Straus and Giroux, 1965), p. 62.

26. Ibid.

27. Ibid., p. 89. Eugene Hillman, in *Polygamy Reconsidered,* p. 113, comments that, "the Christian theology of marriage rests almost entirely upon the Western experience, conception, and institutionalization of marriage and family . . . it is important to note that the typically Western patterns of marriage are unique in the world."

28. Fesquet, *Drama of Vatican II,* p. 551.

29. Joseph Ratzinger, *Theological Highlights of Vatican II,* Deus Book (New York: Paulist Press, 1966), p. 167.

30. Ibid., p. 167, n. 4.

31. Fesquet, *Drama of Vatican II,* p. 479.

32. Ibid., p. 467.

33. Ibid., p. 480.

34. For a brief summary of how this document was developed see Joseph Ratzinger, *Theological Highlights* (pp. 149–150). According to Ratzinger, the first draft of the paper on the Church in the Modern World was written mainly by the Redemptorist Bernard Häring, a moral theologian. It was submitted to the Council for discussion in the fall of 1964. The text was neither biblically precise nor in line with modern thought. The Fathers ordered a thoroughgoing revision. A text was then drafted by the press secretary of the French bishops, Abbé Hauptman (the second part of this new text leaned heavily on Häring's draft). Hauptman's draft prevailed over a text of Polish origin, and was the one distributed to the Fathers of the Council in the fall of 1965 and accepted after some criticism and minor changes. For a complete history of the text see Herbert Vorgrimler, ed., *Commentary on the Documents of Vatican II* (Montreal: Palm Publishers, 1969), V, 1–76.

35. Victor L. Heylen, in "Fostering the Nobility of Marriage and the Family," in *The Church Today,* ed. Group 2000, trans. Denis Barrett (Westminster, Md.: Newman Press, 1967), p. 118, defends the form of the text saying that, "care was taken to give equal emphasis to various cultures and civilizations." (What he means by this is hard to determine, since the text does not speak about different cultural traditions and marriage institutions.)

36. This pressure from the African bishops was pointed out by Edward Schillebeeckx in an interview with the author in December 1969. (Professor Schillebeeckx served as an advisor to the Dutch bishops during the Second Vatican Council. He was a member of the subcommittee that prepared the statement on marriage.) It is also clear from the context that the sentence was inserted later, since it does not flow logically from the previous sentence.

37. "Plures quoque nostrae aetatis homines verum amorem inter maritum et uxorem variis rationibus secundum honestos populorum et temporum mores manifestatum magni faciunt." Vat. II, Const. Past. De Ecclesia, p. 1069. English trans., *The Documents of Vatican II* (GS 49).

38. Heylen, "Nobility of Marriage," p. 118.

39. See the African Writers Series, ed. (advisor) Chinua Achebe, 46 vols. (London, Ibadan, Nairobi: Heinemann Educational Books Ltd.).

40. Bernard Häring, "Marriage and the Family," in *Vatican II: An Interfaith Appraisal,* ed. John H. Miller (Notre Dame, Ind.: University of Notre Dame Press, 1966), p. 440.

41. Bernard Häring, *Road to Renewal* (Montreal: Palm Publishers, 1966), pp. 150–154.

42. Ibid.

43. In the arranged marriages among the Luo people in Tanzania, for example, there are customary ways for a girl to refuse a spouse proposed by her parents: a clear indication that personal choice also plays a part in these marriages.

44. Peter J. Riga, *The Church Made Relevant: A Commentary on the Pastoral Constitution of Vatican II* (Notre Dame, Ind.: Fides, 1967), 177.

45. The vote of the Council Fathers on the whole of Chapter I, "Marriage and the Family" was: 1,569 "acceptable," 72 "unacceptable," 484 "partially acceptable." Moellar, "History of the Constitution," V, p. 74.

46. Hillman, *Polygamy Reconsidered,* pp. 60, 72.

47. Voss, "Missionary Accommodation," p. 45.

48. Murphy, *Teach Ye All Nations,* p. 86–87.

49. Paul IV, "Africae Terrarum," *AAS* 59 (1967), 1092–1093, no. 33. English trans., *The Pope Speaks* 13 (1967) 5–22.

50. Lyndon Harries, "Christian Marriage in African Society," *in Survey of African Marriage and Family Life,* ed. Arthur Phillips (London: Oxford University Press, 1953), p. 337.

51. Cardinal Rugambwa of Tanzania voiced this complaint at the Second Vatican Council. See Fesquet, *Drama of Vatican II,* p. 493.

52. Fesquet, *Drama of Vatican II,* p. 493.

53. Louis Luzbetak (*The Church and Culture,* p. 352) feels that a missionary of this mentality should have his spiritual eyes examined. Moreover, Luzbetak feels that the root of the problem of adaptation is the difference in the *enculturation* of the missionaries and the older churches on the one hand, and the new Christian communities on the other.

54. Stephen Neill (*History of Christian Missions,* p. 515), speaking of the Protestant missionaries, says that they were extraordinarily slow to recognize and trust the gifts of indigenous Christians. Even when ordained to the ministry, they were still regarded as no more than assistants to the missionaries. Similarly, Adrian Hastings, in *Church and Mission in Modern Africa* (London: Burns and Oates, 1967), p. 24, complains that the Catholic Church's unwillingness to ordain sufficient African clergy, while continuing to baptize large numbers of people, has resulted in the creation of large non-Eucharistic communities.

55. An example of this type of belligerency is found in the writings of an Italian missionary, Paolo Mana, *The Conversion of the Pagan World,* trans. Joseph McGlinchey (Cambridge, Mass.: Harvard University Press, 1921), pp. 84–86. Mana speaks of Mohammedanism as closing the African convert's heart to every possible action of the grace of God, and Protestantism as presenting a danger "much greater than is generally believed."

56. Robin Fox, *Kinship and Marriage*, Penguin Books Ltd. (Middlesex: C. Nicholls & Company, 1967), p. 173. Also A. R. Radcliffe-Brown, "Introduction," in *African Systems of Kinship and Marriage*, ed. A. R Radcliffe and Daryll Forde (London: Oxford University Press, 1950), p. 43–54.

"Lineage" and "corporate kin group" are used here interchangeably. Lucy Mair, in *An Introduction to Social Anthropology* (London: Oxford University Press, 1965), p. 64, defines a lineage as a corporate group recruited by descent. Robin Fox (p. 49) writes that the term "lineage" stresses the fact that the actual relationship between the members of the group can be demonstrated and not simply assumed. Aylward Shorter gives a more descriptive definition: a fairly large number of people related by descent in one line from a living (or recently) dead common ancestor (*The African Contribution to World Church: And Other Essays in Pastoral Anthropology*, Gaba Institute Pastoral Papers, No. 22, [Kampala, Uganda: Gaba Publications, 1972], p. 50).

57. John Thomas, in *The Catholic Viewpoint on Marriage and the Family* (New York: Hanover House, 1958), p. 35, distinguished essential unchanging values and a number of changing relative elements. The unchanging being the permanent indissoluble marital union of man and woman and the relative being the various roles concerning the status of wives, parents, offspring, and family unit. John Noonan speaks of *permanent* principles such as those determining Christian marriage in terms of the values of procreation, education, freedom but does not distinguish cultures ("Freedom, Experimentation, and Permanence in the Canon Law on Marriage," in *Law for Liberty*, ed. James Buchler [Baltimore: Helicon, 1967], pp. 52–69). Joseph Fuchs speaks of those elements that belong to or are congruent with only a certain situation of man/woman in a certain period of time or a certain country ("Theology of the Meaning of Marriage Today," in *Marriage in the Light of Vatican II*, ed. J. McHugh [Washington, D. C.: Family Life Bureau, 1968]). Bernard Häring, in *Theology of Protest*, p. 144, distinguishes in marriage ethics and marriage law the specifically Christian elements from those elements which were more or less successful accommodations to European culture.

End of Chapter Six

CHAPTER SEVEN

The African Leviratic Custom in
Catholic Theological Literature

In light of the empirical data presented in Part I and the Catholic Church's "incarnational" approach to cultures, we now return to the question: was the Catholic principle of adaptation reasonably applied by the Church in the case of the levirate?* That is, was the proscription of the African leviratic custom by the Catholic Church the result of a process that carefully examined all the factors surrounding the leviratic issue, factors such as the meaning, role, and function of the levirate regarding the care and treatment of African widows and their children, the relationship of the levirate to Christian marriage and sexual behavior as taught and experienced by Western man? In other words was the pastoral judgment that the leviratic custom was and is radically incompatible with Christian moral behavior the conclusion of a Christian theology of marriage that took into account the underlying African social structures? Furthermore, was there evidence of respect for African leviratic customs and institutions, as demanded by the official teaching magisterium of the Catholic Church? And was there careful theological investigation and discussion preceding the actual pastoral prohibition of the custom? In short was the prohibition of the African leviratic union the result of a skillful and honest effort to adapt Christianity to a non-Western marital institution?

To proceed with a reply to these questions, let us first assess the Catholic theological literature dealing with this issue to see if there was sufficient theological reflection on the nature, meaning, and role of the leviratic custom, and to find out how the theological

---

*See Introduction, p. 2.

arguments (whether pro or con) were formulated about its compatibility with Christianity.

Given the *fact* of the pastoral prohibition of the African leviratic union by the Catholic Church in the East African area under discussion,* one would at least expect to find a body of Catholic writings discussing the theological reasoning behind this position. However, this is not the case. There is no literature in journals, books, or manuscripts that treats the levirate in terms of its uniqueness or that raises the question whether this custom deserves special theological investigation. There are only scattered references to the leviratic custom both acknowledging its existence and describing in an unscientific way its nature and function within African society.[1] There is no discussion as to why the Church deems it necessary to prohibit it.

Not only are theological reflections on the African leviratic union lacking but also there is a great deal of imprecision in the terminology employed in discussing the custom. This terminological imprecision is found not only in the Catholic theological literature but also—perhaps more surprisingly—in the standard anthropological literature. Let us consider evidence for this latter point.

In the anthropological literature dealing with African marriage customs there are described several types of marital adjustments possible to a woman on the death of her husband. In one of them, the widow becomes the legal wife of the inheritor and the relationship becomes one of a simple (or complex) legal marriage.† The children of this union inherit through the new husband, who is their legal father. This kind of custom is called by anthropologists such as Shorter, Radcliffe-Brown, Evans-Pritchard, "widow inheritance," and they distinguish it from another type of marital union with widows that they call the "levirate."[2] In the levirate, the inheritor is merely a *substitute* husband, and any children born of the union are considered the children of the deceased husband, who continues to be the legal father.[3] But, this technical distinction between the terms "widow inheritance" and "levirate" is *not* made

---

*For confirmation of this prohibition see Appendix A, Table 38.

†"Simple" if the marriage is monogamous; "complex" if polygynous. For more details see E. E. Evans-Pritchard, *Kinship and Marriage among the Nuer.*[4]

by other social scientists such as Westermarck and Mair.[5] They use the term "widow inheritance" in a generic sense that includes the "levirate," and do not reserve it for the custom where the widow becomes the legal wife of the inheritor. It is necessary, therefore, when reading anthropological literature to assess the meaning of the term "widow inheritance" since it can refer to two different customs. That is, in anthropological literature, some writers distinguish the terms "widow inheritance" and "levirate" and others do not.*

Because of the possible confusion over terminology, it was decided in the beginning of this study to avoid using the term "widow inheritance" and to identify the custom under study as either the *levirate* or the *leviratic union* or the *leviratic custom*. The qualification "African" is added at times in order to make clear that this study is specifically concerned only with the levirate as it is practiced in the areas studied in East Africa, and not as it has been or is being practiced in other parts of the world.[6]

A second example of terminological imprecision in the anthropological literature relates to the description of the marital status of the leviratic partners. All anthropologists agree that the relationship between the widow and the inheritor in the leviratic union is such that the inheritor does *not* become the legal husband. Thus the inheritor is described as a "substitute for the dead man" (Evans-Pritchard; Mair), "warmer of the house," "proxy father" (Mair); "pro-husband," "he who provides his brother's wife with a hut," "foster father" (Evans-Pritchard); "surrogate" (Radcliffe-Brown.)[7] One sees in these descriptions a careful avoidance of identifying the relation between the widow and her leviratic partner as "marriage." Yet, as with the term "widow inheritance," there is no consistent use of terminology on this matter by anthropologists. For example, Evans-Pritchard uses the phrase "leviratic marriage" (as do Westermarck and Mair); he argues from the practice of the Nuer people that this custom can be regarded as a variety of a legal marriage *only* to the extent that the brother has

---

*This is not to argue that some anthropologists are unaware of this distinction between these two customs, but only that the term "widow inheritance" is used by some anthropologists in a generic sense which *includes* the leviratic custom and by others in a (technical) specific sense that *excludes* the leviratic custom.

the status of legal representative of the husband; namely, he can: (1) demand compensation if anyone commits adultery with the widow; and (2) divorce her under special circumstances.[8] Mair ("African Marriage," p. 54) describes the levirate as a domestic relationship indistinguishable from *marriage*. Others, such as Shorter and Radcliffe-Brown, call the union simply the "levirate."[9]

From the survey data already discussed we can see that the description of the African leviratic union as "marriage" is inaccurate and misleading. The widow in such a relationship does not and cannot make a new marital commitment to her inheritor because her marriage to her deceased husband is seen as continuing. Hence, 80% of the survey respondents, i.e., those who said that a widow cannot and does not want to be remarried, gave as their reason that the widow's marriage was still intact, still continuing despite her husband's death.* The idioms used to express this idea were: "the widow is already married, she can't be married twice"; "the bridewealth can't be paid twice"; "she knows she is the wife of a family"; "her husband didn't divorce her."† The leviratic custom, therefore, is the way of continuing the widow's original marriage. This analysis is further substantiated by anthropological writings. For example, the anthropologist Phillips states that the leviratic custom is based on the idea that the death of the husband does not put an end to the marital relationship; Mair expresses the same idea when she says that the leviratic union is often regarded as a continuation of the previous marriage, requiring no new ceremony; Radcliffe-Brown writes that leviratic unions can be seen to be the continuation or renewal of the existing structures of social relations.[10] On a more theoretical level, anthropologists reason that among patrilineal people where marriage secures children to perpetuate the father's group, and marriage involves lineage groups rather than individuals, the leviratic union can be seen as part of the network preserving the perpetuity of the lineage groups and the security of each individual in them.[11]

There is a great deal of evidence, therefore, supporting the claim that the African leviratic union is not a marriage in any ordinary

---

*The total number of adults who responded in this category was 530.

†See Appendix A, Tables 28 and 31, for frequency distribution of these responses.

sense of the term and should not be described as such. The African leviratic union is more accurately described as a *marital adjustment in a continuing marriage in which a brother-in-law substitutes temporarily for a deceased legal husband.*

We now return to the limited Catholic theological literature discussing the leviratic custom in order to assess (in light of the distinction in terminology made above) the quality and depth of its understanding and evaluation of this kind of marital relationship. The most striking fact about the Catholic literature is that it consistently describes the levirate as a type of *polygynous marriage.* For example, the Catholic theologian, Hastings, calls the taking of a widowed sister-in-law the taking of a *second wife;* Hillman writes that *polygyny* is required by customary law as a form of social security for widows; Luzbetak says that a function of *polygyny* is a way of providing social security for widows; Leclercq characterizes the levirate as *occasional polygyny;* a report from a conference at Leopoldville, Congo, in 1945 of Roman Catholic Ordinaries states that large numbers of Christians who lapse into *polygyny* do so through inheriting a brother's wife; the priest-anthropologist Shorter calls both the levirate and widow inheritance a form of *polygyny;* even the African writers, Cukopela and Bitakaramire, see the levirate as a way of acquiring *wives.*[12]

Moreover, these Catholic writers, with the exception of Shorter, do not make a distinction between the *leviratic union* and *widow inheritance* as discussed above. Apparently, they are not even aware of this distinction even though it is crucial to an understanding of the issue. Which custom then do Catholic writers have in mind? Is it *widow inheritance* or is it the *levirate*? Since they consider the relationship to be a type of polygyny, one can conjecture that they may be writing about "widow inheritance," since only widow inheritance, as defined above, can possibly be a polygynous relationship. However, it would be best to reserve judgment even on this point since the polygyny label would fit widow inheritance only if (1) the inheritor were already married, (2) the widow were to become his legal wife, and (3) such a union would in fact be a univocal case of polygyny (presently an uncertain assumption). If the inheritor were to be single when the widow became his legal wife, how would this be polygyny? Would it not be a simple legal monogamous marriage? The point is that even the custom defined as "widow inheritance" is not inherently polygynous, for it can be practiced by both single and married men. The theologians, therefore, by labelling the relationships between a widow and her brother-in-law as inherently polygynous, overlooked the complexity of the issue, addressing themselves to only one of a number of possible types of unions. Table 23 shows different kinds of customary unions with women by marital status of the male partner.

TABLE 23

CUSTOMARY UNIONS WITH WOMEN BY MARITAL STATUS OF MALE PARTNER

Type of Customary Union	Marital Status of Male Partner	
	Single	Married
a. Legal marriage with a single woman	(1) Monogamous marriage	(2) Polygynous marriage
b. Legal marriage with a widow ("widow inheritance")	(3) Monogamous marriage (?)	(4) Polygnous marriage (?)
c. Leviratic union with a widow	(5) Leviratic union with a single man	(6) Leviratic union with a married man

Given the above possibilities, it is evident that the label "*polygyny*" *clearly* applies in only one of these relationships, namely, number 2, although it appears that it would also apply to number 4. However, it should be realized that to call "widow inheritance" by a married man (number 4), polygynous, is done so on the basis of a still obscure analogy to some normative idea of polygyny. It is not at all certain that "widow inheritance" involving a married man is an univocal case of polygyny (as the theological writings simply assume). Furthermore, number 6 (leviratic union with a married man) could only be considered polygynous if one equated polygyny with a mans' having sexual access to two women simultaneously. This, however, is not the ordinary meaning of the term. Our definition of polygyny requires that the man be considered legally married to two or more women according to traditional customs—a factor not present in the leviratic union.

In the other three relationships, numbers 1, 3, and 5, there is no logical reason for considering them polygynous no matter how one perceives the nature of these relationships, since the male partner is single before the union. Moreover, a question mark is placed after number 3 (a legal marriage with a widow by a single partner), for again it is not entirely clear in the African context whether the first marriage of the widow is ever considered actually terminated. Thus a widow's marriage to a single partner may not be a univocal case of a monogamous union, especially if the new partner is a relative of the deceased husband. In such a case, even though the widow may be considered a legal wife of the new partner, the union, due to a sense of communal identity, may in fact be a special type of the levirate. Or perhaps the new marriage should be discussed as a type of polyandry, since the woman is now considered to have two legal husbands. The physical death of the first husband does not, in fact, return the widow to a single state (as in the Western tradition), just as the death of a wife does not return a monogamous man to a single state or a polygynous man to a monogamous state.

Even in Western societies and traditions there is a certain confusion over the nature of a marital union with a widow. For often the widow continues to interact with her deceased husband through their children in such a way that her new partner actually functions not only as a step father but also as a step husband.

Why do the Catholic theologians not make a clear distinction between the *married* man's and the *single* man's marital relationships with widows? Why do they not distinguish *leviratic union* from *widow inheritance*? The answer to these questions, again, can only be by way of suggestion, since none of the theologians go into detailed discussions about the nature and meaning of marital relationships with African widows. The first suggestion is that the occasional use of the term "marriage" by some (not all) social scientists has led the theologians to assume that every union or relationship with a widow is in essence a type of legal marriage. Hence, if a man were married, the taking of his brother's widow would be the same as his taking a second wife: a polygynous relationship inconsistent with Christian teaching.[13] Moreover, the case where the inheritor is single was overlooked—a situation that would call their whole argument into question.

Another reason why the theologians do not make these distinctions may be that the anthropological descriptions of the different kinds of relationships possible between a widow and her brother-in-law were not *widely* available until the mid 1950s, when works of scholars like Evans-Pritchard, Radcliffe-Brown, and Phillips were published.[14] The impact of these writings has yet to be felt in nonanthropological circles. Likewise, the lack of standardization of technical anthropological terms such as "widow inheritance" and "levirate" makes it difficult for someone from another discipline to grasp the import and meaning of these distinctions.

However, it should be noted that although the theologians do not utilize anthropological categories, they draw on their own theological judgment and are quick to point out that the levirate does not have the full "malice" of polygyny (this is a theological way of saying that it is a special kind of polygyny). Moreover, in the most recent theological writings, they describe the leviratic union as having some "redeeming merits" and as deserving special pastoral consideration. Thus, Hastings writes that the levirate should be understood with the *greatest sympathy*, and it should not be impossible to receive the widow and her married inheritor back to the Church in a double union.[15] Bernard Häring in *Theology of Protest* softens his previous position by saying that the levirate is aimed at procreation and not sexual indiscipline. He is upset that the missionaries continue to apply ecclesiastical sanctions against the leviratic custom without consideration of the hardships this creates. He writes angrily:

> Must the missionary obey the moralist and deny the sacraments to a Christian married man who with considerable sacrifice fulfills his levirate duty towards the widow of his brother, and to the widow who adheres to this order demanded by tribal custom in order that she may not be robbed of her children and lose her place in the tribe? He will do this even when conjugal intercourse is reduced to a radical minimum.[16]

Häring goes on to say that the primary question of those who protest this rigid morality is: "Have you moralists thought as earnestly about this question as about the imposition of the smallest rubrical instruction?"[17]

Hillman calls the levirate a form of *social security* for a widow and her children required by customary law; Shorter calls the custom a way of *catering to unsupported women* and for ensuring the continuation of the line.[18] Leclercq writes that this custom is inspired by the desire to *fulfill the primary purpose of marriage*, and that the error in this custom is that a man is too attached to the material fact of posterity.[19]

However, in spite of all these qualifications, there is no evidence in Catholic theological writings of any careful investigation or discussion of the leviratic custom that would question its characterization as *polygyny*. An analysis of the few writings available shows them to be so imprecise and unscientific that they cannot reasonably be used as a guide to understanding the reasons for the custom's prohibition. These writings presuppose, unjustifiably, that the levirate is always a legal polygynous marriage, even though it is admitted that the levirate does have some redeeming features and should be given special pastoral considerations. Furthermore, these writings show no awareness of the massive opposition to the prohibition of the leviratic custom by the African people together with the Catholic Church leaders both missionary and indigenous. The inescapable conclusion is that the prohibition of the African leviratic union as incompatible with Roman Catholic marital behavior *cannot* be justified by means of the arguments and discussions presented in Catholic theological literature.

Let us now proceed to the next chapter, where the theological issues raised by the empirical data will be articulated and discussed. It is felt that it is these issues that will determine whether the leviratic union is truly compatible with Christian marital and moral behavior.

NOTES

1. See Bernard Häring, *Marriage in the Modern World* (Westminster, Md.: Newman, 1966), p. 262; Alyward Shorter, "Christians and African Marriage and Family Life," *The African Contributions to World Church and Other Essays in Pastoral Anthropology* (Kampala, Uganda: Gaba Publications, 1972), p. 16; George Hayward Joyce, *Christian Marriage* (London: Sheed and Ward, 1948), pp. 570–608; Joseph Mullin, *The Catholic Church in Modern Africa* (London: Geoffrey Chapman, 1965), p. 154; Adrian Hastings, "Report on Marriage," *New Blackfriars* 54 (June 1973) 255; Alyward Shorter, "Notes on Traditional and Christian Marriage in Africa," Church's Research Project on Marriage in Africa, No. 11 (Kampala, Uganda: Gaba Publications), p. 2; Alyward Shorter, *Essays in Pastoral Anthropology,*

Gaba Institute Pastoral Papers, No. 5 (Kampala, Uganda: Gaba Publications, 1969), p. 16; Eugene Hillman, *Polygamy Reconsidered,* pp. 120–121; Luzbetak, *The Church and Culture,* p. 247; Jacques Leclercq, *Marriage and the Family,* trans. Thomas Hanley (New York and Cincinnati: Frederick Pustet, 1942), p. 67; Henry Bitarkaramire, *Traditional and Christian Marriage,* Gaba Institute Pastoral Papers, No. 9 (Kampala, Uganda: Gaba Publications, l969), p. 20; E. K. Cukopela, "Marriage Commitment," *African Ecclesiastical Review* 14 (1972) 328; H. Ulbrich and F. Van Driessche, "Some Elements for Possible Solution of the Actual Crisis in Christian Marriage Life in Africa and Especially Rhodesia" (mimeographed, 1971); Adrian Hastings, *Christian Marriage in Africa* (London: S.P.C.K., 1973), p. 99.

In general, the Protestant writings on this issue are of the same caliber and quality as the Catholics'. See Gerhard Jasper, "Polygamy in the Old Testament," *African Theological Journal* No. 2 (February 1969) 39; M. D. W. Jeffreys, "Polygamy in the Christian Fold," *Practical Anthropology* 19 (1972) 85; John S. Mbiti, *African Religion and Philosophy* (New York: Praeger, 1969), p. 149; Alan Tippet, "Polygamy as a Missionary Problem: The Anthropological Issues," *Church Growth Bulletin* 5 (March 1969) 77; Kenneth Hughes, "The Church and Marriage in Africa," *The Christian Century* 82 (February 17, 1965) 205; T. T. T. Nabeta, "Mutual Dependence and Church Growth," *Church Growth Bulletin* 5 (March 1969) 59-60; H. W. Turner, "Monogamy: A Mark of the Church?" *International Review of Mission* 31 (April 1942) 220–223; N. G. N. Inyamah, "Polygamy and the Christian Church," *Concordia Theological Monthly* 43 (March 1972) 138–143.

2. Evans-Pritchard, *Kinship,* p. 112; Shorter, "Notes," p. 2; A. R. Radcliffe-Brown, "Introduction," p. 64. There are other marital adjustments practiced, such as widow concubinate and remarriage, but they are not relevant to this discussion; see Evans-Pritchard, *Kinship,* pp. 116 ff.

3. Edward Westermarck in his *History of Human Marriage* (London: Macmillan, 1891), I, p. 510, discusses the theory proposed by McLennon that the levirate derives from polyandry—this he rejects. In Vol. III, p. 262, he argues against Franzer's thesis that the levirate originated in group marriage. Westermarck is also aware of the distinction between the levirate as a duty and the levirate as a right (I, p. 511). Likewise, citing McLennon, he calls attention to the fact that among certain people the children begotten by the brother are accounted the children of the deceased (I, p. 513). In his fifth re-written edition he gives as a subsidiary motive for the levirate fear of the deceased husband's jealous ghost (III, p. 217).

Jan Cunnison in *The Luapula Peoples of Northern Rhodesia: Custom and History in Tribal Politics* (Manchester: Manchester University Press, 1959), pp. 96–98, discusses an interesting type of leviratic custom where the new husband of the widow loses his former name and takes the name of the dead man aş do his children by his other wives. He calls this custom "positional succession."

4. E. E. Evans-Pritchard, *Kinship and Marriage among the Nuer* (London: Oxford University Press, 1951), pp. 108 ff.

5. Edward Westermarck, *A Short History of Marriage* (New York: Humanities Press, 1926), pp. 264–65; Lucy Mair, "African Marriage and Social Change," in

Survey of African Marriage and Family Life, ed. Arthur Phillips (London: Oxford University Press, 1953), p. 15.

6. For an extensive bibliography on the leviratic custom as it is practiced in other parts of the world, see Edward Westermarck, *The History of Human Marriage,* 5th ed. (New York: The Allerton Book Company, 1922), pp. 208–211, n. 1. Also, David Mace and Vera Mace, *Marriage East and West,* Dolphin Books (Garden City, N.Y.: Doubleday, 1957), p. 279.

7. Mair, "African Marriage," pp. 54–55; Evans-Pritchard, *Kinship,* p. 112. Radcliffe-Brown, "Introduction," p. 64; E. E. Evans-Pritchard, *Some Aspects of Marriage and Family among the Nuer,* The Rhodes-Livingstone Papers, No. 11 (Livingstone, Northern Rhodesia:The Rhodes-Livingstone Institute, 1945), p. 14.

8. Evans-Pritchard, *Kinship,* p. 113; Mair, "African Marriage," p. 3; Westermarck, *A Short History of Marriage,* p. 265.

9. Shorter, "Notes," p. 2; Radcliffe-Brown, "Introduction," p. 64.

10. Arthur Phillips, "Marriage Laws in Africa," in *Survey of African Marriage and Family Life,* ed. Arthur Phillips (London: Oxford University Press, 1953), p. 287; Mair, "African Marriage," p. 3; Radcliffe-Brown, "Introduction," p. 64.

11. See Mair, "African Marriage," pp. 44, 70, 98; Lucy Mair, *An Introduction to Social Anthropology* (London: Oxford University Press, 1965), p. 84; Sylvia Leith-Ross, *African Women* (London: Routledge & Kegan Paul, 1965), p. 102; Tippet, "Polygamy as a Missionary Problem: The Anthropological Issues," *Church Growth Bullentin* 5 (1968) 60; Joseph Mullin, *The Catholic Church in Modern Africa* (London: Geoffrey Chapman, 1965), p. 154.

12. Hastings, "Report on Marriage," p. 255; Hillman, *Polygamy Reconsidered,* p. 118; Luzbetak, *The Church and Culture,* p. 247; Leclercq, *Marriage and the Family,* p. 67; Shorter, "Notes," p. 13; Cukopela, "Marriage Commitment," p. 328; Bitakaramire, *Traditional and Christian Marriage,* p. 20; Lyndon Harries, "Christian Marriage in African Society," *Survey of African Marriage and Family Life,* ed. Arthur Phillips (London: Oxford University Press, 1953), p. 410.

Harries (p. 410) reports that the Roman Catholic Ordinaries in that 1945 meeting at Leopoldville sought the support of the government in freeing the parties to a Christian marriage from the obligation of receiving and protecting a deceased brother's widow.

13. This would be accurate perhaps, if a man were practicing the custom we have defined as "widow inheritance"—a common practice of some African peoples. See Narâná Coissoró, *The Customary Law of Succession in Central Africa,* Estudo de Ciências Políticas e Socials, No. 78 (Lisbon:Technical University of Lisbon, 1966), *passim.* Polygyny was officially condemned by the Catholic Church in the twenty-fourth session of the Council of Trent, November 11, 1563—Canon no. 2 of the *Canone de Sacramento Matrimonii.* See Henrici Denzinger, *Enchiridion Symbolorum,* ed. Karl Rahner, 31st ed. (Barcelona: Herder, 1960), p. 340. Eugene Hillman in *Polygamy Reconsidered,* pp. 226, 228–229, writes that the condemnation of polygamy by the Council of Trent was directed against Luther's efforts to justify his friend and supporter Philip of Hess and did not in fact consider the missionary and pastoral question of simultaneous polygyny. See Harries, "Christian Marriage in African Society," pp. 355–356 for a description of how the polygyny prohibition was applied in the mission countries.

14. Phillips' work was published in 1953; Radcliffe-Brown's "Introduction" in 1950; Evans-Pritchard's *Nuer* in 1951. Adrian Hastings in "The Church's Response to African Marriage," *African Ecclesiastical Review* 13 (1971) 196, offers a similar explanation, saying, "Nor did they [missionaries] have much help from anthropologists as a scientific anthropology of marriage did not develop until well into the twentieth century."

15. Hastings, "Report on Marriage," p. 252.

16. Häring, *Theology of Protest,* pp. 146–47.

17. Ibid., p. 147.

18. Hillman, *Polygamy Reconsidered,* pp. 120–121; Shorter, "Christians and African Marriage," p. 57.

19. Leclercq, *Marriage and the Family,* p. 62.

CHAPTER EIGHT

The Theological Implications of
The Empirical Leviratic Data

Implications Regarding the Nature of the Levirate

The data presented in Part I show that the marital relationship between the widow and her brother-in-law under consideration is the leviratic union and not widow inheritance—in no place is mention made of the widow becoming the legal wife of her brother-in-law through a traditional marriage. Hence, the whole moral and theological issue of the levirate as polygyny is inapplicable and irrelevant to our study. The data deal only with the widow and her relationship to one man: whether the man is married or single is of no consequence. Furthermore, the data show that the leviratic custom is only *one* way of caring for widows and is by no means a universal pattern for all African societies. Indeed, among the four peoples surveyed (taken as a whole) it is only one of four possible ways for their care.* Moreover, in the societies where the levirate is present, it is not practiced without variation. The analysis of the data in Part I makes it clear that the leviratic custom arises only in the context of certain presuppositions about the nature and function of marriage in particular societies. These presuppositions must be the starting point for the theologian if he is to properly understand, discuss, and evaluate the leviratic custom in the light of Christian marital principles.

---

*A widow may: (1) be divorced and then seek to be remarried; (2) return home with her children; (3) remain single in her husband's homestead; (4) enter into a leviratic union.

174

The first presupposition is that marriage (according to the patrilineal rules of inheritance and descent) is a group-oriented relationship involving not only the bride and the groom but also their lineages. Hence, the bride is seen as both the wife of her husband and the wife of his lineage. She is, therefore, called by her husband's lineage (e.g., in the Luo language) both "our brother's wife" (*chi owadwa*) and "our wife" (*chiwa*). She is seen as married only once in her lifetime. The bridewealth paid to her father's lineage comes from the joint effort of her husband's lineage. There is no dissolution of her marriage legally or otherwise due to the death of her husband; the widow continues to be regarded as a functioning wife.

This continuation of the widow's marriage in the patrilineal tradition happens because the marriage is coextensive with the existence of the husband's lineage as well as the existence of the husband. Theoretically, therefore, the marriage would terminate automatically only if the husband died and the husband's lineage also died out. There is no "till physical death do us part" agreement between the bride and groom as in the Western and matrilineal marriage traditions. Rather, the lineage of the husband agrees in covenant at the beginning of the marriage to support and care for the new bride and her children (yet to be born) if death should remove the husband. Thus, the maintenance of the family, the continuing fertility of the wife, the socialization of the children, and the place of the husband and his family in the lineage are implicitly guaranteed by all male relatives of the husband's lineage as part of the marriage alliance.

Marriage in this patrilineal corporate kin-group context is dissoluble or terminated only by means of a traditional divorce; i.e., the breaking of the alliance between the woman's lineage and the husband's lineage (whether the husband is alive or dead is of no consequence). A traditional divorce in this context entails, as we have seen: (1) the return of the bridewealth; (2) the return of the woman to her father's home; and (3) the separation of the woman from her children, who remain with the husband's family. There is no other way for a *widow* (or any woman for that matter) in such a system to terminate a marriage in order to be seen as "free" to remarry. Only divorcees can remarry. Hence a widow, if she wishes to remarry, must get a divorce from her deceased husband and his lineage.* To promote remarriage of widows in such a situation is tantamount to promoting a divorce that will destroy the basic family unit and separate the children from their mothers.

The leviratic union, therefore, is a rather sophisticated answer to the question of how marriages involving patrilineal corporate kin-groups can continue to function once the husbands are dead. It represents an adjustment in the lineage's relationship to the widow made in the name of the dead husband because of the original marriage alliance. This adjustment is such that one of the brothers takes full responsibility (temporarily) for the widow and her children; he *stands* or *substitutes* for the deceased in all the activities and functions of the bereaved family. Thus the deceased's name and family can *continue on* just as if he were alive. This aspect of the leviratic union raises the *basic* theological issue of the nature and meaning of "marriage" and "indissolubility" in marriage institutions entwined with a lineage ideology, i.e., systems which involve both individuals and lineages.

The second patrilineal presupposition underlying the leviratic union is that perpetuation of the father's lineage through his children is of utmost importance, indeed, is essential to the marriage. Hence children born of the marriage belong *in perpetuum* to the lineage of the father and the mother does not have legal control over them even though the father is dead. If a marriage is terminated by divorce, the woman has no legal way of retaining control over her children; she would have to leave them behind in the care of her husband's lineage—a powerful argument against divorce. This control over the children by the husband's lineage is possible because the husband and his lineage have rights over the procreative powers of the wife as well as over her sexual and domestic powers.† These rights are part of the marriage alliance. They determine that any offspring of the marriage both continue the husband's lineage and bear his name, ensuring him of a place in the

---

*Remarriage of a widow, in the eyes of the Luo people, means that the woman has a bad reputation: she has failed to live up to her commitments to her husband's family. One respondent said, "Those who remarry are called prostitutes."

†If rights over the procreative powers of the woman are not given over to the husband's lineage, as in the case of the Kwaya marriage following matrilineal rules of inheritance and descent, there is usually no leviratic relationship.

lineage. The leviratic custom in this aspect, therefore, enables the widow to remain with her children while ensuring her continuing fertility. This aspect of the custom raises the *basic* theological issues of "family," "identity," and "inheritance" in marriage systems where children are recruited only to their fathers' lineages.

The third presupposition underlying the leviratic custom is that the brother-in-law's relationship with the widow is one of *substitution*. He does not become her legal husband nor is she his legal wife. He merely acts for or substitutes for her deceased husband. There is no new marital commitment to the widow apart from what was made at the time of the marriage, namely a promise and guarantee to do all to ensure the growth and continuance of the family if her husband should die; the brother-in-law's agreement to "play" the role of the husband is the way these promises are fulfilled. The widow, therefore, experiences her husband in the ministrations of his brother. Even in her sexual relations with the brother-in-law, it is her husband's interests and wishes that are being served. The actions of the brother-in-law maintain the husband's identity, the integrity of his family, and his presence within the family. The brother-in-law's concern for his brother's family contains an implicit statement about the possibility of life and relationships lasting beyond the grave: this is a second reason why marriages in such a system are not terminated by death. The deceased husband is seen as still "present" and capable of influencing the living. For example, according to the Luo tradition a dead husband can cause his widow serious misfortunes such as sicknesses and sterility if she angers him by remarrying. He can, as they say, "put the evil eye on her."

The evidence that the leviratic relationship is merely one of substitution can be seen from the following facts. 1. Children born of the union are born in the name of the dead husband. 2. The widow is still called and related to as the wife of her dead husband and not as the wife of her inheritor.* 3. Once the widow is past child-bearing age (Luo tradition), she leaves the homestead of her inheritor and moves into the homestead set up by her eldest

---

*The brother-in-law is not his own person in this relationship; he is ritually and legally the dead brother.

son—an arrangement identical to the situation of a woman widowed in old age. 4. The leviratic relationship is not permanent and the widow *can* and *will* leave one inheritor for another— something not possible were she considered a legal wife.* 5. Only the sexual relationship with the inheriting brother-in-law is seen as moral and good; if the widow enters into other sexual relation- ships, they are seen as adulterous and the leviratic husband can demand compensation. 6. There are no rewards for the brother- in-law in terms of "building up" his homestead or increasing the number of his children; rather the levirate adds many serious responsibilities in the social, moral, and economic orders.† This aspect of the leviratic union raises the basic theological issues of "sexuality" and "life after death."

Another issue raised by the data is the nature of the relationship between the leviratic union and the payment of bridewealth. It might appear that the payment of bridewealth is also a prerequisite in creating the kind of marriage system necessary for the existence of the leviratic union (this is certainly the case of the four peoples surveyed). The problem with this judgment is its assumption that the payment of bridewealth and a patrilineal descent system are inseparably entwined. This is not necessarily true. There are societies where a patrilineal descent pattern is followed without any bridewealth payments or with only token payments, e.g., societies where there is an exchange of sisters in alternating generations.‡ Hence, the patrilineal descent system that underpins the leviratic custom may or may not involve the payment of bridewealth. Con- sequently, the payment of bridewealth is not an essential element of the African leviratic union.

The final issue raised by the data is the *quality* of the relationship between the widow and her inheritor. The data show that over 70% of those sampled felt that a widow is usually not treated as one

---

*About 30% of the Kuria and Luo widows had cohabited with more than one inheritor. See Appendix A, Table 41.

†One respondent in the survey stated, "There is no advantage in this custom to the (inheriting) brother; it is done only out of respect for the deceased."

‡For further elaboration of this point see Robin Fox, *Kinship and Marriage* (Middlesex: C. Nicholls and Company, 1967), pp. 200 ff.

should treat a wife.* The general reason given for this lack of proper attention was that it is difficult to care for one who is not your *real* wife. This issue, even though it is not essential to an understanding of the leviratic union, would have important pastoral implications if this custom were accepted within a Christian context.

In summary, the basic theological issues raised by the data in Part I concerning the leviratic institution are as follows: (1) the nature of divorce in a marriage system where the woman is seen as both the wife of her husband and the wife of his lineage, i.e., the theological problem of "marriage" and "indissolubility"; (2) the nature of the relationships between mothers and children in marriage systems where children are recruited only to the father's lineage, i.e., the theological problems of "identity" "inheritance" and "family"; and (3) the nature of the sexual relationship between a widow and her brother-in-law in a marriage system where the brother-in-law is seen as only a substitute for the deceased husband, i.e., the theological problems of "sexuality" and "life after death." These are the essential theological issues that must eventually be discussed, analyzed, and evaluated if one is to understand the leviratic custom within its own social system. What one says about these issues determines what one will say about the leviratic union and its compatibility or incompatibility with Christian marital values and practices.†

Furthermore, it is clear from the previous chapter that the information and insights presented here concerning the leviratic custom were not known by the theologians writing about this custom. Likewise, as will be shown in the following chapter, the missionaries were unaware of these issues. Thus, neither the theologians nor the missionaries were in a position to make any reasonable assessment of the Christian acceptability of this custom. What is prohibited by the Church, therefore, cannot be the true levirate in the context of an African marriage system. The true African leviratic custom has yet to be theologically assessed.

---

*See Appendix A, Table 33.

†It is, of course, impossible to adequately discuss these issues within the scope of this study, since that would involve extensive theoretical work. However, some reflections on these issues are presented in the final chapters.

Implications Regarding the Christian Prohibition of the Levirate

The empirical data relating to the effects of the prohibition of the leviratic custom by the Christian churches raises five major issues of interest to the theologians. These are discussed in order.

First, the African respondents articulated only one major *marital* reason as the cause of the churches' prohibition of the leviratic union, namely, that the widow is not the brother-in-law's wife.* This reason was given by 430 people representing 35% of the entire sample.† On the basis of the frequency and distribution of this response, it appears that this response must be the *ordinary* marital reason specifically preached and taught by the Church leaders as justification for prohibiting the leviratic custom. At least, it is the one reason that a large number of African people understood and could articulate. There is no evidence that the Church leaders, in the areas surveyed, link the prohibition of the levirate with the prohibition of polygyny (as has been done by the Catholic theologians): not even one respondent mentioned polygyny in this context. The Church leaders, therefore, must have assessed the leviratic custom as unlawful precisely because there is no possibility of a marriage between the two partners, even though they insist on cohabiting. How ironic this is! The Catholic theologians find the leviratic custom to be unlawful because it is a marriage (a polygynous marriage) while the Catholic Church leaders find it unlawful because it is not a marriage.

Second, there is massive opposition to the churches' prohibition

---

*Typical expressions underlying this category are: "there are no marriage promises"; "the Church wants marriage"; "she remains the wife of her dead husband"; "she is like a second wife."

The comments written-in on this response stated that a widow in such a relationship is a "prostitute," "like a second wife," "one who is sinning sexually," "one who spoils another's sacrament of matrimony."

†See Appendix A, Table 34, for statistical details. In point of fact, 40% of the people said that the prohibition was merely a part of the rules and regulations of the Church. Another 12% said that they did not know why the churches prohibited the custom.

among the people who follow the rules of patrilineal succession and inheritance (54% of the Kuria; 65% of the Sukuma; 74% of the Luo). Their arguments against the prohibition are threefold. The first concerns the personal moral situation of the widow. It argues that the widow cannot be remarried; that she is not responsible for her husband's death; that she is not a prostitute; that she is in need and should be helped.

The second concerns the meaning of the custom within the society. It argues that this custom builds the deceased brother's house; that it is a sign of love for one's deceased brother; that it is an old tradition; that it keeps the bridewealth from being wasted; that it functions because of the sympathy of the brothers-in-law.

The third concerns the religious commitment of the widow. It argues that the widow is still a member of the Church, that she still prays and loves God, that she was not forbidden by divine law to follow this custom.

All three of these arguments imply the African conviction that the leviratic widow remains the wife of her deceased husband. Taken together, these arguments form a comprehensive rebuttal to the Christian churches' prohibition of the levirate. They present a serious challenge to the churches' position from the moral, religious, and social points of view. These three arguments must be answered if the churches, in particular the Catholic Church, are to claim to be taking into account the indigenous forms of social structures when presenting Christian moral teachings.

Third, the Catholic Church leaders generally agree that the leviratic custom is not a marriage but a way of caring for widows; likewise, over half of them ask that the prohibition be removed and the custom accepted since they find no adequate reason for declaring it to be un-Christian. This shows how the Catholic leaders in the areas surveyed, no doubt observing and reflecting on the workings of the levirate in the concrete have understood the leviratic union differently than the Catholic theologians: there is little evidence to suggest that the theologians' polygynous analysis of the leviratic union has been accepted as true and accurate by the leaders. Thus, the influence of Catholic theological writings on the Catholic Church leaders in Africa must be judged to be minimal. Table 24 illustrates the Catholic Church leaders' opinions on the nature of the leviratic union.

TABLE 24

CATHOLIC CHURCH LEADERS' OPINIONS ON THE LEVIRATIC UNION (%)

Opinion	% Catholic Leaders
Way of caring for a widow	79
In between a marriage and caring	5
A real marriage	8
Other	8
Total %	100
Number	(115)

Furthermore, the number of Catholic Church leaders opposing the prohibition of the leviratic custom is correlated with the number of Christian people affected by it in each area. That is, in the Luo and Kuria areas, where the prohibition is most acutely felt, 60-70% of the leaders ask that the custom be accepted and the prohibition dropped. On the other hand, in the Kwaya and Sukuma areas where there is less of a problem, only 30-40% of the leaders ask that it be accepted. It is to be noted that this opposition to the leviratic prohibition, with the exception of the African leaders in the Sukuma area, is on the part of both the African and missionary leaders a clear indication that they have a similar assessment of the leviratic issue. Further, the very opposition to the prohibition by the Catholic Church leaders is one more piece of evidence against the Catholic Church's claim that it has taken into account all the pertinent factors before deciding on a pastoral position regarding the levirate.

Fourth, the acceptance of the Christian prohibition of the leviratic custom is highly conditioned by *nonreligious* factors such as (a) the the type of descent pattern followed, (b) the presence in the society of other options for the care of widows, (c) the amount of independence given to women. Likewise, there are almost no correlations between membership in a Christian religion (or formal education) and approval of the Christian leviratic prohibition (the one exception is the Luo people). It must be humbling to missionaries to see that initiation into a Christian religion or formal education, two of their high-priority activities, have had so little influence on traditional leviratic attitudes and customs. This points up how unrealistic it is to expect to directly influence and change customs and attitudes through either religious conversion or formal education.

Those who approve of the churches' prohibition have accepted the churches' moral objection to the leviratic union as their own reason for opposing this custom; i.e., they now claim that the widow in such a relationship is like a second wife, is committing sin, is destroying the inheritors' sacramental marriage. These negative moral judgments, of course, were not present in the traditional culture. The question this raises is: are these moral judgments based on an informed evaluation of the leviratic custom vis-à-vis Christian moral teachings?

Fifth, the prohibition of this custom has in fact resulted in a large number of Christians being censured by their churches for long periods of time, especially in the Luo area. There 10% of all adult Luo Christians (both men and women) have been censured by their churches for entering into leviratic unions.* Many of these people have been excluded from full participation in their churches' activities and worship for periods of ten years or more. Furthermore, the data indicate that most of the censured widows are young women with dependent children. In the other three areas there is not as serious a problem, but there are indications in two of these areas that this problem will become increasingly more frequent. These indications are the aging of the Christian community (Kuria area) and the greater number of people following rules of patrilineal inheritance and descent (Kwaya area).†

In summary, the issues raised by the pastoral data regarding the levirate show the theologian how the moralistic response of the

---

*In the Catholic Church the censure imposed on those who enter into a leviratic union is exclusion from the sacraments.

†In the Kwaya area, the Catholic Church is in the peculiar situation of promoting a marriage system that cares for its widows by means of the levirate and, at the same time, of declaring the leviratic relationship immoral and un-Christian.

churches to the complex leviratic relationships is in no way pastorally adequate or theologically justified. The very approval of the churches' position, in general, is shown to be due to its harmony with patterns of behavior already existing within the society and not due to any widespread change in attitudes or practices caused by religious conversion. The majority of the Catholic leaders and the majority of the African peoples, both Christian and non-Christian, see little reason for continuing this prohibition and ask that the leviratic custom be accepted within a Christian context.

In conclusion, the pastoral and anthropological insights, information, and issues presented in Part I of this study have not been known by the Christian theologians and, consequently, have not influenced their judgments and reflections about the leviratic custom. The theologians have been unaware of the true nature of the leviratic custom, the pastoral effects of the prohibition, the reasons for the prohibition's acceptance by some and rejection by others and the massive opposition to the prohibition on the part of both clerics and laity. The missionaries, on the other hand, aware that the theologians were wrong, had a surprisingly accurate grasp of the nature of the leviratic union. However, they were left to grapple with this custom on their own; they had to fall back on the Western models of Christian marital and sexual behavior taught them in the seminaries as the framework in which to understand and deal with the levirate pastorally. As a result, they too distorted the theological and pastoral implications of this custom.

Let us now proceed to the next chapter where the models of marital and sexual behavior taught to the Western missionaries are described and applied to the leviratic custom.

CHAPTER NINE

The Models of Christian Marriage and Sexuality Taught to Western Missionaries

Catholic missionaries sent to Africa from Europe and North America prior to the Second Vatican Council (1962–1965) were formed in their thinking about marriage and sexuality by a theology, known as the "manualist" theology that was taught in the standard (seminary) canon law, moral theology, and dogmatic theology textbooks.[1] These texts, products of nineteenth-century neoscholastic theology, presented models of Christian marital and sexual behavior that were regarded as normative for all Christian peoples no matter what their culture or their social situation. The manualist theology claimed to teach and present all the essential elements necessary for understanding and entering into Christian marriages and lawful sexual unions.*

In the manualist model of Christian marriage, there are four issues of relevance to the discussion of the levirate: they are presented in order. First, the manualist model defines Christian marriage as an individualistic contract or alliance between two people. The purpose of the contract is primarily the procreation and education of children, and secondarily mutual aid and the easing of concupiscence.[2]

The contract itself, furthermore, is asserted to be a sacrament—this is taught as a doctrine of faith.[3] Hence, there can

---

*It is difficult for the non-Catholic theologian or lay reader to appreciate the power of the Catholic manualist theology in shaping the thinking of generations of Catholic clergy. This theology was precisely regulated in form and content by Rome; it was required in all seminaries. Hence, in discussing the manualist models, one can be safely assured of their pervading influence.

be no marriage between Christians that is not sacramental;* to try to exclude the sacrament would exclude the marriage contract and render the marriage invalid.[4]

The contract is described in Canon 1881, no. 2, as: "an act of the will by which each party surrenders and accepts a perpetual and exclusive bodily right to the end that acts may be performed which are as such adequate for the generation of offspring."[5] The procreation principle is seen as so essential that if it is positively excluded, there can be no valid marriage.† The surprising thing is that although conjugal affection is presumed, it is not seen as essential for validity.[6]

Second, marriage has two essential properties in the manualist model. The one is unity, the other indissolubility. According to the property of unity, a valid marriage can be contracted only between one man and one woman. If this is positively excluded, there can be no valid marriage (Abbo, *Sacred Canons,* II, p. 165). "Unity" therefore requires that polygamy in all of its forms be forbidden. Indeed, the property is seen to apply even to the marriages of non-Christians.[7] The reasoning behind this prohibition of polygamy according to the canonist John Abbo (*Sacred Canons,* II, p. 166), is that polygamy undermines the secondary purpose of marriage by its *interference* with mutual aid between the spouses in the attainment of marital happiness and the education of children.

The second property, indissolubility, makes the marital agreement a perpetual partnership, a permanent bond, which can neither be broken by the parties themselves nor by their superiors. It is so essential to Christian marriage that just an intention to violate it is sufficient to render the marriage invalid.[8] Further, the bond is such that it can be broken only by dying. [9]

---

*This point is disputed by José Montserrat-Torrents in *The Abandoned Spouse* (Milwaukee: Bruce, 1969). He claims that what is taught as faith is only that the sacrament of marriage lies in the bond or contract of marriage, and that the teaching that every contract of marriage by baptized Christians is thereby sacramental is a theological opinion that cannot be logically deduced from the first premise.

†Abbo, *Sacred Canons,* (II, p. 165) states that this position is based on the principle that exclusion of children *in perpetuum* means the exclusion of the right to conjugal relations.

The scriptural basis for the dissolution of marriage by death is found in 1 Cor. 7:39, "A wife is bound to her husband as long as he lives. But if the husband dies, she is free to marry whom she will." Also, Romans 7:2–3, "For example, a married woman is by law bound to her husband while he lives; but if her husband dies, she is discharged from the obligations of the marriage law."[10]

The intrinsic reasons for indissolubility, according to Ludwig Ott (*Fundamentals of Catholic Dogma,* p. 462), are the assuring of the physical and moral education of the children, the protection of marital fidelity, the imitation of the indissoluble connection of Christ and his Church, and consideration for the welfare of the family and society.

Third, the Catholic Church, according to the manualist model, has authority over all marriages of baptized people by virtue of its Canon Law (cn. 1016) without prejudice to the competence of the civil powers.[11] This gives the Catholic Church power to regulate the form and conditions for a valid marriage. We read in Abbo and Hannan:

> In virtue of it [ecclesiastical authority] the Church is authorized within the limits of the natural and the divine law to impose, within those limits, prohibiting and invalidating impediments to marriage. . . Finally, as a natural complement to the foregoing competence, the Church possesses the power to punish those of its subjects who violate the laws affecting marriage. [12]

Fourth, there are numerous impediments to a marriage described in Canons 1058–1080. Some of them render a marriage invalid, others, illicit. Some are of ecclesiastical origin and can be dispensed, others are of divine origin and cannot be dispensed. Only one of them is of special interest to this discussion, namely, the impediment of "affinity." This states that one cannot validly marry one's affines in a direct line in all degrees, e.g., one's father-in-law, or in the collateral line to the second degree, e.g., one's brother-in-law. This impediment is seen to be of Church origin and can be dispensed.[13] (If applied in Africa, a Church marriage between a widow and her brother-in-law would require a dispensation.)

As a further note, Canon 1142 states that although chaste widowhood is said to be a more honorable situation, it is *lawful* for a widow to enter into a second or even additional marriages.[14]

In brief, the manualist model of Christian marriage presupposes a social structure where two people, legally independent of their families, enter into a marital alliance that functions as a new social unit in the society. For a valid *Christian* marriage all that is demanded is (1) they be baptized; (2) they be free of all invalidating impediments; and (3) they freely consent to cohabit as husband and wife exclusively and permanently, primarily to procreate and educate children and secondarily to aid each other and ease concupiscence. There is no other model of Christian marriage hinted at or suggested. There is no consideration given to a social structure where marriage is not only an alliance between individuals but also an alliance between lineages (corporate kin-groups).

The manualist model of Christian marriage, therefore, is relevant only to a particular system of marriage such as the one presently followed by most people in Europe and North America.[15] It is not applicable to nor does it fit systems of marriage operating in the African societies south of the Sahara. Thus, the training the Western missionaries received regarding the nature of Christian marriage in no way prepared them to deal with the bewildering variety of customs and institutions they encountered in Africa. Moreover, they mistakenly believed that the manualist model of Christian marriage was supracultural and universally applicable. Consequently, they were not open to accepting other (non-Western) marriage institutions and customs as valid and moral for Christians.

Turning now to the manualist model of Christian sexuality taught to missionaries, we find that it is also very precise and definite.[16] It teaches that any directly willed consent to venereal pleasure outside of marriage is always mortally sinful and never admits of slight matter.* [17] The reason given for this position is that all venereal pleasure is related to the act of procreation, and the act of procreation is forbidden outside of the marriage bond. To use this generative faculty in any other circumstances is to use it against its end.[18] McHugh writes:

---

*Slight matter is that which is not by its very nature seriously evil; e.g., reading a "slightly" suggestive novel.

> Coition itself is lawful in the married state and this legitimatizes all the preparatory or accessory endearments. Hence, the rule as to married persons is that venereal kisses and other such acts are lawful when given with a view to the exercise of the lawful marriage act and kept within the bounds of decency and moderation.[19]

There are a number of different types of unlawful sexual unions distinguished in these manuals. One of them, fornication, defined as sexual copulation between unmarried people, is declared by faith to be a "mortal" sin: this is presented as the teachings of the Church Fathers, the Old and New Testaments and the declarations of the Catholic Church.[20] Interestingly, the malice of fornication is said to be its injury to a new potential life, i.e., the life is deprived of legitimacy and protection of both parents and education in the home circle. The moralist McHugh acknowledges that there may be exceptional cases where there is provision for the rearing of the child, but, he writes, the morality of any act must be judged, "not by the exceptional and accidental, but by the usual and natural. [Furthermore] those who commit fornication are thinking of their own pleasure rather than of duty, and will generally shirk the difficult burdens of parenthood."[21]

Could one not argue on the basis of McHugh's "exceptional" cases (cases that are in fact "usual" in an African context) that there is no malice in the African leviratic relationship between a single man and a widow? The children are "usually and naturally" provided for and reared; the parties involved are acting out of duty rather than desire for sexual release; there is no shirking of the burdens of parenthood.

Moreover there are three forms of fornication distinguished in the manualist model. The first, "ordinary fornication," is committed with a woman who is neither a harlot nor a concubine; the second, "whoremongering," is committed with a harlot; the third, "free love," is committed with a mistress. (A woman is labeled a mistress if she has a personal contract with a man for habitual sexual intercourse as if they were husband and wife: this kind of relationship is often called "concubinage.") There is said to be a further malice attached to the last type of fornication, for the two people are seen as living in a proximate occasion of sin, and cannot be absolved from their sins unless they break the alliance.[22] Ultimately, as we shall see, the missionaries justified their opposition to the leviratic union on the ground that it was either this last type of fornication; i.e., concubinage, or if the brother-in-law was already married, a type of adulterous concubinage.

A second type of unlawful sexual union distinguished in these manuals is "adultery," i.e., intercourse where one or both parties are already married. Adultery, like fornication, is termed a grave sin; it has the added malice of violating the faith pledged in the contract and sacrament of marriage, and is an injury to the rights of one's spouse.[23]

The case where a husband or wife gives permission for an adulterous relationship is also discussed. The decision is that no one has the right to give such a permission since it is opposed to the sacredness of the marriage vows. The judgment is that even though the individual is not formally injured, the married state is injured.[24]

One can again raise the question of giving permission for an "adulterous" relationship in the context of the African leviratic custom. According to the custom, the women implicitly give permission to their spouses for leviratic unions—adulterous relationships according to the manualist model of Christian sexuality. The question asked is: Does this permission, in fact, injure the marriage state? From the point of view of the widow, at least, this permission clearly protects her married state and helps her maintain her marriage alliance with her deceased husband and his lineage. Further, there was no indication in the empirical data that this permission in fact injures or destroys the marriage state of the brother-in-law.

In brief, the manualist model of Christian sexuality, like the model of Christian marriage, was individualistic, Western and, therefore, incapable of dealing with forms of traditional African sexual behavior. Hence, this model impeded any real adjustments by the missionaries to the non-Western African sexual customs and institutions. The fact that the manualist model grew out of and reflected Western social structures that are not necessarily repeatable in other parts of the world was not understood; the model was taught as the norm for all cultures rather than as a particular example relevant to the Western experience of sexuality.

The Western missionaries, therefore, had no flexible speculative or practical tools for dealing with non-Western types of sexual institutions and behavior. They had no way of evaluating custom such as the "substitutional sexuality" present in the leviratic union. Thus they had to dismiss as un-Christian any type of behavior that did not fit into their predetermined modes of lawful sexual behavior.

In the light of the manualist theology, taught to the missionaries sent to Africa, it is becoming clearer why they felt no need or incentive to investigate, evaluate, and understand non-Western forms of sexual and marital relationships. Adrian Hastings writes:

> Nineteenth-century missionaries. . .had very little theology of marriage. . .and also little historical sense of the relativity of social patterns. Christian marriage was as they had known it at home, as they endeavoured to practice it in their own little compounds, and the conflicts between this and the confusing reality they witnessed in the world is and was extreme indeed.[25]

The pastoral training of the missionaries, therefore, preempted the possibility of any radical adaptations to non-Western social structures. The "correct" decisions about marriage and sexual relationships had already been made, and these decisions were taught in such a way that the cultural presuppositions behind them were never called into question. Indeed, each missionary saw it to be his task to achieve universal conformity in these matters no matter what the consequences.[26]

Thus, in spite of the theological recognition of cultural plurality taught in many official Catholic documents, the Catholic Church has held a fixed ethnocentric position on the pastoral level, a position that in practice has denied the principle of cultural plurality. In other words, after stating theologically that all cultures are equal and have equal rights to an independent existence with Christianity, the Catholic Church has operated on the pastoral level with the view that there is only one culture compatible with Christianity, namely, the culture of the Western missionaries. Consequently, the missionaries have been under no pressure to see if there were factors that would enable them to accept non-Western customs in a Christian context. Customs like the levirate, therefore, since they do not fit the manualist model of Christian marital behavior, were ruled out, in principle, before being examined.

From the evidence presented, it appears that the missionaries' judgment against accepting the leviratic custom has been based, *in fact,* on the following casuistic moral argument:* the leviratic union cannot be considered a type of Christian marriage since the partners do not marry one another even though they insist on cohabiting as man and wife;† thus, the conjugal intercourse has to be seen as unlawful and the relationship categorized as (adulterous) concubinage; concubinage places the leviratic partners in a proximate occasion of mortal sin, which automatically excludes them from the sacraments of the Church.

For all practical purposes, the *complex, responsible* leviratic union has been simplified by the missionaries to the level of the potentially exploitative relationship between a man and his mistress—a custom practiced in the Western world—and then dismissed as un-Christian. In other words, it appears that the missionaries have had to imagine the levirate as resembling a sexual union experienced in their own culture, namely, "concubinage" (whether adulterous or otherwise) in order to give the levirate a moral label. Confirmatory evidence on this point is contained in the usual response given in the survey as to why the churches are opposed to the levirate, namely: "The widow is not the brother-in-law's wife." This response feeds back to the missionaries what the African people heard them saying about the nature and morality of the leviratic custom. It contains both the missionaries' marital and moral objections: *marital,* in that the widow is not a proper wife, i.e., she is not married (hence the union is one of concubinage); *moral,* in that she is *acting* in the relationship as if she were a wife (hence unlawful sexual behavior).

The curious thing about the missionaries' position on the levirate is that they do not object to the leviratic institution as such but only to the unlawful sexual relations; i.e., they can accept a nonsexual leviratic relationship. Hence, if two partners involved in a

---

*This is not to suggest that each and every missionary justified the prohibition by such casuistic reasoning. For many, no doubt, factors such as cultural repugnance as well as unquestioned acceptance of pastoral practices already being followed were sufficient reasons.

†As already pointed out, there are a few cases where "patrilineal" widows are married by single men in Church ceremonies, but only under the most unusual circumstances.

leviratic relationship make a public sign indicating that they are not going to have sexual relations, e.g., building the widow a special house outside the compound, both partners would be allowed to receive the sacraments and the ecclesiastical censure would be lifted. The fact that the widow would still be actually an inherited woman in a leviratic relationship was of no consequence: they judged in terms of Western customs.

In summary, there is no evidence to suggest that there has been any attempt by the missionaries to work out the morality of the leviratic relationship in terms of the theological issues raised in this study, namely, the nature of "family," "identity," "inheritance," "marriage," "indissolubility," "sexuality," and "life after death" in African leviratic marriage systems. The Catholic missionaries forbade the leviratic custom because it did not seem to fit their Western manualist models of Christian marital and sexual behavior. Thus, the African leviratic custom has not been prohibited by the missionaries in terms of its own social structures. What has been prohibited is the leviratic custom stripped of its African value and meaning and misconstrued as a Western-style unlawful alliance.

Let us now go on to the final section of this book, where theological and anthropological reflections are presented on the issues raised by the leviratic prohibitions.

NOTES

1. The following are representative examples of these textbooks (the page numbers refer to the sections treating marriage): John A. Abbo and Jerome Hannon, *The Sacred Canons,* 2nd ed., 2 vols. (St. Louis: B. Herder Book Co., 1960), II, pp. 160–412; H. Noldin and A. Schmitt, *Summa Theologiae Moralis,* ed. G. Heinsel, 30th ed., 3 vols. (Austria: Feliciani Rauch, 1954), III, pp. 426–580; *Codex Juris Canonici* (Rome: Typis Polyglottis Vaticanis, 1917), pp. 192–214; A. H. van Vliet and C. D. Breed, *Marriage and Canon Law* (London: Burns and Oates, 1964): George Hayward Joyce, *Christian Marriage: An Historical Doctrinal Study* (London: Sheed and Ward, 1948); L. Ott, *Fundamentals of Catholic Dogma,* ed. J. C. Bastible, trans. P. Lynch (Cork: Mercier, 1955); R. Divine, *The Law of Christian Marriage* (London: R. & T. Washbourne, 1908). J. McHugh and Charles Callan, *Moral Theology,* 2 vols. (New York: Joseph F. Wagner, 1960), II, pp. 751–781; A. D. Tanquerey, *Synopsis Theologiae Moralis et Pastoralis,* 7th ed., 3 vols. (Rome: Desclée et Socii, 1920).

2. Canon 1013 No. 1 of the Code of Canon Law reads: "Matrimonii finis primarius est procreatio atque educatio prolis: secundarius mutuum adjutorium et remedium concupiscentiae" (*Codex Juris Canonici*, p. 192, hereafter noted as *Codex*). Also Abbo, *Sacred Canons*, II, p. 161; Noldin, *Summa*, III, p. 426.

3. Denzinger, *Enchiridion*, p. 340, no. 971.

4. Abbo, *Sacred Canons*, II, p. 163.

5. Ibid., p. 301, No. 2. "Consensus matrimonialis est actus voluntatis quo utraque pars tradit et acceptat jus in corpus, perpetuum et exclusivum, ordine ad actus per se aptos ad prolis generationem" (*Codex*, p. 202).

6. For a reference to this issue, see Van Vliet and Breed, *Marriage and Canon Law*, p. 3, No.1.

7. We read in Noldin, *Summa* (III, p. 440) the following: "etiam inter infideles secundem matrimonium durante priore invalidum sit." Also Abbo, *Sacred Canons*, II, p. 259, especially No. 18.

8. Abbo, *Sacred Canons*, II, p. 167.

9. Ibid., II, pp. 165 ff., 377. Also Ott, *Fundamentals*, p. 462; *Codex*, cn. 1118, p. 210.

10. See also Noldin, *Summa*, III, p. 440.

11. *Codex*, p. 193, "Baptizatorum matrimonium regitur jure non solum divino, sed etiam canonico, salva competentia civilis potestatis circa mere civiles eiusdem matrimonii effectus." See also Noldin, *Summa*, III, p. 436.

12. Abbo, *Sacred Canons*, II, p. 171.

13. *Codex*, cns. 1058–1080, pp. 199-203, cn. 1077, p. 202; McHugh and Callan, *Moral Theology*, II, p. 773; Noldin, *Summa*, III, pp. 504–506.

14. *Codex*, p. 214.

15. Josef Fuchs, "Theology of the Meaning of Marriage Today," in *Marriage in the Light of the Vatican II*, ed. J. McHugh (Washington, D.C.: Family Life Bureau, 1968), p. 20, raises the question of whether the marriage institutions we have discovered belong in fact only to our given culture.

16. The following are representative examples of the moral theology textbooks used in the seminaries; the page numbers refer to the sections treating of sexual morality. H. Davis, *Moral and Pastoral Theology* (London:Sheed and Ward, 1951), pp. 70-81; McHugh and Callan, *Moral Theology*, II, pp. 512–558; Dominic M. Prummer, *Handbook of Moral Theology*, trans. Gerald Shelton (Cork:Mercier Press, 1956), pp. 229–238; Noldin, *Summa*, I, Appendix: *De Castitate*, 35th ed., pp. 1-94; Denzinger, *Enchiridion, passim*.

17. Prummer, *Handbook*, p. 230; McHugh and Callan, *Moral Theology*, II, p. 520; Davis, *Moral and Pastoral Theology*, p. 71.

18. Noldin, *Summa*, I, Appendix, p. 16; Prummer, *Handbook*, p. 230.

19. McHugh and Callan, *Moral Theology*, II, p. 532.

20. Ibid., p. 543; Prummer, *Handbook*, p. 234.

21. McHugh and Callan, *Moral Theology*, II, p. 544.

22. Ibid., p. 547.

23. Ibid., p. 548; Prummer, *Handbook*, p. 235; Noldin, *Summa*, Appendix, p. 24.

24. McHugh and Callan, *Moral Theology*, II, p. 549; Noldin, *Summa*, Appendix, p. 5; Denzinger, *Enchiridion*, p. 372, no. 1200.

25. Adrian Hastings, "The Church's Response to African Marriage," p. 196. In the same vein, Charles Taber in "The Missionary: Wrecker, Builder, or Catalyst?" *Practical Anthropology* 17 (July–August 1970) 149, comments, "The average missionary is no better equipped to perform cultural surgery than I am to perform open-heart surgery."

26. Hillman, in *Polygamy Reconsidered,* p. 22 writes that legions of missionaries, sent out from the Western world, have acted on the assumption that non-Roman ways and laws of marriage are somehow less appropriate for Christians.

PART THREE

*A Reassessment of
the Christian Prohibition of
the African Leviratic Custom*

CHAPTER TEN

Towards a Theology of the Leviratic Union

Given the analysis of the leviratic custom through the theological literature and the survey data, it can be seen that the Catholic Church's prohibition of the custom has been based on erroneous judgments as to the levirate's nature, value, and purpose. Thus, the answer to the question posed in the Introduction—whether or not the principle of adaptation was reasonably applied in the process which led up to the prohibition of this custom—is an unqualified No! We have provided extensive evidence that the Catholic Church has misunderstood both the sexual involvement as well as the marital relationship inherent in the leviratic union. We have seen that the Catholic Church promotes remarriage of widows, oblivious of the fact that among people following a patrilineal descent pattern, such a solution causes divorce, break-up of the family unit, and the denial of solemn promises. Thus, the Catholic Church by encouraging widows in "leviratic" marriage systems to remarry, is, in fact, encouraging them to violate the Catholic teaching on divorce and remarriage. This puts the whole confused situation in a rather poignant light, revealing the self-contradictory character of the Catholic Church's position on the African leviratic union.

The reasons given by the Catholic Church for its prohibition of this custom do not stand up as either anthropologically or theologically valid. These reasons show little understanding of the delicate interweaving of relationships involved in this custom; moreover they are shown to be based on misinformation, a lack of understanding of marriage among people who follow a patrilineal descent pattern, and an application of ethnocentric "manualist" principles of sexual and marital morality. The real theological issues involved (e.g., the nature of "sexuality," "family," "inheritance," and "identity" in African leviratic marriage systems) have not yet been discussed by Catholic theologians.

The Catholic Church's prohibition of the African leviratic cus-

199

tom, therefore, is not based on any serious attempt to evaluate the custom in its own social milieu. That is, the prohibition does not fulfill the Church's own announced pastoral approach to non-Western marriage customs and institutions. Moreover, the prohibition reveals the Church's insensitivity to the hardships it has created in the lives of many Christians, and to the clerical and lay opposition to its position. Further, the *fact* of the prohibition suggests that the Catholic Church has no theology or model of marriage for a marriage system that involves both *individuals and their lineages.* It also suggests that there is no Catholic pastoral theology dealing with problems such as divorce, marital and sexual fidelity, care of widows, sexuality, and identity in the African traditional marriage systems.

The conclusion of the preceding analysis is that *the principle of adaptation was not operative or applied in the decision-making process that led up to the Catholic Church's prohibition of the African leviratic union. Thus the Catholic Church today, in terms of its own theological position on adaptation, has no informed opinion as to the compatibility or incompatibility of the African leviratic custom with Christianity.*

An adequate reassessment of the African leviratic custom within a Christian theology of marriage is beyond the scope of this book. Such a reassessment would involve extensive theoretical exploration of the nature of Christian marriage in marriage systems entwined with an "extended" (lineal) family institution in which descent is traced through the men alone. In such systems, marriages are alliances between both the individual partners and their lineages ("extended" families); the marital partners do not create a juridically independent family unit apart or separate from the man's lineage; the lineages of both partners are intimately involved in the inception, continuance, and termination of the marriage.

Unfortunately, there exists at present no Catholic theology systematically reflecting on or discussing the meaning of marriage in these larger kinship units. However, in order to begin the discussion, some theological reflections are offered here on several of the issues raised by the leviratic custom. These reflections grow out of the material of this study together with the author's seven years of pastoral experience among the Luo, a people who practice the leviratic custom as the ordinary way of caring for widows. These reflections, of course, do not pretend to offer a definitive theological statement about the African levirate institution; rather they seek to initiate the necessary dialogue.

The following problems with respect to marriage systems entwined with patrilineal corporate kin-groups would seem to be crucial to a systematic discussion of the leviratic custom: (1) the nature and meaning of the surrogate marital relationship between a widow and her brother-in-law in a leviratic union; (2) the nature and meaning of divorce and indissolubility in a patrilineal marriage system; (3) the nature and meaning of unilineal descent and inheritance patterns in which children are recruited only into their fathers' lineages; and (4) the nature and meaning of the "incarnational" adaptation of Christianity as applied to the African leviratic union. We shall treat each of these in order.

Preliminary Considerations

Given the understanding of the African leviratic custom as delineated in previous chapters, it can be seen that this custom, from an overall viewpoint, is in radical agreement with what is most essential to Christian marriage, namely, permanence, stability, responsible socialization of children, fidelity, loyalty (even beyond the grave), and unbreakable covenants between individuals and lineages. The levirate is, in fact, a way of preserving marriages and can be seen, therefore, as a type of institution supporting rather than destroying legitimate unions.

The ultimate basis of this custom is a marriage alliance in which the woman becomes the wife of both her husband and his lineage. This alliance is such that the husband and his lineage have full rights over the wife's procreative powers. Consequently, any children born of the marriage belong *in perpetuum* to the husband and his lineage. If this type of alliance is not part of the marriage agreement, as happens with the people following matrilineal patterns of descent, the leviratic custom does not arise.

The purpose of the leviratic custom is to continue the marriage of a "widow"* and bring her family to full fruition in the name of

---

* The word "widow" in this context connotes that a woman is still a functioning *wife*. She is called, for example, in the Luo language *chi liel,* i.e., wife of a grave. It is in this sense that it will be used in reference to the leviratic custom.

her deceased husband. There is no dissolution of a marriage legally or otherwise because of a husband's "physical death."* The custom arises out of a social system which ensures that each and every marriage maintains its identity and achieves its goals even in the face of physical death. Thus, if physical death should remove the father of a family, a temporary adjustment is made in the family relationships, in the name of the dead person, so that the deceased's family can maintain its identity and continue to grow and develop. In this adjustment, the brother of the dead man takes full responsibility for the widow and her children. Moreover, he substitutes for the deceased in all the activities of the bereaved family.

From the point of view of the *social dislocation* caused by death, the African societies that practice the leviratic custom offer a better alternative to the problem of the care of widows than the Western societies based on the nuclear family unit. The former readily provide the widow with a position in society where she can continue her marriage and raise her family in security and stability, whereas the latter leave the widow to struggle alone, dependent on government agencies for assistance. And, if she wants to remarry, sends her into the marketplace searching for a new marital partner.

The Catholic Church, through its missionaries, misunderstood the leviratic union as a type of cohabitational relationship already forbidden by Catholic moral teachings.† For the missionaries,

---

* The meaning of physical death in this context is very different from that ordinarily given it by Western theologians. For the African, physical death is only the *beginning* of a process which gradually removes a person from the "present" to the "past" period. After physical death, the person continues to exist in the *present period* and is capable of influencing the living. Thus, the African does not equate physical death with the kind of "death" understood by the expression "till death do us part" of the Western marriage vows. John S. Mbiti, an African theologian, writes that as long as the person is remembered by name, he is not really dead but in a state of personal immortality; he is called by Mbiti the "living-dead." The African understanding of death has such immediate relevance to the custom of the leviratic union that Mbiti's discussion of the topic, entitled "Death and Immortality," is the subject matter of the following chapter. [1]

† On the other hand, the Catholic theological writings, as we have seen, misunderstood the leviratic custom as a type of polygyny, an assessment shown to be false in Chapter VII.

therefore, the problem of the leviratic union was one of personal moral behavior; i.e., the levirate entailed unlawful sexual activity. The data from the survey do not support the missionaries' position; they show the following: 1. The leviratic union, from the Africans' perspective, is a respectable social institution for the care of widows, and is not considered to be a sexually immoral (adulterous) union. 2. The conflict between the leviratic custom and Christianity does not arise because the leviratic custom as such violates any moral principles; rather the leviratic union is rejected because of an assertion that it is intimately linked with a type of unlawful cohabitation. Thus, any adequate theological assessment of the levirate must consider it primarily in terms of its institutional role within African societies and only secondarily in terms of its effects on personal moral behavior.

For the Catholic Church to reject the leviratic custom as a cultural institution would be for it to attack the very heart of the patrilineal marriage system underlying the levirate, and would demand such radical changes in the culture as to effectively entail a rejection of the culture as a whole.* (This may seem to be an extreme statement of the effects of rejecting the levirate. However, we have already seen, in the case of the Kwaya, how the rejection of certain institutions within Kwaya society contributed to the general disruption of the entire social order.) Moreover, the rejection of the levirate would involve the Catholic Church in a contradiction with its own theological position on the need for and the necessity of adaptation, and the right of each people to maintain its own cultural traditions intact when converting to Christianity.

For the Catholic Church to avoid contradicting the principle of adaptation, while still rejecting the levirate, would require demonstration that: (1) The levirate is truly inconsistent with the Christian doctrine on marriage; and (2) the religious ideas underlying the levirate are inextricably bound up with error and are themselves incompatible with Christianity—an extremely difficult position to argue in light of the many positive values found in the

---

* Louis Luzbetak, points out that all cultural institutions are interrelated and held together and cannot be changed, piecemeal, without disturbing the whole system. [2]

African "leviratic" cultures. The conclusion must be that a rejection of the levirate as a cultural institution involves, in fact, a rejection of African marriage systems entwined with a patrilineal corporate kin-group, since the two are fundamentally related. But nowhere does the Catholic Church reject such marriage systems; rather, the Second Vatican Council openly proclaimed that non-Western cultures (and this must include their marriage systems) have a right to an independent existence within the Church. Therefore, from a systematic point of view, the Catholic Church should accept the consequence of its theological position on non-Western cultures and marriage systems and allow the leviratic custom.

Moreover, the African social system underlying the levirate does not destroy personal freedom, initiative, and other individualistic values, as it is often criticized for doing.* Rather, it allows personal goals and desires to be lived out in the context of a vital kinship community; i.e., where people know one another personally, and where there are complex social institutions interrelating people and defining roles. Thus, the response of the corporate kinship group to the needs of its widows does not represent an unusual or irresponsible pattern of behavior. It is a logical and necessary response flowing from its understanding of the communal (corporate) dimension of its marriages, and its understanding of itself as the larger responsible community.

Marital Relationships with Widows

In discussing the marital relationship of the widow with the brother-in-law in the leviratic union (a major issue of contention with the Catholic ethic), it is clear that the sexual union cannot be equated with any *lawful* or *unlawful* sexual unions practiced in the Western world. It cannot be classified as adultery or fornication, plural marriage or monogamy, or even cohabitation. The union does not arise out of lust or desire for sexual release—a necessary

---

* Neither does the Western individualistic social system represent the triumph of individualistic values over communal pressures and responsibilities. Indeed, according to some critics of Western society, personal freedom and individualistic values have been seriously eroded by the communal pressures of "mass" culture. See Martin Jay, *The Dialectical Imagination* (Boston: Little, Brown, 1973).

condition if the relationship is to be classified as either adultery or fornication. It does not arise from a desire to possess a second wife for purposes of status and power—a necessary condition for plural marriage. There is no unlawful agreement to have sexual intercourse as if married—a necessary condition for cohabitation. There are no marriage vows—a necessary condition for a valid marriage. The leviratic union arises out of a covenant, a solemn pledge made to the bride and groom at the time of the marriage by the lineage of the groom. It is part of the mutual agreement, based on love and respect, to do all to continue the family of the groom if he should be removed by death. The sexual union with the widow in these circumstances is a unique type. It is a symbolic union with the physically dead husband, in his name, with his implied permission, and for his interests.

To object that the sexual involvement of unmarried people is always and everywhere prohibited by the Catholic ethic, no matter what the circumstances, * fails to take seriously the fact that this union continues the widow's conjugal relationship with her husband; it is a lawful sexual union based on the covenant of her original marriage.

To further object that this "substitutional" explanation is just a quibble on words, for the brother-in-law, in fact, physically desires and possesses the woman in a sexual embrace, reduces sexuality to the level of physical expression and denies the role of intention and purpose in human actions. On this point, Peter Riga, in *Sexuality and Marriage in Recent Catholic Thought,* writes that, traditionally, Catholic theologians have approached human sexuality from the perspective of biological naturalism. However, he says if there is to be a balanced view of human sexuality, cultural and social considerations must be added to biological concepts. [3]

In a strictly "biological" analysis, a woman who has intercourse with a man whom she mistakenly thinks is her husband, would be guilty of unlawful sexual behavior—an untenable moral position

---

* This objection is a direct application of natural-law principles regarding sexuality (discussed in a previous chapter) that were taught in the standard manualist moral theology textbooks. These texts were in use in the Catholic seminaries up until the Second Vatican Council (1963). See Noldin, *Summa,* Appendix, I, 22–25.

even to the manualist theologians.* Her action would be judged lawful on the grounds that she *intends* her husband. So also, the widow's *intention* to have intercourse with her deceased husband and the brother-in-law's *intention to be* the deceased husband are what make it possible for the leviratic sexual union to be judged as lawful. The only difference from the first example is that the widow's husband is present by way of *substitution* and not by way of *mistaken identity.* The leviratic sexual union, therefore, can be seen as part of the widow's marital commitment to her husband—there is no parallel marital relationship of this type in Western cultures, although this kind of substitutional identity is possible in certain legal arrangements.

Continuing the discussion of the sexual relationship from another angle, it is clear that sexual relations, outside of a particular spouse, do not in themselves destroy or terminate a marriage. The real sins against marriage are not sexual sins but sins against the lifelong commitments and obligations of perpetual involvement agreed to by the partners. In the leviratic union there is no attempt to supplant the brother-in-law's wife (wives). There is no threat to the brother-in-law's lifetime marital commitment to his wife. There is no question of the widow's children competing with the brother-in-law's children for the inheritance. There may be competition for scarce material resources such as food and clothing, but this competition is part of the more general problem of communal sharing of resources in a rural homestead, and would happen whether the husband were alive or dead.

The leviratic relationship does not set up a new household. It is usually only for a time. Thus a widow who has a son, whether widowed in her old age or in her youth, ends up her life in the care of that son. † Likewise the leviratic relationship rather than the leviratic brother-in-law is what is important. If a widow feels that

---

* The manualist moral theologians discuss this case under the heading of invincible antecedent ignorance. The judgment is that "ignorance excuses" since one cannot will what is not known. This type of ignorance also removes the guilt associated with the voluntary act. An example cited is that of a hunter, who having used reasonable diligence, kills a man whom he mistook for a deer.[4]

†In the leviratic institutions studied in Part I, the widow usually goes to live with her eldest son after he has moved out and set up his own homestead.

she is not being properly cared for, she has the right to break that union and be cared for by another leviratic partner. Thus, the particular leviratic relationship depends on both partners' fulfilling the terms of the original marriage covenant. When that is not done, either can terminate the union without the legal and social consequences associated with divorce. The reason for the above is that the widow's marriage to her deceased husband remains her only stable and permanent relationship.

The objection that the leviratic relationship disrupts the marriage of the brother-in-law and his wife, causing jealousy and domestic quarrelling, is valid only if these allegations are, in fact, true. But, turning to the survey data relating to the causes of domestic strife, one finds no specific mention of the levirate as the cause of either divorce or problems within a marriage. Rather the data show that the conflicts that arise are due to personal misunderstandings in the relationship between the widow and the brother-in-law.* This is understandable, since even in a Western culture, domestic strife or peace tends to arise out of the quality of the interpersonal relationships among the individuals in the home (homestead) and not out of their marital status. For example, one can find among the Luo people some monogamous homesteads that are filled with unhappiness and quarrelling and others that are filled with peace and serenity; this is similarly true of polygynous homesteads. This is not to argue that there are *no* situations where a widow, in a leviratic union, causes conflicts with the other wives of her partner, rather it is to argue that such conflicts generally arise out of the ordinary misunderstandings between the women, and not because one of the women happens to be a widow in a leviratic union with the husband.

Moreover, it appears that the women, knowing that they will always be cared for by their brothers-in-law, and expecting the same treatment in the event of their husband's deaths, tend to be sympathetic towards their husbands' undertaking the obligation of caring for widows. They know that this is part of the agreement between the lineages, indeed, it is part of their own marriage alliances. They do not consider the sexual involvement to be adulterous nor the relationship to be an attempt to supplant them as wives.

---

* See Appendix A, Table 52.

In summary, there is no clear evidence that the leviratic union as such disturbs a brother-in-law's marriage and causes domestic strife. The source of domestic troubles is usually the poor quality of the interpersonal relationships between the men and women in the homestead. Nor does the sexual relationship with the brother-in-law threaten the stability of his marriage. The sexual union is a unique type; it can be understood as an expression of the widow's lawful marital rights with her husband.

Divorce and Indissolubility

The leviratic union, from the point of view of the lineage involvement in the marriage system, shows that the men of the lineage take full responsibility for the women they marry. There is a subtle interaction between the lineage and each of its wives in the continuance and stability of their marriages. Thus the widow can continue her marriage with her deceased husband through the ministrations and support of the corporate kinship group. This support has been institutionalized in the leviratic custom. The levirate is proof that marriages are not terminated or dissolved by the physical death of the husband. The levirate protects the *indissoluble* quality of the original marriage alliance; it enables the original marriage to continue to function socially, economically, and reproductively.

To oppose the leviratic custom on the grounds that it treats widows as mere chattel, the property of the lineage, and is a serious obstacle to the development of Christian attitudes towards women,[5] shows no understanding of the elements of liberation, freedom, unity, security, and happiness present within the leviratic institution. Arguments of this kind against the levirate arise out of an individualistic approach to marriage. Indeed, the survey data show clearly that widows in these situations do not want to be remarried.* They see their marriages within their husbands' lineages as indissoluble lifetime commitments that will function, at least corporately, i.e., through the assistance of the lineage, until they die.

---

*See Appendix A, Table 29.

To further object that the leviratic custom denies a widow her right to remarry ignores the fact that she is not *free* to remarry—her original marriage is not dissolved by her husband's physical death. Moreover, such an objection denies the reality of the corporate kinship structures surrounding the original marriage alliance, and argues as if they do not exist, and as if the widow does not have a corporate identity. In order for a widow (in such a marriage system) to remarry, as we have seen in Part I, she must first be divorced from her dead husband and his lineage; i.e., the marriage covenant between the two lineages must be broken, the bridewealth paid back, the children left behind in their father's homestead. Under these conditions, it is no wonder that the ordinary widow is not at all interested in remarriage, especially since it involves her lineage in divorce litigation.* Moreover, divorce usually means that the woman loses her reputation and respect in the eyes of the people.

The Western theology on divorce and indissolubility is not adequate for the African marriage systems. It discusses divorce and indissolubility the same way it discusses marriage, i.e., in individualistic categories. Hence the Church, faced with the leviratic problem and ignoring both the communal (corporate) aspects of the African marriage systems and the fact that the Africans do not accept the premise of the dissolubility of marriage by physical death, declare a widow in a leviratic system to be free to remarry. As a consequence, the Church, in violation of its own moral teaching about the indissolubility of marriage, actually promotes *divorce* when it promotes the remarriage of widows in these patrilineal marriage systems.

The Church's teaching, in effect, asks the widow, in the name of Christian rights, freedom, and dignity, (1) to repudiate her sacred marital obligations to her husband and his lineage; (2) to separate herself from her children; and (3) to lay a heavy social and financial burden on her own lineage, which must pay back the bridewealth and break the marriage alliance.

---

* According to the experience of the author, the Luo widows who divorced their dead spouses and remarried were marginal women; i.e., women of such bizarre and unattractive behavior that the husbands' lineages were happy to see them leave.

In light of these factors, one should probably argue that it would be much more reasonable, moral, and defensible for the Church to promote the *levirate* rather than divorce and remarriage. The reason for this is not just the evils caused by divorce in the African system, but principally the Church's own teaching on the indissolubility of marriage and its firm opposition to divorce in any form or circumstance. This latter is probably the most cogent reason why the Church should accept and affirm the African leviratic custom; otherwise it contradicts its own teaching on the indissoluble nature of Christian marriage.

Patrilineal Rules of Descent

Another difficulty with the Church's promotion of remarriage for widows in patrilineal cultures is that such remarriages, as we have seen, separate a widow from her children—the children always belong to the husband's lineage. The missionaries have also felt obliged to oppose such separations. They maintain that a woman has a right to take her children with her into a new marriage even though this would change the rules of inheritance and descent. This problem brings up the issue of the place of children in these marriage alliances, and their relationship to their parents.

In unilineal systems of descent, children cannot belong to both of their parents, as in the Western systems, since their parents at the time of marriage do not create a new juridically independent social unit for the purpose of inheritance and descent. Thus, the children must belong either to their mother's lineage or to their father's lineage. To speak of a woman "losing" legal rights over her children, without distinguishing the type of marriage system, does not adequately define the problem. Children belonging to lineages are not under the private jurisdiction of their parents. They belong to the larger kinship group and are socialized into that group. To say, therefore, that a woman has no legal rights over her children, means only that she is married into a lineage following patrilineal rules of descent. On the other hand, among people following matrilineal rules of descent, it is the father who "loses" legal control over his children, i.e., they belong to the mother's lineage. The fact that a woman's children build up only her husband's family presupposes that there are other women giving the same kind of services to her father's lineage. Thus there is a mutual exchange of children and marital services between lineages creating alliances between these larger social groups.

In light of this understanding of recruitment of children into a particular lineage, the women's "loss" of legal control over their children is not immoral and can be seen to be a type of cultural value compatible with Christian principles. Moreover, this kind of recruitment has a number of beneficial effects. First, the children are not tied to the personal fortunes of their parents. They are immediately located in a community that supports, cares for, and gives them an identity. If a particular parent is emotionally unstable, sick, inadequate, there is the larger community helping to ensure a "normal" development. There are no abandoned children or orphans; every child has a place in the community and is wanted. Second, no child is deprived of an inheritance, as happens in Western societies. Every child's patrimony, e.g., land, cattle for marriage, are guaranteed by the lineage. Third, by means of the leviratic union, the children are not separated from their mothers even if their fathers should die. The mothers, along with the children, are insured a place within the larger kinship grouping.

In summary, the legal control of parents over children, so important in the Western systems of marriage, presupposes an individualistic Western approach to marriage. In many traditional African marriage systems, legal control over children is in the hands of the lineage and not of the individuals. There is nothing objectionable to Christian principles in this kind of social arrangement; rather it shows an intelligent understanding of the necessity for children to be socialized by a group larger than the nuclear family unit. The Church can easily endorse such a tradition without hesitation or fear of compromise. The missionaries' opposition to the separation of the "divorced" widow from her children is evidently based on a lack of insight into the rules of patrilineal inheritance and descent and the nature of lineage family and is not a valid reason for opposing this kind of social structure. Indeed, the children of the remarried widow according to the Church's policy, would have grown up without lineage identity; they would have been effectively orphaned and lacking a place in society at large.

One of the effects of Western marriage is to produce orphans and widows—for when the husband dies or both parents die, the wife or the children no longer belong to a family. In African lineage marriage, there are no *orphans* or *widows* in the ordinary Western meaning of the terms. In fact, as already described, the terms "widow" and "orphan" are applied in the African context only by way of analogy. The death of a husband or of either or both parents in Africa does not dissolve the lineage family to which the children or wife truly belong—everybody has lineage identity. In Western societies by way of contrast, identity is through "nuclear" style families. Yet too many members of Western societies are without families: some through choice, some through lack of a suitable partner, some through divorce or death, others because of youth or financial difficulties. These members, therefore, exist in society as anonymous people—a truly vicious and tragic situation, and are discriminated against by a familial-oriented moral code that does not take into account their circumstances.

The Catholic Church and Adaptation to the Levirate

There is a growing number of Church leaders who are, in fact, aware that the Church has often been wrong in its approach to these cultures. But, many of them now argue that it is too late to adapt to customs like the levirate. They feel that the missionaries have committed the Church for so long and with such intensity to opposition to certain customs, that to change now would cause greater harm and bring into question the credibility of the Church's leadership. It would also, they say, scandalize faithful Christians, especially those who have resisted, with great fortitude, intense social pressure to follow certain proscribed customs.[6] Besides, they argue, the trend towards adopting and accepting Western customs and social institutions has already started and the old ways and traditions are beginning to die out.[7] To support these traditions now, even though they are not un-Christian, would be merely a rear guard action, doomed to failure.

Implicit in this "nonadaptive" argument is a lack of confidence in the African Church's ability to understand, articulate, and explain conflicts, and to accept the necessary changes no matter how painful they might be. Moreover, it expresses the questionable assumptions that Westernization is inevitable.

The fear on the part of the Church leaders over the reactions of the African Christians does not seem realistic. For example, 54% of the sampled population oppose the present policy of the Catholic Church in the matter of the leviratic custom. Moreover, 62% of the Catholic leaders see the levirate as compatible with the demands of Christian morality. In fact, in the areas where the conflict over the levirate is most serious, there is also the greatest resistance to the Church's prohibition. The conclusion is that most of the people would welcome the acceptance of the leviratic custom with undisguised relief. The greater and more intolerable evil would be refusal to change the pastoral policy regarding this custom, knowing that the present prohibition is untenable.

Also, implicit in this nonadaptive argument of Church leaders, is an ethnocentric position that regards Western forms of social and marital behavior as inherently better and more Christian. This perspective sees the work of the missionaries as building for the future, trusting that slowly people will be "brought around" to proper and more fitting customs (of a Western Christian variety). From this point of view, to adapt Christianity to the leviratic custom, no matter what the morality of the situation, would only prolong the "search" for "authentic" "modern" customs, and hold back the new Christian people from necessary social development.*

Another argument of the Church leaders against accepting the leviratic custom is based on the supposition that one cannot make the solution of a small localized problem a part of the pastoral policy of a whole national church. This leviratic problem, they say, is a Luo and Kuria problem and does not have any relevance to the rest of the Church in Tanzania and East Africa, hence it should be ignored. The response to this argument is that the leviratic custom, although it varies in frequency from area to area, is in fact wide-

---

* This kind of attitude has raised in missiological circles the question of whether people who cannot or will not accept basic Christian precepts such as monogamy should be baptized. One proposed solution (pre-evangelization) was to leave these people in a permanent precatechumenate until such a time as they would be able to accept and live by these precepts. According to this argument, to baptize people knowing that they are unable to fulfill the obligations demanded is immoral and creates not only frustrations and anxiety on the part of the people concerned, but also does irreparable damage to their religious and moral instincts.[8]

spread throughout East Africa. Moreover, the principle underlying the acceptance of the levirate is stated in the following general terms: *the leviratic custom is compatible with Christian doctrine on marriage no matter where or how frequently it occurs; it promotes Christian marital values and is an acceptable relationship within and by members of Christian communities.*

General Conclusions

In summary, this study does not argue for a new radical pastoral theology for the African Church; rather it argues that if the Catholic Church were consistent and serious about the application of its own self-proclaimed theology on "incarnational adaptation" and Christian marriage, it both could and would, without hesitations or fear, adapt itself to a vast number of non-Western cultures together with their marriage customs and institutions. Our analysis has shown that the basic pastoral problem on marrriage in the African Church does not arise out of a Christian *theology* of marriage, but out of a failure to adapt Christian *theology* to non-Western cultural situations.

In the case of the leviratic custom studied in this book, the Catholic Church contradicts its doctrines on both "incarnational adaptation" and on indissolubility of Christian marriage when it promotes widow remarriage and opposes the levirate. In contradicting its principle of incarnational adaptation the Church ignores the integrity and values of the leviratic institutions operative within the African social structures. It presupposes Western marital institutions as the universal models and forms for Christian behavior. Such an approach is in direct violation of the Church's clearly stated theological position that all peoples within the family of man have an inalienable right to "convert" to Christianity without being disinherited from their cultural traditions and institutions. Likewise, in contradicting its principle of marital indissolubility, the Church promotes traditional divorces that break up family units and disinherit children from their fathers' lineage. And this is done while ignoring the communal dimensions of the African marriage institutions as well as the communal identity of the people. Again this approach is in contradiction to the Church's teachings on the permanence and indissolubility of Christian marriage.

Thus, it seems that the Catholic Church, as it expressed itself in the Second Vatican Council, has no option but to accept the consequences of its own theology of adaptation and liberate itself and its members throughout the world from its narrow Western preoccupations and its ethnocentric pastoral position vis-à-vis non-Western cultures. Otherwise, it will continue to distort, in the pastoral order, the rich and varied cultural systems and institutions of the vast majority of mankind, leaving non-Western people no options but (1) to reject the Church as irrelevant and unrepresentative of the "community of the people of God," and (2) to call the Church to task for its own inner contradictions and ambivalence towards non-Western peoples.

NOTES

1. John S. Mbiti, *African Religions and Philosophy* (New York: Praeger, 1969), pp. 25–27.

2. Luzbetak, *The Church and Culture,* p. 346.

3. Peter J. Riga, *Sexuality and Marriage in Recent Catholic Thought,* Corpus Papers (Washington:Corpus Books, 1969), pp. 58–60.

4. See Karl Horman, *An Introduction to Moral Theology,* trans. Edward Quinn (London:Burns and Oates, 1961), p. 103; McHugh and Callan, *Moral Theology,* I, pp. 14–15; Noldin, *Summa,* I, pp. 52–53.

5. For examples of this kind of argument, see Joan Dilworth, "Unexploited Riches in African Families," *African Ecclesiastical Review* 1 (1959) 59; Joan Dilworth, "Marriage Education," *African Ecclesiastical Review* 4 (1962) 236; Hugh Dinwiddy, "Christian Marriage," *African Ecclesiastical Review* 3 (1961) 124.

6. For a discussion of this same concern about scandal in relation to plural marriage, see Hillman, *Polygamy Reconsidered,* pp. 192–195.

7. Ibid., pp. 190–191. Also Henri Maurier, *The Other Covenant: A Theology of Paganism,* trans. Charles McGrath (Glen Rock, N. J.: Newman Press, 1968), p. 241.

8. For a discussion of pre-evangelization, see Alfonso Nebreda, *Kerygma in Crisis?* (Chicago:Loyola University Press, 1964), chs. 4–6, especially p. 104; P. A. Liégé, "Avant le Catéchuménat, la Mission," *Parole et Mission* 5 (1962) 23–32; Maurier, *The Other Covenant,* pp. 239–246; Joseph Mullin, *The Catholic Church in Modern Africa* (London: Geoffrey Chapman, 1965).

CHAPTER ELEVEN

Death and Immortality: An African View

We have referred on a number of occasions to the fact that the Africans have a different understanding than Westerners of the meaning and nature of physical death. This understanding, as we have seen, makes it possible for Africans to conceive of marital relationships continuing beyond the grave—an important element in making the leviratic union possible. Indeed, the African concept of death is so interesting, unique, and rich in social implications that a further discussion of it is here presented by an African theologian, John S. Mbiti.* He explains:

> As the individual gets older, he is in effect moving gradually from the Sasa [present] to the Zamani [past]. His birth is a slow process which is finalized long after the person has been physically born. In many societies, a person is not considered a full human being until he has gone through the whole process of physical birth, naming ceremonies, puberty and initiation rites, and finally marriage (or even procreation). Then he is fully 'born', he is a complete person.
>
> Similarly, death is a process which removes a person gradually from the Sasa period to the Zamani. After the physical death, the individual continues to exist in the Sasa and does not immediately disappear from it. He is *remembered* by relatives and friends who knew him in this life and who have survived him. They recall him by name, though not necessarily mentioning it, they remember his personality, his character, his words and incidents of his life. If he

---

*Quoted from *African Religions and Philosophy*, by John S. Mbiti. Copyright © 1969 by J. S. Mbiti. Reprinted by permission of Praeger Publishers, New York City, a Division of Holt, Rinehart and Winston, CBS, Inc. Professor Mbiti was born in Kenya. From Makerere University College, he went on to Barrington College, Rhode Island, and the University of Cambridge. After obtaining his doctorate in theology at Cambridge he served for a period in a parish in England. Since 1964 he has been working as a lecturer at Makerere University College in Uganda, in 1968 being appointed Professor of Religious Studies.

'appears' (as people believe), he is recognized *by name*. The departed appear mainly to the older members of their surviving families and rarely or never to children. They appear to people whose Sasa period is the longest.

This recognition by name is extremely important. The appearance of the departed, and his being recognized by name, may continue for up to four or five generations, so long as someone is alive who once knew the departed personally and by name. When, however, the last person who knew the departed also dies, then the former passes out of the horizon of the Sasa period; and in effect he now becomes completely *dead* as far as family ties are concerned. He has sunk into the Zamani period. But while the departed person is remembered by name, he is not really dead, he is alive, and such a person I would call the *living-dead*. The living-dead is a person who is physically dead but alive in the memory of those who knew him in his life as well as being alive in the world of the spirits. So long as the living-dead is thus remembered, he is in the state of *personal immortality*. This personal immortality is externalized in the physical continuation of the individual through procreation, so that the children bear the traits of their parents or progenitors. From the point of view of the survivors, personal immortality is expressed or externalized in acts like respecting the departed, giving bits of food to them, pouring out libation and carrying out instructions given by them either while they lived or when they appear.

This concept of personal immortality should help us to understand the religious significance of marriage in African societies. Unless a person has close relatives to remember him when he has physically died, then he is nobody and simply vanishes out of human existence like a flame when it is extinguished. Therefore it is a duty, religious and ontological, for everyone to get married; and if a man has no children or only daughters, he finds another wife so that through her, children (or sons) may be born who would survive him and keep him (with the other living-dead of the family) in personal immortality. Procreation is the absolute way of insuring that a person is not cut off from personal immortality.

The acts of pouring out libation (of beer, milk or water), or giving portions of food to the living-dead, are symbols of communion, fellowship and remembrance. They are the mystical ties that bind the living-dead to their surviving relatives. Therefore these acts are performed within the family. The oldest member of the family is the one who has the longest Sasa period, and therefore the one who has the longest memory of the departed. He it is who performs or supervises these acts of remembrance on behalf of the entire family, addressing (when the occasion demands it) the symbolic meal to all the departed (living-dead) of the family, even if only one or two of the departed may be mentioned by name or position (e.g., father, grandfather). There is nothing here about so-called 'ancestor worship', even if these acts may so seem to the outsiders who do not understand the situation.

With the passing of time, the living-dead sink beyond the horizon of the *Sasa* period. This point is reached when there is no longer anyone alive who remembers them personally by name. Then the process of dying is completed. But the living-dead do not vanish out of existence: they now enter into the state of *collective immortality*. This is the state of the spirits who are no longer formal members of the human families. People lose personal contact with them. The departed in this state become members of the family or community of the spirits, and if they appear to human beings they are not recognized by name and may cause dread and fear. Their names may still be mentioned by human beings, especially in genealogies, but they are *empty names* which are more or less without a personality or at best with only a mythological personality built around fact and fiction. Such spirits have no personal communication with human families; in some societies, however, they might speak through a medium or become guardians of the clan or nation, and may be mentioned or appealed to in religious rites of local or national significance. In other societies such spirits are incorporated into the body of intermediaries between God and man, and human beings approach God through them or seek other help from them. In reality, these spirits of the departed, together with other spirits which may or may not have been once human beings, occupy the ontological state between God and men. Beyond the state of the spirits, men cannot go or develop. This then is the destiny of man, as far as African ontology is concerned. African religious activities are chiefly focused upon the relationship between human beings and the departed; which really means that man tries to penetrate or project himself into the world of what remains of him after this physical life. If the living-dead are suddenly forgotten, this means that they are cast out of the Sasa period, and are in effect excommunicated, their personal immortality is destroyed and they are turned into a state of non-existence. And this is the worst possible punishment for anyone. The departed resent it, and the living do all they can to avoid it because it is feared that it would bring illness and misfortunes to those who forget their departed relatives. Paradoxically, death lies 'in front' of the individual, it is still a 'future' event; but when one dies, one enters the state of personal immortality which lies not in the future but in the Zamani.

The above passage from Professor Mbiti makes us keenly aware that there is a whole religious outlook underlying the leviratic custom. It is an outlook that sees deceased persons as living on in a "communion of saints," a communion that is still active and present to the living, still part of their emotional and psychological lives. Indeed, if one presses hard enough, it will be found that all the institutions of African society, not just the levirate, arise out of its specific religious and spiritual aspirations. This is another way of arguing that one cannot change piecemeal particular social customs without in fact disrupting the underlying spiritual unity of a culture so that it begins to fragment and disintegrate.

The need, therefore, is not simply to study particular institutions within a society, but also the religious ideas that are part and parcel of the society. These religious ideas give each institution its ultimate meaning and value. Thus we see that the heart of the levirate is actually the African view on *immortality*. Would we be willing or able to judge that this view of immortality is un-Christian, and, therefore, that the customs it underpins are also un-Christian and invalid? Yet by attacking the leviratic custom, the Church, indirectly, has called into question the African view of immortality.

Moreover, at first glance, the African view of immortality, as presented by Mbiti, shows itself to be not only very interesting but also very complicated, and, in some ways, even more sophisticated and human than the view of immortality present in Western Christian thought and life. Could one not argue that the African view is closer to and a more adequate expression of "essential" Christian notions about death than the Western view? Especially since it institutionalizes emotional and psychological relations with the "communion of saints"—the dead who are alive—thus giving the dead an existence and a right that are denied to them by Western Christian thought. Under this assumption, would it not be the Western view of immortality along with the customs and institutions it has spawned that could be called into question and judged to be inadequate for expressing an essential Christian view of death? Johann Baptist Metz has recently spoken out against the Western Church's failure to be sensitive to the *life* and claims of the dead. "Who," he asks, "responds to cries for freedom in past sufferings and hopes? Who answers the challenge of the dead and makes conscience sensitive to their freedom? Who cultivates solidarity with the dead to whom we ourselves shall belong the day after tomorrow?" [1]

Thanks to the insights presented by Professor Mbiti, we have now come full circle: from challenging African assumptions about the nature of marriage to challenging Western Christian assumptions about immortality and our communion with the dead. Mbiti's work, of course, is the kind of theoretical work that must be done on all aspects of African symbols, mythology, and values before one can begin to discuss the "incarnational" adaptation of Christianity to African cultures. For just as the present "Western" expression of Christianity was formulated and shaped through the world-view of the Greek philosophers in such a way that it is now indigenous to Western culture, so also must the African expression of Christianity be allowed to be shaped and modified by African philosophy until it too becomes indigenous to African cultures.

Moreover, the "incarnational" adaptation of Christianity, as a rule, cannot be done by people who are not members of a particular culture. It must be done by people like Mbiti. This is perhaps the major reason why the missionary movement into Africa for the past three hundred years has had such a poor performance in this area. Not that there were no attempts on the part of the missionaries at a more harmonious mix of African and Christian things, but that foreign missionaries, ultimately, are not the ones who can instigate, control, or shape adaptation vis-à-vis African cultures.

The African Church is now beginning to speak out in defense of its traditional values and religious aspirations. It is beginning to sort out the essential from the nonessential elements of Western Christianity. It is beginning to articulate the Christian truths in terms of its own non-Western world view. I, therefore, call upon my fellow missionaries all over Africa as well as all African Church leaders, to do nothing to hinder this search for an authentic indigenous Christian identity, and to accept without fear or hesitation the inevitable changes in style, manner, and customs of the African Church. What is *wanted* and *needed* and to which we must pledge ourselves is an African Christian Church that is truly liberated, free, and able to touch in a radical way the religious sensibilities of the African peoples. Only then will the mysteries of Christ be "incarnationally adapted" to the African cultures.

I would like to close on a personal note. I worked for seven years, from 1963 to 1970, in a rural African mission unaware of many of the things discussed in this book. Indeed, after the seven years I was still unable to accurately identify traditional religious leaders much less know in a systematic way the traditional religious beliefs, values, and aspirations. (There was of course no pressing need to know these things, nor did I have the training to search them out.) However, the African people in their own gentle ways constantly reminded me that I was ignorant of their traditions. People like Victoria Akech said openly that I did not understand African customs or way of life.

This criticism by the African people made me and my co-missionaries aware that we were not responding adequately to their religious needs, sensibilities, and aspirations. And it was in response to this criticism that I was asked by my confreres to do this study of African marriage—a study that has now opened up the whole issue of the adaptation of Christianity to African cultures. I would like, therefore, to thank in a special way all the African critics as well all those who so graciously answered the survey questions, funishing me with the empirical data of this study. Indeed, it was really their own understanding of their religious values and traditions and their ability to express them, that has made this study possible. They are its co-authors and, in large measure, this is their book.

NOTE

1. J. B. Metz, "Prophetic Authority," in Jürgen Moltmann et al., *Religion and Political Society* (New York:Harper & Row, 1974), p. 206.

APPENDIX A
STATISTICAL TABLES

TABLE 25

NUMBER OF WOMEN WHO HAVE BEEN WIDOWED
BY ETHNIC GROUP SURVEYED (%)

Were You Ever a Widow?	Ethnic Group				%Total
	%Luo	%Kuria	%Kwaya	%Sukuma	
Yes................	22	19	20	27	22
No................	78	79	80	73	78
No answer...........	-	2	-	-	-
Total %	100	100	100	100	100
Number	(118)	(115)	(115)	(89)	(437)

TABLE 26

WIDOWS WHO HAVE REMARRIED, BY ETHNIC GROUP SURVEYED (%)

Have You Remarried?	Ethnic Group				%Total
	%Luo	%Kuria	%Kwaya	%Sukuma	
Yes................	-	9	13	21	10
No................	96	82	83	75	84
No answer...........	4	9	4	4	6
Total %	100	100	100	100	100
Number	(26)	(30)	(23)	(24)	(106)

TABLE 27

REASONS GIVEN WHY WIDOWS CAN REMARRY
BY ETHNIC GROUP SURVEYED (%)

Reasons Given	Ethnic Group				%Total
	%Luo	%Kuria	%Kwaya	%Sukuma	
If no child.........	-	41	11	9	14
If she wants she can.................	36	10	76	30	46
Husband already dead, nothing to oppose it...........	27	21	6	46	26
If she can't live on her own..........	27	23 (35)[a]	5	14	12
Other...............	9	4	2	1	2
Total %	100	100	100	100	100
Number	(11)	(99)	(289)	(295)	(694)

[a]Given as a second reason by 12 respondents.

TABLE 28

REASONS GIVEN WHY WIDOWS CANNOT REMARRY
BY ETHNIC GROUP SURVEYED (%)

Reasons Given	Ethnic Group				%Total
	%Luo	%Kuria	%Kwaya	%Sukuma	
Already married, cannot be married twice, she is some-one's wife...............	50	79	75	29	62
Bridewealth paid, cannot be paid twice	22	8 (26)[a]	15	57	21
Always "taken" by brother-in-law or finds someone to care for her..............	23	1	-	-	13
Other.....................	5	2	10	14	5
Total %	100	100	100	100	100
Number	(286)	(202)	(20)	(7)	(515)

[a]Given as a second reason by 15 respondents.

TABLE 29

OPINIONS REGARDING THE WIDOWS' DESIRE FOR REMARRIAGE
BY ETHNIC GROUPS SURVEYED (%)

Do Widows Want Remarriage?	Ethnic Group				%Total
	%Luo	%Kuria	%Kwaya	%Sukuma	
Yes...............	3	11	89	95	50
(Now) yes[a].........	3	3	5.5	3	4
No.....................	94	86	5.5	2	46
Total %	100	100	100	100	100
Number	(289)	(295)	(309)	(301)	(1,194)

[a]Formerly did not want to remarry (a recent change).

TABLE 30

REASONS GIVEN WHY WIDOWS WANT TO REMARRY
BY ETHNIC GROUP SURVEYED (%)

Reasons Given	Ethnic Group				%Total
	%Luo	%Kuria	%Kwaya	%Sukuma	
If no one to care for her....................	14	36	35	6	22
If she still wants a husband.................	-	24	52	11	30
Young widows want to remarry...............		12	7	25	16
Difficult to live without a husband...............	14	14	5	56	30
Other...........................	10	14	1	2	3
Total %	100	100	100	100	100
Number	(21)	(42)	(291)	(29)	(648)

TABLE 31

REASONS GIVEN WHY WIDOWS DO NOT WANT TO REMARRY
BY ETHNIC GROUP SURVEYED (%)

Reasons Given	Ethnic Group				%Total
	%Luo	%Kuria.	%Kwaya	%Sukuma	
Knows she is wife of a family; already married..................	56	77	33	14	60
Bad luck that husband died; did not divorce her.....................	15	20 (24)[a]	17	43	18
"Evil eye" of dead husband; men would stop her.....................	19	2	-	-	10
Would not want to leave her children	6	6 (18)[a]	39	-	7
Other...................	4	5	-	-	5
Total % Number	100 (270)	100 (257)	100 (18)	100 (7)	100 (552)

[a]Given as second reason by respondents.

TABLE 32

THE INDIVIDUAL BEST ABLE TO CARE FOR A WIDOW WHO CANNOT REMARRY BY ETHNIC GROUP SURVEYED (%)

Individual	Ethnic Group				%Total
	%Luo	%Kuria	%Kwaya	%Sukuma	
Brother-in-law...........	86	46	81	48	65
Husband's relative............	9	38	15	15	20
Friend if no understanding with brother-in-law................	2	14	1	9	6
Unmarried man.................	1	-	2	7	2
Her own family..............	-	-	-	19	5
Other.................	2	2	1	5	2
Total % Number	100 (304)	100 (303)	100 (309)	100 (301)	100 (1,217)

TABLE 33

THE FREQUENCY WITH WHICH WIDOWS IN LEVIRATIC UNIONS ARE TREATED JUST LIKE WIVES, BY ETHNIC GROUP SURVEYED (%)

Frequency	Ethnic Group				%Total
	%Luo	%Kuria	%Kwaya	%Sukuma	
Always................	6	28	11	23	17
Frequently............	5	10	16	19	13
Sometimes.............	21	35	47	19	30
Rarely................	15	23	22	18	20
Never.................	53	4	4	21	20
Total % Number	100 (303)	100 (294)	100 (306)	100 (299)	100 (1,202)

TABLE 34

REASONS GIVEN FOR THE CHRISTIAN PROHIBITION OF THE LEVIRATIC UNION
BY ETHNIC GROUPS SURVEYED (%)

Reasons for Prohibition	Ethnic Groups				%Total
	%Luo	%Kuria	%Kwaya	%Sukuma	
Custom of Christians	44	4	67	43	40
Widow is not his wife	18	57	27	39	35
God forbids the levirate..................	8	9	3	15	9
Do not know church discipline...........	19	26	1	2	12
Other....................	11	4	2	1	4
Total %	100	100	100	100	100
Number	(304)	(303)	(309)	(301)	(1,217)

TABLE 35

REASONS GIVEN FOR APPROVING THE CHRISTIAN PROHIBITION OF THE LEVIRATE
BY ETHNIC GROUP SURVEYED (%)

Reasons for Approval	Ethnic Group				%Total
	%Luo	%Kuria	%Kwaya	%Sukuma	
Against church law	25	15	30	35	27
Widow is like a second wife............	31	43	55	32	45
Widow has sinned.......	8	8	2	9	5
Widow destroys another's sacrament of matrimony.......	18	21	10	18	15
Widow is like a prostitute..........	-	4	-	6	2
Other...............	18	9	3	-	6
Total %	100	100	100	100	100
Number	(51)	(108)	(229)	(104)	(492)

TABLE 36

REASONS GIVEN FOR OPPOSING THE CHURCHES' PROHIBITION
OF THE LEVIRATE, BY ETHNIC GROUP SURVEYED (%)

Reasons for Opposing Prohibition	Ethnic Group				Total
	%Luo	%Kuria	%Kwaya	%Sukuma	
Widow still loves God...............	8	2	5	7	6
Widow is still a member of the Church	13	4	12	15	11
God did not forbid this custom.......	20	11	22	17	17
The widow is not a prostitute........	12	64	21	45	32
She did not kill her husband, there is no reason to reject her	12	12 (19)[a]	15	13	13
Widow is in need and should be helped....	16	-	11	-	7
Church would have us throw away the bride-wealth...............	9	1 (11)[a]	1	-	3
Other.................	-	6	12	3	11
Total %	100	100	100	100	100
Number	(223)	(163)	(81)	(194)	(661)

[a]Given as a second reason by respondents.

TABLE 37

ATTITUDES TOWARDS WIDOW REMARRIAGE OF CATHOLIC CHURCH LEADERS
IN THE FOUR AREAS SURVEYED (%)

| Attitudes | Catholic Church Leaders | | | | %Total |
	%Luo	%Kuria	%Kwaya	%Sukuma	
Yes.................	13	-	79	75	40
Depends.............	3	-	5	6	3
No..................	84	31	16	8	36
Yes, but do not like remarriage..........	-	66	-	-	17
Other..........	-	3	-	11	4
Total %	100	100	100	100	100
Number	(31)	(29)	(19)	(36)	(115)

TABLE 38

POSSIBILITY OF WIDOWS IN LEVIRATIC UNIONS RECEIVING THE SACRAMENTS
BY CATHOLIC CHURCH LEADERS IN AREAS SURVEYED (%)

| Can Widows Receive the Sacraments? | Leaders in Areas Surveyed | | | | %Total |
	%Luo	%Kuria	%Kwaya	%Sukuma	
Yes..............	32	4	32	28	24
Depends...............	32	17	37	25	27
No....................	36	79	31	33	45
Other.................	-	-	-	14	4
Total %	100	100	100	100	100
Number	(31)	(29)	(19)	(36)	(115)

TABLE 39

CATHOLIC CHURCH LEADERS' OPINIONS ON THE NATURE OF THE LEVIRATIC UNION
BY AREAS SURVEYED (%)

Nature of the Leviratic Union	Leaders in Areas Surveyed				%Total
	%Luo	%Kuria	%Kwaya	%Sukuma	
A way of caring for widows.............	94	79	79	67	79
Between marriage and caring..............	3	-	5	11	5
A real marriage....	3	-	11	17	8
A bad friendship.......	-	21	-	3	5
Other.................	-	-	•5	2	3
Total %	100	100	100	100	100
Number	(31)	(29)	(19)	(36)	(115)

TABLE 40

NUMBER OF BRIDEWEALTH COWS PAID FOR FIRST WIFE
BY ETHNIC GROUP SURVEYED (%)

Number of Cows	Ethnic Groups				%Total
	%Luo	%Kuria	%Kwaya	%Sukuma	
None.............	-	-	34	-	8
1-5...................	2	-	16	-	6
6-10..................	14	5	22	6	20
11-15.................	22	2	11	39	17
16-20.................	58	19	8	35	26
21-30.................	4	45	5	20	14
31-40.................	-	28	-	-	7
Over 40...............	-	1	-	-	1
Other.................	-	-	1	-	1
Total %	100	100	100	100	100
Number	(102)	(101)	(94)	(101)	(398)

TABLE 41

NUMBER OF LEVIRATIC UNIONS ENTERED INTO BY WIDOWS SINCE
THEIR HUSBANDS' DEATHS, BY ETHNIC GROUP SURVEYED (%)

Number of Unions	Ethnic Group				%Total
	%Luo	%Kuria	%Kwaya	%Sukuma	
None............	8	45	75	83	50
One.............	54	21	5	9	24
Two.............	23	21	5	-	13
Three...........	8	3	-	-	3
Four............	-	3	-	-	1
No answer.......	8	7	15	9	9
Total %	100	100	100	100	100
Number	(26)	(29)	(20)	(22)	(97)

TABLE 42

NUMBER OF WIDOWS WITH WHOM MEN ARE PRESENTLY COHABITING
IN LEVIRATIC UNIONS, BY ETHNIC GROUP SURVEYED (%)

Number of Widows	Ethnic Group				%Total
	%Luo	%Kuria	%Kwaya	%Sukuma	
None............	82	97	98	100	94
One.............	15	2	-	-	4
Two.............	2	-	-	-	1
No Answer.......	1	1	2	-	1
Total %	100	100	100	100	100
Number	(104)	(102)	(95)	(101)	(402)

TABLE 43

NUMBER OF WIDOWS WITH WHOM MEN HAVE ESTABLISHED LEVIRATIC UNIONS
IN THE PAST, BY ETHNIC GROUP SURVEYED (%)

Number of Widows	Ethnic Group				%Total
	%Luo	%Kuria	%Kwaya	%Sukuma	
None..........	81	95	95	98	92
One...........	14	5	4	2	6
Two...........	1	-	1	-	1
Three.........	2	-	-	-	1
Four..........	1	-	-	-	(.2)
No Answer.....	1	-	-	-	(.2)
Total %	100	100	100	100	100
Number	(104)	(102)	(95)	(101)	(402)

TABLE 44

TYPE OF MARRIAGE OF MEN, BY ETHNIC GROUP SURVEYED (%)

Type of Marriage (Men)	Ethnic Group (Men)				%Total
	%Luo	%Kuria	%Kwaya	%Sukuma	
Monogamous	55	72	87	88	63
Polygynous	45	28	13	12	37
Total %	100	100	100	100	100
Number	(100)	(98)	(85)	(100)	(383)

TABLE 45

Luo Attitudes Towards the Christian Prohibition
of the Leviratic Union, by Sex of Respondents (%)

Attitudes	Sex of Respondent		Total
	Men	Women	
Approve.............	11	24	17
Disapprove..........	78	69	74
Do not know.........	11	7	9
Total %	100	100	100
Number	(159)	(145)	(304)

TABLE 46

The Churches' Treatment of Christian Widows and Leviratic
Brothers-In-Law, by Ethnic Group Surveyed (N=86)

Treatment	Ethnic Group								Total
	Luo		Kuria		Kwaya		Sukuma		
	Bro.	Wid.	Bro.	Wid.	Bro.	Wid.	Bro.	Wid.	
Punished	15	9	-	2	-	-	1	-	27
Not punished	6	13	2	15	5	10	2	6	59
Number	21	22	2	17	5	10	3	6	86

TABLE 47

THE KIND OF PERSONS WITH WHOM WIDOWS ARE PRESENTLY COHABITING
BY ETHNIC GROUP SURVEYED (%)

Kind of Person	Ethnic Group				%Total
	%Luo	%Kuria	%Kwaya	%Sukuma	
No one...........	54	53	75	82	64
Brother-in-law...	35	13	5	9	16
Friend...........	-	27	10	-	10
No answer........	11	7	10	9	9
Total % Number	100 (26)	100 (30)	100 (20)	100 (22)	100 (98)

TABLE 48

RELIGIOUS AFFILIATION, BY ETHNIC GROUP SURVEYED (%)

Religious Affiliation	Ethnic Group				%Total
	%Luo	%Kuria	%Kwaya	%Sukuma	
Traditional.............	16	54	47	58	46
Muslim..................	-	10	2	-	4
Catholic................	41	26	43	24	32
Mennonite..............	12	3	2	-	4
African Inland Church...	-	-	-	10	3
Seventh Day Adventist...	13	6	-	6	6
Pentecostal.............	6	-	-	-	2
Roho Evangelical........	3	-	-	-	1
Nomiya Catholic.........	3	-	-	-	1
Other..................	6	1	2	2	1
Total % Number	100 (304)	100 (303)	100 (309)	100 (301)	100 (1,217)

TABLE 49

TYPE OF KWAYA MARRIAGE ALLIANCE, BY AREAS SURVEYED (%)

Type of Marriage Alliance	Survey Areas					%Total
	%Kama-tico	%Efu-rifu	%Mumu-hari	%Kumu-gongo	%Kaki-sieri	
Bridewealth	79	92	74	43	45	66
Nonbridewealth	21	8	26	57	55	34
Total %	100	100	100	100	100	100
Number	(43)	(38)	(39)	(42)	(42)	(204)

TABLE 50

REASONS FOR THE CHRISTIAN PROHIBITION OF THE LEVIRATE
BY SUKUMA WAGE WORKERS (%)

Reasons for Prohibition	Worked for a Wage (Sukuma)		%Total
	%Yes (N=37)	%No (N=255)	
Customs of the churches.......	19	46	43
The widow is not a wife.......	78	34	39
God has forbidden this custom........................	3	17	15
Other.........................	-	3	3
Total %	100	100	100

TABLE 51

Sukuma Attitudes Towards the Church Prohibition of the Levirate by Urban Residence (%)

Attitudes	Urban Residence		Total
	More than a year	Less than a year	
Approve............	13	36	35
Disapprove...............	87	63	64
Do not know..............	-	1	1
Total % Number	100 (15)	100 (286)	100 (301)

TABLE 52

Reasons Why Leviratic Unions with Widows Ended by Ethnic Group Surveyed (%)

Reasons Given	Ethnic Group				%Total
	%Luo	%Kuria	%Kwaya	%Sukuma	
No understanding.............	45	60	75	100	48
Went to live with her son........................	15 (20)[a]	20	-	-	13
She was old and tired.........................	5	-	-	-	-
Widow died......................	10	20	25	-	13
She loved someone else..........................	5	-	-	-	3
She took up co-habitation with another brother..............	15 (20)[a]	-	-	-	10
No Answer....................	5	-	-	-	3
Total % Number	100 (20)	100 (5)	100 (4)	100 (2)	100 (31)

[a]Given as second reason by two respondents.

TABLE 53

REASONS GIVEN BY SUKUMA FOR DISAPPROVING THE CHRISTIAN PROHIBITION
OF THE LEVIRATE, BY WAGE WORK (%)

Reasons Given	Worked for a Wage		%Total
	Yes	No	
Still loves God............	16	5	7
Still a member of the Church.....................	40	12	16
God did not forbid the levirate...................	8	18	16
Widow is not a prostitute..	24	49	46
Widow did not kill her husband.....................	12	13	13
Other.......................	-	3	2
Total %	100	100	100
Number	(25)	(168)	(193)

TABLE 54

TYPE OF KWAYA MARRIAGE ALLIANCES, BY AGE GROUPS (%)

Marriage Alliances	Age Groups		Total
	Under 45	Over 45	
No bridewealth (matrilineal)	30	43	34
Bridewealth (patrilineal)	70	57	62
Total %	100	100	100
Number	(143)	(61)	(204)

TABLE 55

CATHOLIC CHURCH LEADERS WHO MENTIONED WIDOWS SPECIFICALLY
WHEN QUESTIONED ABOUT GENERAL CHANGES THEY WOULD LIKE
TO SEE IN MARRIAGE DISCIPLINE (N=21)[a]

Changes for Widows	Catholic Leaders				Total
	Luo	Kuria	Kwaya	Sukuma	
Allow the sacrament to levirate partners	6	2	-	3	11
Allow the sacrament if taken by a pagan	1	-	-	-	1
Follow African customs..............	3	-	2	-	5
Promote remarriage	1	-	-	1	2
Investigate problem of widows.............	-	-	-	1	1
Be more lenient with widows................	-	-	-	1	1
Total	11	2	2	6	21

[a]This table shows the relative importance of the problem of widows among the four peoples surveyed.

TABLE 56

ATTITUDE TOWARDS THE PROHIBITION OF THE LEVIRATE
BY TYPE OF CHRISTIAN RELIGION (%)

Attitude	Type of Christian Religion						%Total
	%Cath	%SDA	%Menn	%AIC	%CMS	%Indep.	
Approve...........	50	42	21	31	29	10	42
Disapprove........	48	54	73	69	57	82	54
Do not know.......	2	4	6	-	14	8	4
Total %	100	100	100	100	100	100	100
Number	(393)	(79)	(52)	(32)	(7)	(48)	(615)

TABLE 57

FLUENCY IN KISWAHILI, BY ETHNIC GROUP (%)

Degree of Fluency	Ethnic Group				%Total
	%Luo	%Kuria	%Kwaya	%Sukuma	
Know well.....................	15	7	12	20	14
Know sufficiently.............	17	7	29	18	18
Know little...................	22	23	23	17	21
Know nothing.................	46	63	35	51	48
Total %	100	100	100	100	100
Number	(304)	(303)	(309)	(301)	(1,217)

APPENDIX B

SELECTED BIBLIOGRAPHY

PART I: THEOLOGICAL WORKS

Aagaard, Johanne. "Some Main Trends in the Renewal of Roman Catholic Missiology." *Challenge and Response: A Protestant Perspective of the Vatican Council*. Edited by Warren Quanbeck. Minneapolis: Augsburg, 1966.

Abbo, John A. and Hannon, Jerome. *The Sacred Canons*. 2 vols. St. Louis: B. Herder Book Co., 1960.

Adam, Karl. *The Spirit of Catholicism*. Translated by Dom Justin McCann. New York: MacMillan, 1929.

African Theological Journal, No. 2 (1969). Nakumira, Tanzania: Lutheran Theological College.

Balina, Aloys, Mayala, Anthony, and Mabula, Justin. *Traditional Marriage in Tanzania Today*. Tabora, Tanzania: Kipalapala Seminary, 1970.

Benedict XIV. "Ex Quo Singulari." *Opera Omnia*. Prate: In Typographica Aldini, 1839. XV, 229–235.

——. "Omnium Solicitudinem." *Opera Omnia*. Prate: In Typographica Aldini, 1839. XV, 229–235.

Benedict XV. "Maximum Illud." *Acta Apostolicae Sedis* 2 (1919) 440–445.

Bitakaramire, Henry. *Traditional and Christian Marriage*. Gaba Institute Pastoral Papers, No. 9. Kampala, Uganda: Gaba Publications, 1969.

Böckle, Franz, ed. *The Future of Marriage as Institution*. Concilium, Vol. 55. New York: Herder, 1970.

Boer, Harry. "Polygamy." *Frontier* 2 (1968) 24–27.

Carney, Joseph. "The History of the Functional Structure of the Maryknoll Mission in Musoma and Shinyanga, Tanzania." Ph.D. dissertation, St. John's University, New York, 1973.

Catholic Missions: Four Great Encyclicals. Edited by Thomas Burke. New York: Fordham University Press, 1957.

Codex Juris Canonici. Rome: Typis Polyglottis Vaticanis, 1917.

Cohen, Paul. *China and Christianity: The Missionary Movement and the Growth of Chinese Antiforeignism 1860–1870*. Cambridge: Harvard University Press, 1963.

Commentary on the Documents of Vatican II. Vol. V. Edited by Herbert Vorgrimler. New York: Herder & Herder, 1969.

243

Cukopela, E. K. "Marriage Commitment." *African Ecclesiastical Review* 14 (1972) 325–330.

Davis, H. *Moral and Pastoral Theology.* London: Sheed and Ward, 1951.

Dilworth, Joan. "Marriage Education." *African Ecclesiasitical Review* 4 (1962) 236–240.

————. "Unexploited Riches in African Families." *African Ecclesiastical Review* 1 (1959) 57–62.

Dinwiddy, Hugh. "Christian Marriage." *African Ecclesiastical Review* 3 (1961) 122–125.

Diop, Alioune. "Colonization and the Christian Conscience." *Cross Currents* 3 (Summer 1953) 353–355.

Divine, R. *The Law of Christian Marriage.* London: R. & T. Washbourne, Ltd., 1908.

The Documents of Vatican II. Edited by Walter M. Abbott. New York: Guild Press, 1966.

Dulles, Avery. *Dimensions of the Church.* Westminster, Md.: Newman Press, 1967.

Enchiridion Symbolorum: Definitionum et Declarationum de Rebus Fidei et Morum. Edited by Heinrich Denzinger. Thirty-first edition edited by Karl Rahner. Barcelona: Herder 1960.

Fesquet, Henri. *The Drama of Vatican II: The Ecumenical Council. June 1962–December 1965.* Translated by Bernard Murchland. New York: Random House, 1967.

Fuchs, Josef. "Is There a Specifically Christian Morality?" *Theology Digest* 19 (1971) 39–42.

————. "Theology of the Meaning of Marriage Today." *Marriage in the Light of Vatican II.* Edited by J. McHugh. Washington, D.C.: Family Life Bureau, 1968.

Häring, Bernard. "Marriage and the Family." *Vatican II: An Interfaith Appraisal.* Edited by John Miller. Notre Dame, Ind.: University of Notre Dame Press, 1966.

————. *Marriage in the Modern World.* Westminster, Md: Newman Press, 1966.

————. *Road to Renewal.* Montreal: Palm Publishers, 1966.

————. *A Theology of Protest.* New York: Farrar, Strauss & Giroux, 1970.

Harries, Lyndon. "Christian Marriage in African Society." *Survey of African Marriage and Family Life.* Edited by Arthur Phillips. London, New York, Toronto: Oxford University Press, 1953.

Hastings, Adrian. *African Christianity.* London: Geoffrey Chapman, 1976, and New York: Seabury Press, 1977.

————. *Christian Marriage in Africa.* London: S.P.C.K., 1973.

————. *Church and Mission in Modern Africa.* London: Burns and Oates, 1967; New York: Fordham University Press, 1968.

————. "The Church's Response to African Marriage." *African Ecclesiastical Review* 13 (1971) 193–204.

————. "Report on Marriage." *New Blackfriers* 54 (1973) 253–260.

Hauben, Marcel. *Contribution à la solution pastorale de la problématique du mariage africain et de son paiement.* Rome: Herder, 1966.

Heylen, Victor L. "Fostering the Nobility of Marriage in the Family." *The Church Today.* Edited by Group 2,000. Translated by Denis Barrett. Westminster, Md.: Newman Press, 1967.

Hillman, Eugene. *Polygamy Reconsidered.* Maryknoll, N.Y.: Orbis Books, 1975.

————. "Polygyny Reconsidered." *The Renewal of Preaching.* Edited by Karl Rahner. Concilium, Vol. 33. New York: Paulist Press, 1968.

Hoffman, Ronan. "The Council and the Missions." *Vatican II: The Theological Dimension.* Edited by Anthony Lee. Washington, D.C.: Thomist Press, 1963.

Horman, Karl. *An Introduction to Moral Theology.* Translated by Edward Quinn. London: Burns and Oates, 1961.

Idowu, E. Bolaji. *African Traditional Religion.* Maryknoll, N.Y.: Orbis Books, 1975.

————. *Towards an Indigenous Church.* London: Oxford University Press, 1965.

Inyamah, Nathaniel G. "Polygamy and the Christian Church." *Concordia Theological Monthly* 43 (1972) 138–143.

Jasper, Gerhard. "Polygamy in the Old Testament." *African Theological Journal* No. 2 (February 1969) 27–57.

Jassy, Marie-France P. *Basic Community in the African Churches.* Maryknoll, N.Y.: Orbis Books, 1973.

Jay, Martin. *The Dialectical Imagination.* Boston: Little, Brown, 1973.

Jeffreys, M. D. W. "Polygamy in the Christian Fold." *Practical Anthropology* 19 (1972) 83–97.

John XXIII. "Princeps Pastorum." *Acta Apostolicae Sedis* 51 (1959) 833–864.

Joyce, George Hayward. *Christian Marriage: An Historical Doctrinal Study.* London: Sheed and Ward, 1948.

Kale, S. I. "Polygamy and the Church in Africa." *International Review of Mission* 31 (1942) 220–223.

Kenyatta, Jomo. *Facing Mount Kenya.* London: Secker & Warburg, 1938.

Latourette, K. S. *A History of the Expansion of Christianity.* 5 vols. London: Harper, 1937–45.

Leclercq, Jacques. *Marriage and the Family.* Translated by Thomas Hanley. New York and Cincinnati: Frederick Pustet, 1942.

Liégé, Pierre André. "Avant le Catéchuménat, la Mission." *Parole et Mission* 5 (1962) 23–32.

Lufoluabo, Francois-Marie. *Mariage coutumier et mariage chrétien indissoluble.* Kinshasa, Zaire: Les Editions St. Paul Afrique, 1968.

Mana, Paolo. *The Conversion of the Pagan World.* Translated by Joseph McGlinchey. Cambridge, Mass.: Harvard University Press, 1921.

Maurier, Henri. *The Other Covenant: A Theology of Paganism.* Translated by Charles McGrath. Glen Rock, N.J.: Newman Press, 1968.

Metz, Johann Baptist. "Prophetic Authority." *Religion and Political Society.* Edited and translated in the Institute of Christian Thought. New York: Harper and Row, 1974.

Moellar, Charles. "History of the Constitution." *Commentary on the Documents of Vatican II.* Edited by Herbert Vorgrimler. Montreal: Palm Publishers, 1969.

Montserrat-Torrents, José. *The Abandoned Spouse.* Milwaukee: The Bruce Publishing Company, 1969.

Mourret, F. *A History of the Catholic Church.* Translated by N. Thompson. St. Louis: B. Herder Book Company, 1936.

Mullin, Joseph, *The Catholic Church in Modern Africa.* London: Geoffrey Chapman, 1965.

Murphy, Edward L. *Teach Ye All Nations: The Principles of Catholic Missionary Work.* New York: Benziger Brothers, 1957.

McGrath, Mark C. "The Constitution on the Church in the Modern World." *Vatican II: An Interfaith Appraisal.* Edited by John Miller. Notre Dame, Ind.: University of Notre Dame Press, 1966.

McHugh, J. and Callan, Charles. *Moral Theology: A Complete Course Based on St. Thomas Aquinas and the Best Modern Authorities.* 2 vols. New York: Joseph F. Wagner, 1960.

Nabeta, T. T. T. "Mutual Dependence and Church Growth." *Church Growth Bulletin* 5 (March 1969) 59–60.

———. "Mutual Dependence: The Family and Beyond." *African Independence and Christian Freedom.* London: Oxford University Press, 1965.

Nebreda, Alfonso. *Kerygma in Crisis?* Chicago: Loyola University Press, 1964.

Neill, Stephen. *A History of Christian Missions.* Grand Rapids, Mich.: Eerdmans Publishing Co., 1965.

Noldin, H. and Schmitt, A. *Summa Theologiae Moralis.* 3 vols. 2nd ed. Edited by G. Heinzel. Innsbruck: Feliciani Rauch, 1954.

Noonan, John T. "Freedom, Experimentation, and Permanence in the

Canon Law on Marriage." *Law for Liberty.* Edited by James E. Buchler. Baltimore: Helicon Press, 1967.

Nyamiti, Charles. *African Theology: Its Nature, Problems and Method.* Gaba Institute Pastoral Papers, No. 19. Kampala, Uganda: Gaba Publications [n.d.].

Oldham, J. H. "The Missionary and His Task." *International Review of Mission* 3 (1941) 512–514.

Ott, Ludwig. *Fundamentals of Catholic Dogma.* Edited by J. C. Bastible. Translated by P. Lynch. Cork: The Mercier Press, 1955.

Paul VI, Pope. "Africae Terrarum." *Acta Apostolicae Sedis* 59 (1967) 1073–1097.

Parrinder, Geoffrey. *The Bible and Polygamy.* London: S.P.C.K., 1950.

——————. *Religion in an African City.* London: Oxford University Press, 1953.

Pius XII. "Evangelii Praecones." *Acta Apostolicae Sedis* 43 (1951) 497–528.

Prummer, Dominic M. *Handbook of Moral Theology.* Translated by Gerald Shelton. Cork: The Mercier Press, 1956.

Ratzinger, Joseph. *Theological Highlights of Vatican II.* New York: Paulist Press, 1966.

Riga, Peter J. *The Church Made Relevant: A Commentary on the Pastoral Constitution of Vatican II.* Notre Dame, Ind.: Fides Publishers, 1967.

——————. *Sexuality and Marriage in Recent Catholic Thought.* Corpus Papers. Washington: Corpus Books, 1969.

Robinson, John M. *The Family Apostolate and Africa.* Dublin: The Helicon Press, 1964.

Roy, Rustum and Roy, Della. *Honest Sex.* Signet Book. Toronto: New American Library, 1968.

Rynne, Xavier. *The Fourth Session.* New York: Farrar, Straus & Giroux, 1965.

Schlette, Heinz. "Theological Problems of Adaptation." *Sacramentum Mundi: An Encyclopedia of Theology.* Edited by Karl Rahner. Montreal: Palm Publishers, 1969. IV, 81–84.

——————. *Towards a Theology of Religion.* Quaestiones Disputatae, No. 14. New York: Herder and Herder, 1966.

Schillebeeckx, Edward. *Marriage: Human Reality and Saving Mystery.* 2 vols. New York: Sheed and Ward, 1965.

Schmidlin, J. *Catholic Mission History.* Techny, Ill.: Mission Press, Society of the Divine Word, 1931.

Seligman, C. G. *Races of Africa.* London: Oxford University Press, 1957.

Shorter, Alyward. *African Culture and the Christian Church: An Introduction to Social and Pastoral Anthropology.* London: Geoffrey Chapman, 1973, and Maryknoll, N.Y.: Orbis Books, 1974.

————. "Christian and African Marriage and Family Life." *The African Contribution to World Church and Other Essays in Pastoral Anthropology.* Gaba Institute Pastoral Papers, No. 22. Kampala, Uganda: Gaba Publications, 1972.

————. *Essays in Pastoral Anthropology.* Gaba Institute Pastoral Papers, No. 5. Kampala, Uganda: Gaba Publications, 1969.

————. *Theology of Mission.* Notre Dame, Ind.: Fides, 1972.

Ssennyonga, J. W. "Christianity as a Factor in African Marriage Patterns." Churches' Research Project on Marriage in Africa. No. 17. Gaba Pastoral Institute, Kampala, Uganda, March 1972.

Taber, Charles. "The Missionary: Wrecker, Builder, or Catalyst." *Practical Anthropology* 17 (1970) 145–152.

Tanquerey, A. D. *Synopsis Theologiae Moralis et Pastoralis.* 3 vols. 7th ed. Rome: Desclée, 1920.

Third Session: Council Speeches of Vatican II. Edited by William K. Keahy. Deus Book. Glen Rock, N.J.: Paulist Press, 1966.

Thomas, John. *The Catholic Viewpoint on Marriage and the Family.* New York: Hanover House, 1958.

Thompson, William. "Rahner's Theology of Pluralism." *The Ecumenist* 11 (1973) 17–32.

Tippet, Alan. "Polygamy as a Missionary Problem: The Anthropological Issues." *Church Growth Bulletin* 5 (1968) 60–67.

Turner, H. W. "Monogamy: A Mark of the Church?" *International Review of Mission* 55 (1966) 313–321.

Ulbrich, H. F. and van Driessche, J. "Some Elements for Possible Solution of the Actual Crisis in Christian Marriage Life in Africa and Especially Rhodesia." Churches' Research Project, No. 16. Kampala, Uganda: Gaba Pastoral Institute. Mimeographed. 1971.

Van Gennep, Arnold. *The Rites of Passage.* Translated by Monika B. Vizedom and Gabrielle L. Caffee. Chicago: University of Chicago Press, 1960.

Van Vliet, A. H. and Breed, C. G. *Marriage and Canon Law.* London: Burns and Oates, 1964.

Voss, Gustav. "Missionary Accommodation: A Study of Its History, Theology, and Present Needs." *Missionary Academic Study,* No. 4. New York: Society for the Propagation of the Faith, 1946.

Vriens, Livinus. *Critical Bibliography of Missiology. Bibliographis ad Usum Seminariorum.* Vol. E2. Translated by Deodatus Tummers. Nijmegen: Bestelcentrale Der V.S.K.B. Publishers, 1960.

PART II: SOCIOLOGICAL WORKS

African Systems of Kinship and Marriage. Edited by A. Radcliffe-Brown and Daryll Forde. International African Institute. Toronto: Oxford University Press, 1950.

African Writers Series. 46 vols. Edited by Chinua Achebe. London, Ibadan, Nairobi: Heinemann Educational Books Ltd.

Baker, E. C. "The Ba-Girango." Manuscript in Africana Collection, University of Dar es Salaam, Tanzania [n.d.].

——————. "The Bakuria of N.M. Tarime Tanganyika Territory." Manuscript in the Library of East African Institute of Social Research. Kampala, Uganda [n.d.].

Blalock, Herbert M. *Social Statistics.* Toronto: McGraw-Hill Book Co., 1972.

Clignet, Remi. *Many Wives, Many Powers: Authority and Power in Polygynous Families.* Evanston, Ill.: Northwestern University Press, 1970.

Cohen, Ronald. "Warring Epistemologies: Quality and Quantity in African Research." *Survey Research in Africa.* Edited by William M. O'Barr et al. Evanston, Ill.: Northwestern University Press, 1973. 36–47.

Coissoró, Narâná. *The Customary Law of Succession in Central Africa.* Estudos de Ciências Políticas e Socials, No. 78. Lisbon: Technical University of Lisbon, 1966.

Cory, Hans. "The Customary Law of Inheritance in Bukwaya." Letter to District Commissioner, Musoma, Tanzania, 1945. The Cory Collection, University of Dar es Salaam, Tanzania.

——————. "A Few Notes About the General Introduction of Brideprice in Bukwaya." Letter to the District Commissioner of Musoma, Tanzania, Sept. 1945. The Cory Collection, University of Dar es Salaam, Tanzania.

——————. "Kuria Bridewealth." Manuscript, Mwanza, Tanzania, 1958. The Cory Collection, University of Dar es Salaam, Tanzania.

——————. "Kuria Law and Custom." Manuscript, 1945. Re-edited by E. B. Dobson. The Cory Collection, University of Dar es Salaam, Tanzania.

——————. "Land Tenure in Bukuria." *Tanganyika Notes and Records* 23 (1947) 70–79.

——————. "The Law and the Family in Usukuma." Manuscript [n.d.]. The Cory Collection, University of Dar es Salaam, Tanzania.

————. "Questionnaire Pertaining to Bantu Customary Law." Manuscript [n.d.]. The Cory Collection, University of Dar es Salaam, Tanzania.

————. "Religious Beliefs and Practices of the Sukuma-Nyamwezi Tribal Group." *Tanganyika Notes and Records* 54 (March 1960) 14–16.

————. *Sukuma Law and Custom.* London: Oxford University Press, 1953.

The Craft of Social Anthropology. Edited by A. L. Epstein. Social Science Paperbacks. London: Tabistock Publications, 1967.

Cunnison, Jan. *The Luapala People of Northern Rhodesia: Custom and History in Tribal Politics.* Manchester: Manchester University Press, 1959.

DuPre, Carole D. *The Luo of Kenya: An Annotated Bibliography.* Washington, D.C.: The Institute for Cross-Cultural Research, 1968.

East African High Commission. East African Statistical Department. *Tanganyika Population Census 1957: General African Census, August 1957: Tribal Analysis.* Dar es Salaam: Government Printers, 1958.

Ehrenfels, U. R. "Mother-Right in East Africa." Manuscript [n.d.]. University of Dar es Salaam, Tanzania.

Evans-Pritchard, E. E. *Kinship and Marriage among the Nuer.* Oxford: The Clarendon Press, 1951.

————. "Luo Tribes and Clans." *The Position of Women in Primitive Societies and Other Essays in Social Anthropology.* London: Faber and Faber, 1965.

————. "Marriage Customs of the Luo of Kenya." *The Position of Women in Primitive Societies and Other Essays in Social Anthropology.* London: Faber and Faber, 1965.

————. *Some Aspects of Marriage and Family among the Nuer.* The Rhodes-Livingstone Paper, No. 11. Livingstone, Northern Rhodesia: The Rhodes-Livingstone Institute, 1945.

Fabian, Johannes. *Jamaa: A Charismatic Movement in Katanga.* Evanston, Ill.: Northwestern University Press, 1971.

Fortes, Meyer. *African Systems of Thought.* International African Institute. London: Oxford University Press, 1965.

————. "The Structure of Unilineal Descent Groups." *Readings in Kinship and Social Structure.* Edited by Nelson H. Graburn. New York: Harper & Row, 1971.

Fox, Robin. *Kinship and Marriage.* Middlesex: C. Nicholls and Co., 1967.

Frake, Charles O. "The Ethnographic Study of Cognitive Systems." *Readings in Anthropology.* Edited by Morton Fried. New York: Thomas Y. Crowell Company, 1968.

Hartmann, Rev. "Some Customs of the Luwo Living in South Kavirondo." *Anthropos* 23 (1928) 263–275.

Huber, Hugo. *Marriage and the Family in Rural Bukwaya.* Studia Ethnographica Friburgensia, Vol. 2. Fribourg, Switzerland: The University Press, 1973.

————. "The Wakwaya of Musoma." Manuscript. Switzerland: University of Fribourg [c. 1968].

Hughes, Kenneth. "The Church and Marriage in Africa." *The Christian Century* 82 (1965) 204–208.

Kuria Law Panel. "The Kuria Law of Succession." Unpublished report of meeting held at Kisii, Kenya, June 1963. East African Institute of Social Research, Kampala, Uganda.

————. "The Kuria Law of Succession." Manuscript, 1945. Re-edited by E. B. Dobson. The Cory Collection, University of Dar es Salaam, Tanzania.

Levi-Strauss, Claude. *The Elementary Structures of Kinship.* Edited by E. Rodney Needham. Translated by James Bell and John Richard von Strumer. Boston: Beacon Press, 1969.

Linton, Ralph. "The Natural History of the Family." *Readings in Anthropology.* Edited by Morton Fried. 2nd. ed. New York: Thomas Y. Crowell, 1968.

Luo Law Panel. "The Law of Marriage and Divorce." Unpublished report of a meeting held at Kisumu, Kenya, April 1962. East African Institute of Social Research, Kampala, Uganda.

Luzbetak, Louis. *The Church and Culture: An Applied Anthropology for the Religious Worker.* Techny, Ill.: Divine Word Publications, 1963.

Mace, David and Mace, Vera. *Marriage, East and West.* Dolphin Books. Garden City, N. Y.: Doubleday, 1957.

Mair, Lucy. "African Marriage and Social Change." *Survey of African Marriage and Family Life.* Edited by Arthur Phillips. London: Oxford University Press, 1953.

————. *An Introduction to Social Anthropology.* London: Oxford University Press, 1965.

Malcolm, D. W. *Sukumaland: An African People and Their Country.* London: Oxford University Press for The International African Institute, 1953.

Malo, Shadrack. *Dhoudi mag Central Nyanza* [Clans of Central Nyanza]. Nairobi: Eagle Press, 1953.

Mauss, Marcel. *The Gift.* Translated by Ian Cunnison. New York: W. W. Norton, 1954.

Mayer, Philip. *Gusii Bridewealth Law and Custom.* London: Oxford University Press, 1950.

Mbiti, John S. *African Religion and Philosophy.* New York: Praeger, 1969.

Mboya, Paul. *Luo Kitgi Gi Timbgi* [Luo Customs and Traditions]. Kendu

Bay, Kenya: African Herald Publishing House, 1965.

————. *Thuond Weche* [Important Customs: (Luos)]. Manuscript, Kendu Bay, Kenya [c. 1965].

Mitchell, Clyde J. "On the Quantification in Social Anthropology." *The Craft of Social Anthropology.* Edited by A. L. Epstein. London: Associated Book Publishers, 1967.

Moris, Jon R. "Multi-Subject Farm Surveys Reconsidered: Some Methodological Lessons." Conference Proceedings, East African Agricultural Economics Society, University College, Dar es Salaam, Tanzania, 1970.

Odinga, Oginga. *Not Yet Uhuru.* London: Heinemann Educational Books, 1967.

Ogot, Bethwell A. *Peoples of East Africa: History of the Southern Luo.* Nairobi: East African Publishing House, 1967.

p'Bitek, Okot. *African Religions in Western Scholarship.* Kampala, Nairobi, Dar es Salaam: East African Literature Bureau, 1970.

Phillips, Arthur, ed., "Introductory Essay." *Survey of African Marriage and Family Life.* Edited by Arthur Phillips. London: Oxford University Press, 1953.

————. "Marriage Laws in Africa." *Survey of African Marriage and Family Life.* Edited by Arthur Phillips. London: Oxford University Press, 1953.

Piaget, Jean. *Six Psychological Studies.* Edited by David Elkind. Translated by Anita Tenzer. Vintage Books, New York: Random House,1968.

Radcliffe-Brown, A. R. "Introduction." *African Systems of Kinship and Marriage.* Edited by A. R. Radcliffe-Brown and Daryll Forde. London: Oxford University Press, 1950.

Republic of Kenya. *Kenya Population Census, 1969.* 5 vols. Nairobi, Government Printer, 1970.

Ruel, Malcolm J. "Kuria Generation Classes." *Africa* 23 (1953) 14–37.

————. "Piercing." Conference Proceedings, East African Institute of Social Research, Makerere University College, Kampala, Uganda, June 1958.

————. "Religion and Society among the Kuria of East Africa." *Africa* 40 (July 1956) 295–306.

————. "Some Problems of Change amongst the Kuria." Conference Proceedings, East African Institute of Social Research, Makerere University College, Kampala, Uganda, June 1957.

Shaw, K. C. "Some Preliminary Notes on Luo Marriage Customs." *Journal of East Africa and Uganda Natural History Society* 2 (1932) 45–46.

Sillery, A. "Notes for a Grammar of the Kuria Language." *Bantu Studies* 10 (1936) 9–26.

————. "A Sketch of the Kikwaya Language." *Bantu Studies* 6 (1932) 273–307.

Tanner, Ralph E. S. "Maturity and Marriage among the Northern Basukuma of Tanganyika." *African Studies* 14 (1955) 153–160.

————. "Sukuma Ancestor Worship and Its Relation to Social Structure." *Tanganyika Notes and Records* 5 (June 1958) 52–62.

The United Republic of Tanzania. *The Law of Marriage Act, 5. (May 1, 1971).* Dar es Salaam: Government Printers, 1971.

————. *1967 Population Census.* 5 vols. Dar es Salaam: Government Printers, 1969.

————. *Tanzania Second Five-Year Plan for Economic and Social Development 1st July, 1969–30th June, 1974.* 5 vols. Dar es Salaam: Government Printers, 1969.

van Pelt, P. *Bantu Customs in Mainland Tanzania.* Tabora, Tanzania: T.M.P Book Department, 1971.

Westermarck, Edward. *The History of Human Marriage.* 3 vols. New York: MacMillan, 1891; 5th ed. New York: Allerton Book Co., 1922.

————. A Short History of Marriage. New York: Humanities Press, 1926.

Whisson, Michael. *Change and Challenge.* Nairobi, Kenya: Acme Press, 1964.

————. "The Will of God and the Wiles of Men." Conference Proceedings, East African Institute of Social Research. Makerere University College, Kampala,Uganda, 1962.

Whorf, Benjamin Lee. "Science and Linguistics." *Make Men of Them.* Edited by Charles Hughes. Chicago: Rand McNally, 1972.

Wilson, G. *Chik gi Tim Luo,* (Laws and Customs of the Luos). Nairobi, Kenya: Government Printers, 1961.